PRAISE FOR *Crunch Time*

"*Crunch Time* is an eye-opening book about the ways in which economic insecurity reverberates into family life. In gripping detail, Rao illuminates family dynamics of unemployed professional women and men. Her book shows the surprising ways that gender inequality persists. Highly recommended!"

Annette Lareau, author of *Unequal Childhoods*

"In this deeply researched book, Rao takes us into the lives of professional couples dealing with unemployment and finds that even among these modern-day couples, traditional gender norms about breadwinning endure. A husband's unemployment is experienced as a big problem that needs to be rectified, while a wife's unemployment is experienced as an opportunity for her to spend more time at home—even when she is the primary earner. Rao's insightful examination reveals that when job loss strikes, gender inequalities are reinforced by couples' old-school responses to a new-economy problem."

Marianne Cooper, Stanford University, author of *Cut Adrift: Families in Insecure Times*

"*Cruch Time* is masterful. I picked up the book and could not put it down! A tale of two unemployments, *CrunchTime* details how unemployed men and women adopt an ideal job-seeker norm in divergently gendered ways in the face of economic precarity. A heartwrenching, hopeful, and captivating book, this is a must-read."

Kimberly Kay Hoang, University of Chicago, and author of *Dealing in Desire*

"Aliya Rao's meticulously designed study takes us into the deeply uncertain lives of the affluent as they experience unemployment. Rao's attention to the families profiled in this book is exacting and multifaceted, resisting any platitudes about privilege, unemployment, and especially gender. She illuminates how couples' responses to unemployment are shaped by entrenched understandings of what husbands and wives ought to do. She offers compelling explanations for variations in these gendered responses, expertly linking her findings to broader patterns of social inequalities."

Shelley Correll, Stanford University, Director of Stanford VMWare Women's Leadership Innovation Lab

"Dual-career marriages signal increasing gender equality, but what happens when one member of the couple becomes unemployed? Aliya Rao's surprising research finds that they revert to outdated gender norms. Through intimate portraits of unemployed professionals, Rao deftly exposes how society pushes men and women into traditional gender roles."

Christine Williams, University of Texas at Austin

"This is a beautifully written, well-organized, and meticulously researched book that breaks new ground."

Ofer Sharone, University of Massachusetts Amherst, and author of *Flawed System/Flawed Self*

"Rao's ideas are fresh, and an examination of unemployment and the different strategies between men and women and how their spouses react is welcome in the field."

Rosanna Hertz, Wellesley College

Crunch Time

Crunch Time

HOW MARRIED COUPLES CONFRONT UNEMPLOYMENT

Aliya Hamid Rao

UNIVERSITY OF CALIFORNIA PRESS

University of California Press
Oakland, California

Library of Congress Cataloging-in-Publication Data

Names: Rao, Aliya Hamid, author.
Title: Crunch time : how married couples confront unlemployment /
    Aliya Hamid Rao.
Description: Oakland, California : University of California
    Press, [2020] | Includes bibliographical references and index.
Identifiers: LCCN 2019059486 (print) | LCCN 2019059487 (ebook) |
    ISBN 9780520298606 (cloth) | ISBN 9780520298613 (paperback) |
    ISBN 9780520970670 (ebook)
Subjects: LCSH: Unemployed—Sex differences. | Unemployed—Family
    relationships—Social aspects. | Married people—Employment—
    Psychological aspects. | Upper class families—Economic aspects.
Classification: LCC HD5708 .R37 2020 (print) | LCC HD5708 (ebook) |
    DDC 331.13/708655—dc23
LC record available at https://lccn.loc.gov/2019059486
LC ebook record available at https://lccn.loc.gov/2019059487

29 28 27 26 25 24 23 22 21 20
10 9 8 7 6 5 4 3 2 1

Contents

Tables

Acknowledgments

A tremendous achievement of neoliberalism is how people continue to feel morally deficient after encountering pervasive economic events, such as layoffs and downsizings that are now built into organizational logics. This uncertainty at work occurs alongside a glorification of employment—the belief that what you do is who you are. So, unemployment is a difficult, even if expected, feature of contemporary life. It catalyzes individuals to question themselves, their professional worth, and even their morality as people. It can be hard to talk about. For this reason, and for many others, I am immensely grateful to the unemployed women and men and their spouses who chose to share their experiences of this often dispiriting time with me. My sincerest thanks especially to the Smith, Bach, Jansson, and Mason (all pseudonyms) families who let me into their homes and allowed me to see how unemployment shaped the rhythm of their daily lives. The magnanimity with which they shared some of these most intimate, emotional, and heart-wrenching experiences continues to astound me.

The material realm is enormously powerful in shaping intellectual life. Virginia Woolf recognized this obvious fact when she stated that "a woman must have money and a room of her own if she is to write." While Woolf referred to fiction, nonfiction, too, is not easily written without either of these two things. This book would not have been possible without the extraordinary financial support and intellectual feedback that I have received at three institutions: the University of Pennsylvania, Stanford University, and Singapore Management University (SMU). I've been privileged to be a part of these institutions in the process from the inception of this study to the completion of this book.

As a graduate student at Penn, I had the great fortune to have Annette Lareau as my intellectual mentor and dissertation chair. Annette's insightful and meticulous feedback has pushed me to think deeply about how to contribute to broader sociological questions and to do so with appropriate—and rich—data. Her support has been unparalleled as this study has developed from a dissertation and into a first book. Thank you for the many, many discussions over countless cups of tea at McNeil, in your home, and even over Skype.

My other committee members at Penn—Kristen Harknett, Robin Leidner, and Frank Furstenberg—have been instrumental to both my own intellectual development and that of this study. They provided indispensable feedback through crucial steps of my graduate school journey. I am so very grateful for the hours you have spent reading my writing and discussing my argument with me. I am always awed by Kristen Harknett's quiet, unwavering encouragement. In conversations from Philadelphia to California she has been a fantastic mentor, and I can only hope to emulate her finely honed balance of gentle encouragement and insightful critique. I also benefitted tremendously from conversations with other faculty members at Penn, specifically Melissa Wilde, Randall Collins, Jerry Jacobs, and Demie Kurz. The office staff at Penn went above and beyond to solve tricky and at times seemingly intractable bureaucratic questions with efficient aplomb. Thanks to Aline Rowens, Nancy Bolinski, Marcus Wright and Kathleen Paone, who have answered innumerable questions over the years. Many, *many* thanks to Audra Rodgers in particular.

At Penn, I received a number of fellowships that greatly expedited work on this project. These include: the Benjamin Franklin Fellowship, the Judith Rodin Fellowship, the Teece Fellowship for Dissertation Research, the Ortner Center Seed Grant for Graduate Research, Critical Writing Teaching Fellowship, and three summer fellowships funded by the Otto and Gertrude K. Pollak Scholarship Foundation. I also worked closely with the grants office at Penn, which resulted in a National Science Foundation Doctoral Dissertation Research Improvement Grant.

At Penn, I was lucky to start out with the—no overstatement—"best cohort ever": Rachel Ellis, Hyejeong Jo, Valerio Baćak, and Juliana Truesdale. Although we have moved in wildly different directions (and geographies) I continue to look forward to our annual ASA meetings. Thanks especially to Rachel Ellis (see you with "lunch in hand?") who has been a boon as a friend while navigating the post–graduate school life. Thanks for making life in Philadelphia and at Penn so unforgettable: Junhow Wei, Patricia Tevington, Betsie Garner, Doga Kerestecioglu, Esen Pence, Yi-lin Elim Chiang, Sarah Spell, Bethany Weed, Radha Modi, Tugce Ellialti, Seher Ahmad, Pete Harvey, Andrea Alvarado Urbina, Sebastian Cherng, Nora Gross, Raj Patel, Apoorva Jadhav, Tomás Larroucau de Magalhaes-Calvet, Luca Maria Pesando, Nikkil Sudharsanan, Alejandra Abufhele, and Michael Collins.

I was extraordinarily fortunate to move from a city and a community I adored in Philadelphia and at Penn to the Clayman Institute at Stanford. This was a crucial two years where the dissertation transformed into the book. Here, under Shelley Correll's singular leadership, I had the honor to be part of group of women committed to using sociological research not just to illuminate the stubborn barriers to gender equality—itself a worthy goal—but to devise solutions. My deepest thanks for welcoming me into this community and for being such champions (in every meaning of the word): Shelley Correll, Marianne Cooper, Megan Tobias Neely, Caroline Simard, Lori Nishiura Mackenzie, Alison Dahl-Crossley, Wendy Skidmore, Melissa Abad, JoAnne Wehner, Shannon Gilmartin, Shivani Mehta, Natalie Mason, Jennifer Portillo, Marcie Bianco, Sandra Brenner, Erika Gallegos-Contreras, Karen How, Sara Jordan-Bloch, Sofia Kennedy, Kristine Pederson, Alison Wynn, and Kristine Kilanski.

I imposed the role of intellectual mentor onto Marianne several years before I would even join the Clayman Institute, and it is my luck that she so gracefully accepted it. Marianne's help with developing this book manuscript, from early conversations about my findings to guiding me on the book proposal and reading the manuscript, has been crucial. Megan and I overlapped for one year at Clayman, and while that is a short time, it was enough for us to instate several enriching traditions. My favorite one remains talking sociology over our precariously held wine glasses on the Caltrain from Palo Alto back to San Francisco. It made the otherwise dull journey something to anticipate with excitement. I am deeply thankful for your friendship. The Clayman Institute was truly an idyllic experience where the feminist ethos was translated into a feminist practice. Although I was supported in ways too extensive to recount here, one of the most generous forms of support for this study was my book conference that the Institute hosted. It was an honor—and a joy—to have this work thoughtfully discussed by scholars I so admire. Many thanks to Raka Ray, Myra Strober, David Pedulla, as well as Shelley, Marianne, Alison, and Megan for taking the time to read the manuscript and to engage in a lively discussion on how to chart a way forward for this book.

Life in San Francisco (and before that, Sunnyvale) was immeasurably better because of cherished friendships with Fatma Alam (and our one-and-runs), as well as Dinsha Mistree, Jafar Alam, Vanessa de Conceiçao, Sriram Vaidyanathan, Arvind Chavali, and Juan Pablo. Large sections of this book were written when I lived in a beautiful apartment in San Francisco, where I had not just a room of my own but the whole apartment. My roommates, Diana Yu and Lummi Bae would go off to work each day, and the entire apartment became mine for the writing. Thank you for filling it with plants and light. When I ventured to our rooftop, I had an unobstructed view of the Golden Gate Bridge. This was a gorgeous and peaceful place from where to write parts of the book.

Finally, the last phase of this book's development—the polishing of a manuscript into a book—has taken place halfway across the world from where the study was conducted: in Singapore, at the School of Social Sciences at the Singapore Management University. Here, Chandran Kukuthas and Yoo Guan generously supported the book through a book development grant. Colleagues, particularly Yasmin Ortiga, Ijlal Naqvi, Forrest Zhang, and Ishani Mukherjee have been fantastic in discussing selections of the book, and of course, other pressing matters too! Jancy Poon and Serena Wong smoothed out administrative procedures.

Beyond Penn, Stanford, and SMU, I have had the privilege of discussing this study with scholars whose feedback has shaped this book. Thanks to Ofer Sharone, Rhacel Parreñas, Leslie Salzinger, Julia Behrman, Poulami Roychowdhury Jordanna Matlon, Laurel Westbrook, Savina

Balasubramian, Rosanna Hertz, Marjorie DeVault, Allison Pugh, Arlie Hochschild, David Grusky, Cristobal Young, Kimberly Kay Hoang, and Christine Williams.

I have benefitted tremendously from Audra Wolfe's editorial advice.

Naomi Schneider, my editor, met with me when this book was only a study in its early stages; her support over the years, and especially when I was ready to transform the study into a book has been extremely valuable. At UC Press, I have had the pleasure to work with Summer Farah and Benjy Mailings, who took the time to demystify all that goes into getting a book from a manuscript to press (and after) for this first-time book author. Finally, the illustration for this book was done by Brian Rea, whose whimsical work I have long admired. Thank you for so beautifully capturing the Sisyphean uncertainty that participants in this study encountered.

Thanks to Kartik Nair, Nilanjana Bose, Claire Anderson-Wheeler (my dear, oldest friend!), Pallavi Pinakin, Muliha Khan, Parker Ramey, Imad Khan, Ayat Khan, Jens Jensen, Jens Junaid Jensen, and Thor Hafeez Jensen for your friendship through the years. Thanks to my parents, Asiya and Hamid. My mother has provided unconditional support and exhibited such evident pride in this project, which has been both heartwarming and an important source of encouragement for me.

My biggest cheerleaders through this long journey have been my sister, Alvira, and my dearest friend, Faseeha Khan-Jensen, whom I met when we were still tweens. In recent years, I have not had the pleasure of living close to either of them (or even in the same country), but they have never let space and time difference get in the way of encouraging me and listening to me vent. They have reminded me (when I momentarily forgot) why I was writing this book in the first place. Your love and friendship mitigated my worries during the lows and amplified my joys during the highs of this project.

Thank you.

Introduction

MEET THE BARONS

Todd Baron is a forty-five-year-old marketing manager who has, in the past, worked for candy and cosmetic companies. He is dressed casually in a gray T-shirt and loose black gym shorts. He stands about five feet, nine inches tall, with silver-brown hair, neatly parted on the right. Todd's shoulders stoop as he walks, and while a smile plays at the corners of his mouth, he rubs his index finger nervously against his thumb. His eyes dart around the room. He is friendly, but his rushed manner of speaking suggests a restlessness.

The past five months have been tough for Todd and his family. Todd lost a job he had held for a little over a year. This is the second job loss Todd has experienced in the past four years. His first round of unemployment lasted for ten months, and it dug deeply into the savings Todd and his wife, Kimmie, had amassed. Although Kimmie also works, Todd had been the primary breadwinner in his family, earning a comfortable six-figure salary.

Losing his job was difficult for Todd. There had been rumblings that the candy company was not doing well. Both Todd and Kimmie anticipated

1

that Todd might lose his job. But Kimmie was nevertheless very concerned for Todd when that day finally came. A petite brunette with a face free of makeup, with hazel eyes and long, wavy brown hair, Kimmie knitted her eyebrows as she recounted the telephone call Todd made to her on the day he lost his job, "He was crying. He was upset. I was talking him out of doing something, anything rash ... ending his life or anything like that." Todd was upset, but not as much as Kimmie had initially feared. Still, the past five months have not been easy for them. Todd says, "It's tough sitting alone at home." Todd spends the majority of his time at home, trying to job search so that he can swing back into full employment and the breadwinner role he previously occupied in his family. But staying at home has been difficult, and Todd often feels lonely. He explains, "A good buddy of mine the last couple weeks said, 'Hey, you want to go to lunch?' And I just told him 'I'm tied up.' And I wasn't." Shaking his head, he adds, "I mean, I ate a little sandwich at home." Todd didn't meet his friend for lunch more out of shame than the expense of lunch. He feels that he should be working.

The longer Todd stayed at home, the antsier Kimmie became at his presence. For the first few months after losing his job, Todd weighed his options: he could look for another position, or he could become self-employed by opening up a franchise. He says, "We were looking into the franchise, and I think Kimmie saw that that was getting me a little bit excited." After two months, Kimmie expressed her unease with being in limbo regarding Todd's future earning prospects. Todd says, "I think she stuck with me for the first two months. But she kind of gave me that ulti-matum on New Year's and said 'You've got to stop. We've lost two months. ... Now we're not getting money.'" For her part, Kimmie is reso-lute that Todd should be entirely focused on his job search, with a deeper sense of urgency than she thinks he currently has. She says, "I'm always saying, 'You need to be looking, you need to be looking.' And he's kind of sit-on-his-hands and wait-for-the-other-shoe-to-drop." Kimmie purses her lips into a thin line before continuing, "I'm not a sit-on-my-hands kind of person."

In Kimmie's frustration is a rebuke to Todd: that he is not trying hard enough to find a job. Kimmie recognizes that unemployment is a given in the contemporary world of work; what gnaws at her is her perception of Todd's lackluster effort to find work. She is finding it hard to explain Todd's enduring unemployment as a fact of the contemporary economy; she is beginning to see it as a moral flaw. Todd, according to Kimmie, is not *morally* unemployed, because he is not resolutely focused on job searching.

For Kimmie and Todd, while Todd's job loss was a blow, the more significant experience has been what Todd has done in the months since. From Kimmie's perspective, Todd's priority should be to find a job. Todd agrees with her, but he often finds it difficult to keep searching when he has experienced so many rejections. Sometimes, he does not feel cheerful enough to network—a key aspect of job searching in professional America. At other times, he feels dejected and loses hope that he will ever find a job. On those days, looking for work in the midst of despair seems an impossible task. Yet, for both Kimmie and Todd, the fact that Todd is staying at home is a problem that dominates their marriage and their family life. Todd is ashamed of his unemployment and unable to socialize as he would have previously; Kimmie is worried. For the Barons, Todd's unemployment is a grave problem that needs to be rectified.

MEET THE BROZEKS

Lisa Brozek is a cheerful, athletic fifty-two-year-old. She is so athletic that when we meet, her right arm is in a cast, broken from a martial arts class accident. Her face is scrubbed clean; her cheeks glow pink and her blond hair is tied up in a high ponytail. She smiles widely. She seems relaxed, at ease in the coffee shop where we are meeting, reclining casually on her chair, arm draped around the backrest. She is dressed in a fitted gray zip-up hoodie with a tank top underneath. Her black corduroys are tucked into tan Uggs. Her hands sparkle with jewelry: a large pear-cut diamond on her ring finger and a bracelet of black and white pearls set in silver.

Lisa had been the chief operating officer at a nonprofit. She had spent her entire career in this nonprofit. She started out as a secretary before she even finished college, and worked her way up the ladder, getting a bachelor's degree and eventually an MBA (paid for by the company).

But two years ago, a new CEO instituted dramatic changes that eventually culminated in Lisa losing her job three months ago. Lisa had applied for the position of CEO when it had opened up, but she was passed over in favor of a male outsider. This had hurt Lisa enormously. She thinks that the lingering disappointment of being passed over for CEO in some ways softened the blow of losing her job. Being rejected from the CEO position meant that, as she says, "I've already been in that trench of depression and pain about not being welcome . . . and just getting kind of rejected." Many women in this study, like Lisa, reported that they had felt unwelcome and unfairly treated at their workplaces even before job loss.

Lisa and her husband, Sam, have been married for less than two years. It's the second marriage for both. While Sam and Lisa were dating, and during their marriage, Lisa had been the primary breadwinner, earning a six-figure salary. She also paid for the couple's wedding. Sam Brozek, who has light blond hair that spikes up, a goatee on his ruddy face, and an easy-going smile, is also in his early fifties. He is a self-employed health insurance salesman. In recent years, Sam has been doing well. His income has steadily increased each year, rising from $60,000 the previous year to around $80,000 this year. He anticipates making about $100,000 next year, based on the number of clients whose health care coverage he manages. This is a tremendous change for Sam, who declared personal bankruptcy a decade ago. Nevertheless, at the time of our interview, his income was at about half of Lisa's previous income. Together, the two also own a $200,000 home. Lisa has a savings account with a balance of close to $100,000.

Like any unemployed professional in America, Lisa focuses on networking as part of her job searching strategy. Sam, who dresses casually—usually wearing sweats in the winter and shorts in the summer, unless he has client meetings—explains: "She was trying to network and have coffee with people. Network and find out about jobs and everything. . . . So, that kept her more in the game than anything else. . . . Basically, until she figured out exactly what she wanted, she kept her game up." By "kept her game up," Sam means that Lisa has been diligent about networking. Lisa attributes this to having had lots of support from friends, "My friends have been pretty supportive. . . . We get together. We go to lunch. We go out for drinks." She remains in touch with friends from her previous workplace. Lisa describes these work friends as being unhappy in the toxic environment there, saying: "They're jealous that I don't have to be there. . . . When we go out, they're like, "How are you?" And I'm like, "I'm doing great! How are you guys?" And they're miserable. They're just really unhappy. I feel like the whole dynamic at the [nonprofit] has become a place where people are so unhappy. It's just awful." In contrast to Todd Baron's lonely experience of unemployment, Lisa and Sam both describe hers as being socially rich—she has friends and activities that she is involved in, and her schedule is filled with social and professional appointments. Job searching and networking are important aspects of her life, but neither Lisa nor Sam expect her life to be organized around her job search.

Indeed, Lisa's calendar is full in part because Sam has encouraged Lisa to see her unemployment as an opportunity to figure out how she wants to spend her working life. Sam says: "I've told her, 'If you don't take the time to explore right now, you're never going to have it again and it's going to come back and bite you in the ass. So you take this time . . . to explore . . . because we have money and we have time . . . because if not, you'll be looking back on it the rest of your life and regretting it.'" Lisa, too, explains that Sam's encouragement and support means that "I don't have to leap at anything. I don't have to feel like it's this panic to find a job. . . . And I'm really trying to be careful that I don't get sucked into something that's going to mean more of being unhappy." Lisa and Sam have more of a laissez-faire approach to Lisa's reemployment.

For Lisa and Sam, Lisa's unemployment is not a problem that needs to be rectified, as with the Barons, but rather an opportunity for Lisa to explore a more fulfilling career. Lisa and Sam do not describe Lisa's unemployment in terms that question Lisa's morality. For the Brozeks, that Lisa could opt out of paid work is a viable consideration. Lisa says, "Let's say I started my own . . . shelter for cats. . . . I'm not making any money for a while. . . . And I think Sam would support me in that. . . . We go back and forth about it. And sometimes I'm like, 'No, I have to make money.'" Lisa explains that it's often Sam who pushes her to focus on happiness rather than providing for their family, "Sam's more like, 'Lisa, you gotta do what makes you happy in what you want to be doing. And if that means you take a pay cut to do that . . . then figure that out. To me, it's OK. Whatever you need to do.'"

Sam's support for Lisa is also a way to reassert his masculinity and reclaim the role of the breadwinner. Sam has told Lisa, for example, that

"It's not a big deal. I mean, I work. That's what I do. I work and provide."
Sam frames his economic support of Lisa as his gendered responsibility, as
the man of the house. Lisa echoes this, saying that Sam told her, "'Listen,
I'm going to start making more money, and every year my income's going
to be increased.' It was just, 'Now, *I'll* support you.'" Lisa's unemployment
has become a time when Lisa and Sam reorganize the dynamics in their
family to frame Sam as the primary earner. Her unemployment is not an
ideal situation, but it is not nearly as fraught as Todd's unemployment is
for the Barons.

Why do Todd and Lisa—both the primary earners in their respective
families—have such different experiences of unemployment? Why do
Todd and Kimmie highlight that Todd feels nervous, anxious, lonely, and
that finding a job quickly is paramount for them? In contrast, why do Lisa
and Sam emphasize that Lisa is relaxed, relieved even, to be out of an
unpleasant work situation? Why do the Brozeks explain that Sam supports and encourages Lisa to take the time to explore her options and her
desires, even though it means a considerable cutback in their income?

These questions, all of which essentially ask how professional middle-
class families understand and respond to unemployment, motivate this
book. This book provides a window into the lesser understood, but
increasingly prevalent, phenomenon of unemployment among professionals. What does unemployment look like when it is not mired in poverty? It is my hope that this book will illuminate the delicate negotiations,
self-questioning, and emotional impacts that professionals experience as
they contend with the uncertainties inherent in the current economic
landscape in the United States. As employment insecurity increases,
including for workers who used to be protected from it, and as the cradle-
to-grave job dies its final, inevitable death, we need to understand how
workers and their families contend with it across the economic spectrum.
By focusing on the critical juncture of unemployment—an extreme end of
the spectrum of economic precarity that characterizes labor and employment relations across the board—this account helps us understand how
the status quo of gender inequality at home is reproduced rather than
disrupted. The uncertain labor market does not function in isolation;
rather, workers and their families respond to it. Families have gendered
ideals of marriage and family life that tend to be informed by their racial

and social-class background. As they seek to comply with these ideals, families often afford privileges to unemployed men to facilitate men's participation in this revolving labor market, but not quite to unemployed women.

PRECARITY FOR ALL! PROFESSIONALS CONFRONTING A CHANGING WORKPLACE

Todd Baron and Lisa Brozek are among the millions of Americans who have lost their jobs, or can expect to lose one during the course of their life. Precarity used to be a condition limited to low-wage workers, but it has now become endemic to the organization of work and the American labor market. Of course, precarity looks and feels very different depending on where you are located in the socioeconomic hierarchy; people of different means respond to it through distinctive strategies.[1] For relatively affluent families, such as those in this study, the context of precarity—and the acute instance of unemployment—raises wrenching questions about maintaining their class advantages and, ideally, passing these on to their children. These families are usually not worried about deprivation, since they do not expect that a stint of unemployment will drive them into poverty or homelessness—outcomes that are real possibilities for low-wage workers. Instead, these families are more worried about *relative* deprivation; maintaining their class position and its material and cultural accompaniments as they wrestle with financial downsizing.[2] The responses of advantaged families to their precarity are vested in struggles to sustain their understandings of their own class positions, especially when that class position is threatened. These professionals experiencing unemployment invoke nostalgic ideals of male-breadwinner and female-homemaker families as a class-based response that deploys gendered strategies to affirm their class status. This is an aspirational quest to align themselves with images of familial success at a moment when that success is acutely threatened.

The threat these professionals feel is real: over 92 percent of college-educated men and women can expect to be unemployed at least once during the course of their life. The Bureau of Labor Statistics defines the unemployed as people who "do not have a job, have actively looked for work in the prior four weeks, and are currently available for work."[3] College-educated Americans between the ages of eighteen and fifty experience an average of 4.1 instances of unemployment. But there is variation among groups: White college-educated men experience an average of 3.8 unemployment periods, while Black college-educated men experience an average of 4.9 periods of unemployment over the same lifespan. Both White and Black women experience unemployment more frequently, with an average of 4.2 and 5.7 periods between the ages of eighteen and fifty, respectively.[4] When it comes to deciding which workers to fire or which business units to shut down, management tends to cut job roles and units disproportionately filled with women and minorities.[5] As women and people of color enter certain occupations, those occupations often become devalued, making them more susceptible to layoffs.[6] Since this book draws from a largely White sample, this is a sample that fares somewhat better even under conditions where unemployment has simply become a matter of course for more privileged to more vulnerable groups.

Besides these subtle processes that increase the likelihood that minorities of any gender and women of any race will lose their jobs, bolder patterns of discrimination make it more difficult for these groups to get hired in the first place.[7] Whites continue to have a hiring advantage over Blacks or Latinos. In one field experiment, applicants were given equivalent resumes and then simultaneously sent to apply for hundreds of jobs. The researchers found that Black applicants were half as likely as White applicants to receive a callback or a job offer. Latino applicants with "clean" resumes fared the same as White applicants whose resumes indicated that they had just been released from prison.[8] Employers also discriminate against mothers, as well as potential workers who have stepped out of the workplace for caregiving responsibilities. In practice, this targets more women than men.[9] That being said, research has found that "opting out" for family obligations has starker effects for men than for women, suggesting that men continue to be held more strictly than women to expectations of commitment to work. More generally, employers' hiring practices exclude parents with caregiving responsibilities from the labor force. This has profound ramifications for women's careers, since women in the United States continue to have more family and caregiving responsibilities.

Unemployment has become a prevalent life experience in the United States, permeating the lives of even those workers who, in earlier decades, expected to be protected because of their educational qualifications. But unemployment itself is only the extreme end of labor-market churning, a phenomenon that has characterized the US economic landscape in recent decades. Between the ages of eighteen and fifty, college-educated men now hold an average of 11.4 jobs, while college-educated women hold 12.7 jobs.[10] The duration of jobs is also shrinking. Recent data show that one-third of workers in the middle of their career, those aged thirty-five to forty-four, spent less than a year in any given new job. Three-quarters of jobs end in less than five years.[11]

This form of extreme employment insecurity, even at the higher echelons of work and labor, reached its peak in October 2009. In the midst of the Great Recession of 2007 to 2009, the US national unemployment rate peaked at about 10 percent—more than twice the percentage considered acceptable for a healthy economy.[12] It was the highest unemployment rate in the United States in over twenty-five years. The biggest losers in this recession, as in most recessions and depressions, were noncredentialed workers. Male-dominated industries, such as construction, were especially adversely impacted, leading the popular press to call the Great Recession a "Mancession."[13] But while an increase in unemployment rates during recessions and depressions is nothing new, the Great Recession made clear that no one, not even college-educated workers, was safe.

The Great Recession showed that college-educated workers are now more likely than their counterparts in previous decades to lose jobs.[14] Since the 1970s, the unemployment rate for white-collar workers has increased at a sharper rate than that for less-skilled workers without a college education. When white-collar workers do lose jobs, they tend to be pushed into long-term unemployment, defined as lasting twenty-seven weeks or longer.[15] Some studies have also shown that these workers also face the steepest financial penalties, with most earning less after unemployment than they earned prior to it.[16] Once women lose a job, they experience greater earning losses than men.[17]

The impact of the Great Recession has been vast, solidifying trends in work, employment, and organizations that had been circulating in recent years. Employment practices have shifted decisively from a one life–one career model to greater uncertainty: increases in downsizing, restructuring, outsourcing, and the growth of contract and temporary workers all point to a decline in employment stability.[18] Indeed, these practices have become part of organizations' business models, which have been prioritizing increasing shareholder value above other considerations. This consists of adopting a short-term outlook, including dissolving branches of the business that may be (temporarily) underperforming.[19] Political scientist Jacob Hacker (2006) has called this a "risk shift," where "economic risk has been offloaded by government and corporations onto the increasingly fragile balance sheets of workers and their families."[20] While in earlier decades employers frequently provided a social safety net, often in terms of lifelong careers and associated benefits, now individual workers must manage any risk that they encounter without much government or employer support.

This shift in the employer-employee relationship is the result of a variety of factors, including neoliberal transformations, globalization, and technical change.[21] In her 1977 classic *Men and Women of the Corporation*, Harvard sociologist Rosabeth Moss Kanter describes organizations as operating on the staffing principle that "big is better," which meant greater security for workers, as organizations rarely cut jobs. But in her 1993 afterword to the book, Kanter explains that this principle gave way to the assumption that "smaller is beautiful." As Kanter explains, the shift to a business practice of lean organizations means that "such organizations rely on outsourcing and external suppliers for internal services, and impose overtime and overload on existing staff before adding others."[22]

The diminishing consideration of organizations for their workers means that expectations for worker–employer loyalty are no longer reciprocal. Sociologist Allison Pugh terms this a "one-way honor system."[23] One piece of evidence that workers are committed to their work is that the number of hours that Americans work has increased over the decades, with professionals in particular working exceptionally long hours.[24] But scholars are now questioning whether workers are responding to labor market precarity by shifting their loyalty from specific employers to their broader occupations and industries, perhaps heralding a more individualistic shift as a way of dealing with uncertainty in the economic landscape.[25]

Labor writer Steven Greenhouse explains that workers, including white-collar workers, often get short shrift from their employers under the contemporary organization of work. For instance, the switch from pensions to 401(k)s—which are a defined contribution owned by the worker and contingent on the stock market—represents more precarity for the worker, who is no longer guaranteed an income in retirement, as the more secure pensions had allowed.[26] Many Americans must continue to work beyond retirement to make ends meet.[27] Organizations are also asking workers to do tasks outside of their designated roles and making unpaid overtime work a requisite for maintaining a job (and this work may not even be compensated). For white-collar workers, this might mean a work culture in which workers are expected to be accessible all day, every day, through mobile phones, emails, and other devices; limited benefits packages with the cost of health coverage passed onto workers; and more work for lower wages.[28]

This is the background against which the unemployed men and women in my sample experience unemployment. They live and work in a time when losing a job is not as shocking an event as it once was; it is often expected, even if devastating.[29] Sometimes they have experienced it themselves before, or, at a minimum, seen a friend, spouse, or other family member experience it. They take employment instability as a given of US work culture, and they understand their own experience as being part of it. Yet, the wounds and fractures that unemployment exposes—about self-worth as a worker, about their capabilities as a spouse or a parent, about their role in their community—are raw.

HOW FAMILIES RESPOND TO PRECARITY

Unemployment has become a prevalent experience in American life during this period of late capitalism, something that the bulk of the college-educated population can expect to experience at least once, and usually multiple times. But sociological research continues to treat unemployment as an aberration, an anomalous event. Sociological research has documented the quick pace at which the organization of work is changing, with research spanning the rise of precarity, the gig economy, and the growth of human–artificial intelligence (AI) interactions at work. But how these broad changes intersect with other aspects of social life and institutions, especially workers' personal lives, is little understood.[30] Research on family, especially on more privileged families, has not kept pace with changes in the organization of work that inevitably impact families.

Some recent research has paved the way for conceptualizing how individuals and families, including college-educated workers, respond to the insecurity of work. Sociologist Marianne Cooper shows that in this context of risk, families develop "security projects" through which they seek to protect their families. This emotional management of risk is both classed and gendered. The "upper-class" families in Cooper's study, who are most similar to the participants in this book, respond to economic uncertainty by "upscaling" their needs. As Cooper describes it, these affluent families ratchet up what they need to feel secure, worrying about perfecting their children, aiming only for the top Ivy League universities as acceptable college placements. Even the multimillionaire respondents in her study expressed an acute sense of insecurity. These families bolster their excessive focus on their children's futures through a neo-traditional family organization in which highly educated wives drop out of the labor force (at least until the kids go off to college) to prioritize a close monitoring of their children's education and social and extracurricular development. These families worry that their advantaged class status will be unattainable for their children, and they strive to ward off such a reality. As Cooper explains, risk takes an emotional toll, but rising income inequality and the dearth of social safety nets in the United States means that more privileged families can better manage these risks.

The ether of economic insecurity is especially salient for motherhood. Ana Villalobos argues that in an era of risk in which jobs and relationships dissolve frequently, intensive mothering—a style of parenting where the mother–child bond is culturally prized and expected to take up the mother's emotional energy as well as her time—provides a route for *mothers* to feel secure through this intensive attachment.[31] In *The Tumbleweed Society*, Alison Pugh notes that insecurity at work means that people put extremely high demands on their marriages and personal relationships, erecting a "moral wall" that acquiesces to lower expectations of loyalty at work but amps them up at home.[32]

Taken together, this handful of important studies suggests that economic insecurity, with prevalent unemployment as an extreme manifestation, is a contemporary reality even for affluent American families. Individuals formulate selves that respond to market forces, and specifically to labor-market uncertainty. A variety of subjectivities have emerged in response to the profusion of neoliberal logics in increasing aspects of life; such as selves that are self-reliant, therapeutic, positive, passionate, consciously self-branded, entrepreneurial, and investing.[33] These subjectivities are bolstered, or not, through gendered, class-based strategies in marriages. What happens at home, and the specifics of how market logics reach beyond their ostensible bounds, is instructive for understanding the configuration of gender inequalities in these families. Families in this study, as I show, respond to economic insecurity in ways that sustain gender inequalities.

UNEMPLOYMENT AND FAMILY LIFE

Current understandings of how families respond to unemployment and economic precarity owe an enormous debt to such classic works as Mirra Komarovsky's study of men's unemployment during the Great Depression, the team-based study of the Austrian town of Marienthal, whose population experienced almost total unemployment due to a factory closure during the Great Depression, and Katherine Newman's study of downward mobility in the 1980s.[34] These studies illuminate unemployment as an often emotionally and financially devastating experience. While the unemployed grappled with a profound loss of sense of self, their families, too, evinced deep pain as they reckoned with upended lives and sought to reconstruct new ones. These works provide insights into the gendered meanings that families attribute to both paid and unpaid work—specifically, the power of the ideology of the male-breadwinner.

Several decades later, there is ample evidence that the male-breadwinner ideology continues to flourish. Women still do more of all types of housework than men.[35] In a classic article, Julie Brines finds that breadwinning wives do *more* housework. This finding has been replicated in subsequent studies.[36] Cultural explanations may offer more compelling explanations of this finding than economic ones: The hegemony of the male-breadwinner ideology means that both men and women are flouting gendered expectations when women are the providers. Women do more housework, and men do less, as a way of resetting the gender balance in the home.

Several studies have taken an innovative approach to measuring the power of the male-breadwinner ideology by studying whether couples' division of housework is shaped by men's unemployment. One showed that during unemployment, men's contribution to housework increases by three hours per week, but unemployed women (who are already usually doing more housework than their husbands) do an additional six hours of housework per week.[37] The research on the housework division of labor in terms of race is mixed, with some studies finding a more gender-egalitarian division of labor and others disagreeing.[38] Race is key in shaping different ideologies of motherhood, but does not appear to as conclusively shape the division of labor at home, including during unemployment.

More recent qualitative studies paint a more optimistic picture of couples' attitudes toward paid and unpaid work, including how they cope with job loss. These studies suggest that men's access to new, progressive forms of masculinity means that men no longer experience unemployment as a deep wound to their selfhood. These studies suggest that more gender-egalitarian ideologies may be replacing the older notion of the male-breadwinner and female-homemaker. This is plausible, given that the number of stay-at-home dads has doubled from 1.1 million in 1989 to 2.2 million in 2012. (Although this appears to be explained more by involuntary factors—such as being too ill to work and losing a job rather than choosing to stay at home. In contrast 85 percent of married mothers who stay at home cite caring for the family as a primary reason).[39]

Decades after Komarovsky's and Newman's respective studies, research on how unemployment impacts family life continues to focus on men's unemployment. But given that most women in the United States, including those with young children, work outside the home and contribute an increasing share to the household income, we also need to consider what women's unemployment means for family life. In the United States in

2017, 71.3 percent of mothers with children under the age of eighteen were in the labor force, including 63.1 percent of women with children under three. Close to two million women, or 3.7 percent of the labor force, who were between the ages of twenty-five and fifty-four experienced unemployment in the same year.[40] The impacts of women's unemployment on family life cannot simply be extrapolated from studies of unemployment and theories of economic and emotional stress that have historically centered men's experiences. Nor does existing research fully consider that unemployment now occurs in a risk economy, where it is not just a one-time hurdle to be transcended but is likely a repeated occurrence. These facets of unemployment merit deeper consideration in order to develop a more comprehensive understandings of how families respond to unemployment.

GENDERED IDEALS IN FAMILY LIFE

Sociological research on how families, especially married couples, experience unemployment is typically oriented within a larger body of research that examines work, family, and gender. An underlying theme in this research is how ideals of femininity, masculinity, and parenthood shape how individuals and couples view, and respond to, their unemployment. Culturally dominant ideas of masculinity in America posit economic provision as central to men's roles as husbands and fathers. For women, in contrast, work is often framed as being in conflict with their primary role of motherhood. Ideals of "intensive motherhood," combined with a lack of affordable childcare and workplace hostility to caregiving responsibilities, reinforce this message.[41]

Research also points out that much of existing sociological research on families primarily captures the experiences and values of affluent, White, men and women involved in heterosexual relationships. Several scholars explain how women of color in the United States have integrated their roles as workers with their roles as mothers. Dawn Dow argues that middle-class and upper-middle-class Black women in the United States are less influenced by the ideology of intensive motherhood.[42] They are far more likely to operate within what she calls the "integrated motherhood" model, in which women combine participation in paid work with unpaid work, are financially independent, and expect to draw on kin and community support for caregiving. Given denigrating and controlling images of Black women, the women in Dow's study are extremely concerned about maintaining middle-class respectability through their employment. Paid work is key to, rather than in conflict with, their identity as both women and mothers.

In contrast, the idea that paid work is intertwined with masculinity appears to be consistent across race and class groups in the United States. Some research suggests that affluent, White men, who are especially likely to prize working extremely long hours, are particularly attached to this ideology.[43] The link may not be as strong for other groups of men, particularly those who have a long history of being discriminated against in the US labor market. In a study of Black and White low-income fathers, Kathryn Edin and Timothy Nelson explain that these fathers' fluctuating experiences in the labor market meant that they revised their understandings of providing for their children from economic signifiers to the ability to spend time with and care for them.[44] Other research on low-income families finds some support for these patterns across racial groups.

Ideals of family life in the United States—including the role that each spouse plays in it—are shaped by the blend of aspects of identity, including gender, race, and class. These understandings are important for how couples and individuals respond to unemployment. But these family responses have been minimally understood, even as precarity becomes increasingly common, including in the highest-status occupations. How families' responses to unemployment vary depending on whether the unemployed individual is a husband or wife remains particularly understudied.

THE IDEAL JOB-SEEKER NORM: RESPONDING TO UNEMPLOYMENT IN AN ERA OF INSECURITY

I began this introduction with the Barons and the Brozeks, two families that have responded in distinct ways to the unemployment of one spouse. In this book, I show how professionally similar men and women have sharply divergent experiences of unemployment. The experiences of men and women like Lisa and Todd cannot be explained away by how much the unemployed person earned either in absolute terms or relative to their spouse, by their age, the age of their children, or other such factors that are frequently used to account for gender inequalities at home. Instead, I argue, these different experiences arise from how couples understand who in the family bears the moral responsibility for providing the family's economic security. The income that men and women contribute in these families is not completely fungible; it is assigned different, and gendered, meanings.[45] The meanings assigned to a husband's or wife's income maps onto deeply classed, raced, and gendered expectations about who has the moral responsibility for providing economic security for the family. Couples' understanding of this moral responsibility shapes whether they emphasize or minimize the importance of reemployment for the unemployed spouse as well as whether, and how, couples direct resources to facilitating the unemployed spouse's job search.

The question of how families direct resources to the unemployed spouse is important because job-seeking in white-collar occupations in the United States has become an especially time-consuming and complex web of activities, skills, and personality traits that must be demonstrated to potential employers. Scholars detailing the contemporary world of white-collar job searching have explained that potential workers must demonstrate their devotion to finding a job by networking, working intensively with executive or career coaches (sometimes paying out-of-pocket, other times receiving this coaching as part of their severance package), scouring job boards, paying for job- and skill-related training and certification, and perfecting their résumés. Even basic job applications are time consuming because they require candidates to perform deep research into each job to better demonstrate a "chemistry" with each prospective employer.[46] Collectively, these expectations comprise what I term the *ideal job-seeker norm* (see table 1). The current context of changing work organization and shifting employer-worker relationships, where workers are expected to constantly be in the market for new opportunities, means that the ideal job-seeker norm may apply to many workers, including those who are employed. It is, of course, especially applicable to the unemployed. The ideal job-seeker norm is an expectation imposed primarily by the contemporary labor market.

Table 1	The Ideal Job-Seeker Norm
Characteristics	Devoted to finding work
	Networks extensively
	Works with executive and career coaches
	Spends entire time job searching
	Rebuilds skills/certification
	Works largely from home (except for networking)
Employment conditions	Career trajectories are neither hierarchical nor stable
	Horizontal career trajectories more common
	Devotion to occupation/industry, not to a single employer
Devotion demonstrated	At home, through interactions with spouse
Rewards	
Family	Resources (time, space, money, emotions) directed to job-seeker
Professionally	Receiving an appropriate job

Although seemingly gender neutral, the ideal job-seeker norm is gendered because men are encouraged, expected, and helped in complying with it, while women are not. Compliance with the norm is best possible when other family members also believe that finding a job is important, both financially and in terms of the unemployed family member's sense of self. As I show in this book, an unemployed person's ability to find a job is greatly facilitated by families who support, indeed expect, them to be ideal job-seekers. These families restructure their lives so that the unemployed person—usually a man—can comply with the extensive demands of job searching. Gendered expectations in the family mean that, while men are acknowledged as having a legitimate stake at being an ideal job-seeker, women are not. I argue that men are more able, and more encouraged by their spouse, than women to present themselves as "morally unemployed" persons and thus to access resources—such as time, money, space, and emotions—to facilitate their reemployment. In this study, men gain their moral standing by demonstrating to their wives that they are striving to be ideal job-seekers. Women, in contrast, are far less able to frame themselves as morally unemployed in order to gain similar resources. Instead, women continue to be expected to demonstrate their morality in the realm of domestic rather than paid work. Husbands do not unequivocally encourage their wives' attempts to fulfill the requirements of the ideal job-seekers.

Because this devotion to job searching is *demonstrated at home*, interactions among spouses are key to understanding how the ideal job-seeker norm functions. The ability to claim to be morally unemployed, and thus receive support as an ideal job-seeker, depends on mundane interactions among couples. These interactions are guided by well-understood cultural scripts about how each social actor in a situation should respond.[47] Scholars often refer to this approach as "doing gender."[48] These cultural scripts, as I show, turn on raced and classed ideals that inform gendered expectations. Couples generally lack well-defined scripts for their interactions in uncertain circumstances, such as unemployment.[49] Although social actors—or couples, in this study—could create new scripts to account for their new economic realities, I find that they instead fall into modes of interacting that privilege traditional gender worldviews. These more traditional ideals of family appear to represent aspirational scripts for these couples, who are striving to hold on to their sense of what is symbolically appropriate for their social class, in a context where that social class position is threatened. Throughout this book, I emphasize that couples' interactions are not just the result of preordained beliefs about gender and marriage, but that interactions are crucial to sustaining beliefs and behaviors that end up being far more traditional than the material realities of their lives might otherwise predict.

The concept of the ideal job-seeker as I discuss it here builds upon the related concept of the "ideal worker norm," which has been powerful in explaining how the organization of work is gendered. The ideal worker norm explains that securing stable, well-paying jobs—whether in white-collar work or in blue-collar work—requires workers to demonstrate their commitment to working long hours, working weekends, being able to relocate for paid work, working outside the home, and demonstrating a "devotion" to paid work. As scholar Joan Williams explains, these expectations mean that the implicit ideal worker is understood to be a man who has a wife at home who can free the (male) ideal worker from the brunt of domestic and care work. Couples justify the support that wives provide to the ideal male worker on grounds of the income the worker then earns. In contrast to the ideal job-seeker, who must demonstrate dedication *at home*, the ideal worker shows devotion to work primarily *at paid work*, to superiors and colleagues.[50] The conceptualization of the ideal job-seeker norm illuminates how neoliberal logics, shaped by changes in organizational functioning, permeate the intimate realm of marriage.

A main distinction between the ideal job-seeker norm and the ideal worker norm is the emphasis that the former places on intimate interactions. In the ideal worker norm, institutions of paid work are the key contributors to gender inequalities. The ideal job-seeker norm, in contrast, highlights the role of spousal interactions as a significant driving force in the persistence of gender inequality.[51] The ideal job-seeker norm illuminates how, even in the absence of paid work, the home and family life are structured to comply with the demands of job searching. The intimate realm becomes commodified as a response to the labor market that its members encounter. Men, as I show in this book, are more able than women to adhere to the expectation that they should organize their days around job searching, and more able to protect their time from other tasks. Even when women had been the primary earners before their unemployment, families downplay the importance of women's income and employment.

While some of the men and women profiled in this book often claim to embrace progressive attitudes toward gender and family, in practice, they find it challenging to struggle against traditional expectations of a male-breadwinner. Unemployment is a time of flux. In these dual-earner families, couples with unemployed husbands at home could rewrite gender scripts by embracing stay-at-home fatherhood. Likewise, couples with unemployed women who had been breadwinners could encourage the wife to reenter paid employment. I do not find this. Instead, I find that, in this moment of economic uncertainty, couples do not break out of traditional gender norms. The dominant response is to dig in their heels, recreating gender norms, frequently in defiance of the material realities of their lives. Cultural ideals of the male-breadwinner model prove to be alluring for many of these families, with couples seeing this ideal as the key to maintaining their social status at a time when their social position

Table 2 Sample

	Interviews	Follow-up Interviews	Family Observations
Unemployed men	25	11	2
Wives of unemployed men	13	7	
Unemployed women	23	13	2
Husbands of unemployed women	11	4	
TOTAL	72	35	4

is threatened. Through shared understandings and daily interactions, couples preserve the gender status quo, actively maintaining men's position at the helm of paid work and women's in unpaid work.

THE STUDY

The above argument draws from a deep and unique data set. I conducted in-depth interviews with heterosexual, married, college-educated, unemployed, American men and women who have children (see table 2).[52] About 80 percent of the families in this study are White, with the remaining coming from varied racial and ethnic backgrounds. I also conducted interviews with many spouses of these unemployed men and women. I talked with over seventy people from forty-eight families. Because I talked with many people several times, this book draws from over 110 in-depth interviews. The families were almost evenly split between those of unemployed men and unemployed women. Table 3 contains demographic details, including the age of participants, the length of their marriage, duration of unemployment, household income, and so on.

I focus on this elite sample—as defined by their social class, family structure, and often race—for several reasons. First, while sociological research has been deeply concerned with unemployment and its consequences, the focus has usually been on how unemployment impacts the poor or working classes. This focus made sense in an economy in which

Table 3 Descriptive Data on Unemployed Men, Unemployed Women, and Their Families

	Unemployed Men	Unemployed Women
N =	25	23*
Educational attainment		
Graduate degree	12	19
Bachelor's degree	11	4
Some college	2	0
Age of unemployed individual (years) at first interview		
Median	49	47
Range	37–58	31–61
Annual household income before unemployment (USD)		
Median	150,000	165,000
Range	80,000–500,000	70,000–350,000
Race/ethnicity of unemployed individual		
White	20	19
Black	2	1
Non-White, immigrant citizens	3	3
Duration of unemployment at time of first interview (months)		
Median	6	8
Range	2–13	3 weeks–24

Years married		
Median	17	16
Range	5–27	18 months–40
Spouse's employment status		
Works full-time and earns the same as unemployed individual prior to unemployment	7	6
Works full-time and earns more than unemployed individual prior to unemployment	3	4
Works full-time and earns less than unemployed individual prior to unemployment	10	9
Works part-time and earns less than unemployed individual prior to unemployment	5	0
Unemployed and job searching	0	3

* One unemployed woman declined to provide specific information on household finances, such that some of the figures will add up to twenty-two rather than twenty-three responses.

the middle-classes enjoyed employment stability and economic security, as they did in the United States in the period following World War II. But given the changing economic landscape, in which even the professional classes have started feeling the consequences of economic insecurity, we need to understand how unemployment impacts even those better equipped to cushion the blow. This social class is also significant because higher education and skill levels have traditionally represented the final bulwarks against employment insecurity—but now even this group is feeling the effects of precarity. As people who are generally doing well in American society, these families are also the ones setting social and cultural norms, despite being an empirical minority. They are, as sociologist Pamela Stone (2007) puts it, the "cultural arbiters" who are setting hegemonic parameters for acceptable, perhaps even lauded, ways of organizing family life in the new economy.

Second, there is a dearth of research on unemployed women. I focused on dual-earner families precisely so that I could compare the families of unemployed men and unemployed women, without running into cases that cannot be appropriately compared to each other—for example, how unemployment is experienced in a male-breadwinner home versus in a home led by a single mother. A comparison such as that would not be particularly illuminating for understanding gender norms in marriages.

Finally, the affluence of my sample often shields its members from the worst material impacts of unemployment. These families are primarily concerned with maintaining their social-class status and their privilege, rather than survival, in the wake of economic threats. The symbolic work that connotes their class status is important. Understanding how these families respond to unemployment provides insights into the ramifications of economic precarity at the top of the income distribution. Indeed, their responses to unemployment may contribute to sustaining high income inequality, even in a context of precarity for all.

I spent hours talking with each participant, individually, about their experiences with unemployment. I inquired about their education and career history, about how the process of losing their most recent job unfolded, how they felt about it, how it shaped their relationship with their spouse, children, and extended family and friends. I led our conversations, often held over cups of coffee or over lunch or dinner, into probing how these unemployed individuals spent their time, including how activities such as housework or job searching featured in their daily schedule. In short, my aim was to get a deep sense of what it felt like to be unemployed.

I conducted interviews with spouses separately, because I aimed to get the most transparent replies. For this sensitive topic of unemployment, this was the correct choice. As I note in the methodological appendix, this does not mean that I always got transparent responses—participants were performing for me, as a social actor with whom they interacted. In my interviews with spouses, I asked what their husband's or wife's unemployment had been like for them. I was trying to get a multifaceted picture of how one partner's unemployment is experienced in the family, keeping in mind that different family members might have significantly different experiences.[53] I also spoke with a few of the children of my participants to gain their perspective.

Six months to a year after the first interview with participants, I went back and interviewed them again. Unemployment is a particularly time-sensitive experience, and there can be significant differences between how unemployment feels in the first month and how it feels many months later. In these follow-up interviews, I sought to understand how family members' perspectives and feelings about their experience with unemployment had evolved.

Finally, I conducted "intensive family observations" with four of these families.[54] In two families the women were unemployed—these were the families of Darlene and Larry Bach and Rebecca and Chuck Mason. In the other two, men were unemployed. These were the families of William and Shannon Smith and Robert and Laura Jansson. In keeping with sociological practice, all names of participants in this book are pseudonyms. I hung out with each family for two weeks (in one case, three weeks), usually visiting them daily for an average of four hours per visit. I completed at least fifty hours of observations with each of the four families over the course of these weeks. I ate lunches and dinners with them, attended birthday parties and went on trips to the zoo, library, and grocery stores, helped paint a house, and went on an in-state road-trip with one family. Hanging out with families gave me greater insight into how a spouse's unemployment shaped the daily rhythm of family life, the conversations that couples had with each other, and how they discussed unemployment with their children, friends, and other family members.

This book draws on these interviews and observations that I collected over the course of three years. As I detail in the methodological appendix, because I encountered a range of experiences—with some couples coping far better than others—I can be reasonably certain that this study was not biased toward capturing only those couples who were weathering unemployment well or poorly. While the book is based on this larger sample, in presenting my findings, I purposefully zoom in on one family that is illustrative of broader patterns or, where appropriate, represents an exceptional case in this study. This is so that the reader does not get lost in the detail of who is who, and who said what when. It is also my hope that presenting the data in this way will give the reader a deep sense of what life is like for these unemployed individuals and their families. My hope is that this book adds to our understanding of what unemployment looks and feels like on a daily basis, for this social class.

ORGANIZATION OF THE BOOK

I start this book by meeting unemployed men and women when they are weeks, months, and sometimes even years, into their unemployment. But often, worries about losing a job had started well before the job loss itself. In part 1 of the book, I examine how the space of the home becomes a gendered site of contention for unemployed men, but a haven for unemployed women. In chapter 1, I delve into the cases of two families of unemployed men to show how wives play a crucial part in encouraging husbands to comply with the ideal job-seeker norm, with men's being at home becoming a source of tension for some couples but not others. In chapter 2, I delve into the cases of unemployed women to show how spousal interactions nudge women away from the ideal job-seeker norm. This is the dominant experience that unemployed women in my sample faced. But I also examine a case of a woman who feels uneasy at home. I thus explain the variation that women, but not men, experience in terms of staying at home.

In part 2 of the book, I look at the gendered organization of time around job searching. In chapter 3, I explain how daily interactions among unemployed men and their wives shape the tenor of their relationship. For some couples, men's unemployment becomes a time where they become closer and more bound together. In these cases, husbands and wives work together to enable husbands to comply with the ideal job-seeker norm. Others struggle more, and the ideal job-seeker norm looms unpleasantly over their interactions. Interactions are crucial in consolidating gender-normative responses, which privilege men's employment above all else. In chapter 4, I look at unemployed women. In contrast to the situation with unemployed men, the husbands in these marriages mostly dismiss the idea that women's time needs to be protected for job searching. For the most part, wives do not insist that their time should be protected either. I then delve into two variations: one of a woman who behaves like an ideal job-seeker and another of a woman who does not, but whose husband wishes she would.

In part 3 of the book, I focus on the division of housework. In chapter 5, I consider a question that continues to hover over researchers studying paid and unpaid work among couples: why don't unemployed men do more housework? I present two case studies of families, through which I show how the ideal job-seeker norm protects men's time from housework. Interactions among spouses convey to men that they are not responsible for housework, despite being unemployed. But I also show how and when men are more likely to do more housework. In chapter 6, I assess unemployed women's approach to housework, asking why women, who already do the majority of the housework, take on even more during unemployment. I also consider cases of women who do not take on more housework. These cases, like those of unemployed men who do more housework than the norm, illuminate more gender-egalitarian possibilities when it comes to sharing equally in parenting and providing. The conclusion ends by considering some of the implications of the ideal job-seeker norm for broader inequalities.

PART I

Gender and Space During Unemployment

1 Men at Home

"No man, I'm sorry to say, no man needs to stay at home."

—Emily Bader, wife of an unemployed man

After job loss, the most pressing question concerning unemployed men and their wives is: what next? Unemployment raises the mundane, but critical, question of how men should interact with the space of the home. Is their staying at home considered an anomaly? And how do couples seek to resolve this anomaly? Do the scripts available to stay-at-home moms become available to these unemployed men too?

In this chapter I show that husbands and wives sometimes argue over and other times agree on how men should relate to the space of the home. These negotiations are deeply shaped by the vision of the ideal family that couples hold. At the heart of this vision is often an obsolete—and short-lived—idea of the perfect American family. This ideal family is White, suburban, with two married parents and their children. A wife who focuses on the home and a husband who is able to provide round out this sepia-toned picture. My study participants often laughed nervously when invoking this image. They self-consciously distanced themselves from it. Of course, such a caricatured image does not do justice to the realities of the families in this study. The lives of families in this study have been buffeted by economic setbacks such as the Great Recession, which devastated the savings of many participants. Often, the current bout of unemployment itself was one that followed close on the heels of a prior one. But despite the distance between their own life trajectories and this 1950s touchstone, these couples overwhelmingly evoked these scripts as they contended with men's unemployment, and especially as they tried to figure out what unemployed men should do at home.

I draw on two case studies, Jim and Amelia Radzik, and Terry and Sandy Clarke, to explore this dynamic. Both are dual-earner White families in which the husbands are unemployed. In the case of the Clarkes, Terry has typically earned substantially more than Sandy. In the Radzik family, on the other hand, Amelia's employment and income have been the mainstay. Nonetheless, interactions between the spouses of both couples hinge upon the importance of the husband's reemployment because their family ideal centers on the husband's being able to provide. But this ideal is possible for these families only because White professional men in America continue to be among the best remunerated, in the highest echelons of public and corporate employment, and are the most likely to amass salaries that allow them to be the primary providers.[1] This ideal is more attainable for this sample of families than it would be for most other American families.

I explain how the two families in this chapter have distinctive ways of configuring men's presence in the space of the home. Amelia Radzik is fatigued by Jim's history of fluctuating employment, fearful of downward economic mobility, and worried about his mental health. She finds Jim's presence at home troubling for all these reasons. She responds by emphasizing to him that he is like a *trespasser in his own home*—a body that does not belong there and is infringing on the home. In "The Problem of Jim at Home," Amelia insists that Jim needs to be outside the house to prove himself as an ideal job-seeker. In contrast, Sandy and Terry Clarke both agree that Terry can most effectively become an ideal job-seeker by being at home. In "A Room of Terry's Own," they emphasize how staying at home enables Terry to be exceptionally effective at job searching.

These opposing strategies of framing White, professional men's relationship to the home are two sides of the same coin. Couples emphasize that men need to first and foremost focus on reemployment. Because paid employment has been so central to notions of respectability in White, professional families, cultural scripts for how these men should relate to the home when unemployed are few and vague. Couples work to sustain a gendered organization of the home—tied as this is to race and class-based ideals—through their daily interactions around the management of the men at home.

THE PROBLEM OF JIM AT HOME

At five feet, nine inches, with neatly parted chestnut hair that reveals glints of gray, Jim Radzik dresses in business casuals: black slacks, a crisp Oxford shirt and a dark brown sports coat. On his left wrist, he wears an imposing watch with a gleaming face and a polished leather strap. He exudes an air of confidence and gregariousness; you could see him gently taking the lead in a business meeting. But, on the Thursday morning when I meet him at a café near his home, Jim is not at work. In fact, he has not worked for pay a single day in the past year. A marketing professional, Jim is unemployed. His wife, Amelia Radzik, is extremely bothered by Jim staying at home.

Jim and Amelia are a White couple in their late forties. They have two children, a daughter who is about to start graduate school and a high school–aged son. The Radziks are encountering an obstinate difficulty: The Problem of Jim at Home. The problem, quite simply, is that the couple cannot decide how Jim should behave at home—or whether he should even be there. Amelia insists that Jim needs to "get out of the house." Although Amelia's $200,000 annual income has formed the financial foundation of their family for over a decade, both Jim and Amelia agree that they *need* Jim's income. Amelia additionally resents that the onus to provide an income for their household is squarely on her shoulders.

There are two contradictions embedded in the Problem of Jim at Home. First, Jim doesn't actually spend that much time *at* home, and second, the Radziks' financial situation does not suggest any urgency for income that Jim can provide. So where does this deep belief that Jim does not belong at home come from? How does it shape how the Radziks traverse the terrain of Jim's unemployment?

The Cultural Context of Men Staying at Home

In recent years, it has become more culturally acceptable for men in the United States to stay at home. The pervasiveness of economic precarity has seeped into the social consciousness enough so that short periods of men staying at home no longer cause raised eyebrows. Norms around parenting are also becoming more egalitarian. The gender gap in time spent with children is narrowing.[2] The number of fathers who stay at home, especially with young children, doubled from 1.1 million in 1989 to 2.2 million in 2012.[3] Despite these shifts, staying at home remains a relatively rare and unusual choice for men.

Sociologist Allison Pugh notes how working-class stay-at-home dads are often commended for being progressive, yet these dads often feel irritated that acquaintances don't understand that they are not making a choice, but just making the best of a bad situation.[4] For White, professional men, social status is deeply linked to employment status.[5] Staying at home starkly disrupts this ideal of the gainfully employed man, which is particularly important for these men. Staying at home for men continues to be unique enough that unemployed men and wives do not have cultural scripts to guide them. Cultural scripts provide a framework for how individuals should interact with each other in social relationships as varied as those between casual romantic partners, erotic workers and their clients, doormen and tenants, nannies and their employers, and birth surrogates and parents.[6] Interactions occur within the broad framework of cultural scripts. Flouting them can be socially problematic.

The absence of a cultural script for these men staying at home raises an interactional quandary for unemployed men and their wives: How should unemployed men be expected to relate to the space of the home? Should the relationship remain as it was when men were employed? Should it shift—and if so, how? Should it resemble the relationship that their wives have with the home? For affluent, White families, the home itself has historically been a feminized domain, often in terms of the imagined home-as-haven.[7] The work that goes into keeping up a house, such as the cleaning, decorating, and cooking that goes into reproducing the home, has been managed by White women in their families.[8] Affluent families often outsource this labor, in the past to Black domestic workers and now more commonly to immigrant women.[9] The presence of unemployed men at home, particularly when their wives are employed, turns this cultural script on its head. It is in this new and unscripted context that these unemployed men and their wives negotiate the space of the home.

In social contexts without well-defined cultural scripts, individual actors have two main choices: innovate and produce *new* cultural scripts to match new realities, or resist innovation by falling back on existing scripts, even when those scripts may be misaligned with new realities.[10] In navigating the space of the home, the families of unemployed men in my sample overwhelmingly fall back on, and actively reproduce, tropes vested in gendered, raced, and classed imagery of what a home is, who belongs in it, and the roles that men and women occupy within the home.

How Much Time Does Jim Actually Spend at Home?

Since his unemployment, Jim doesn't actually spend that much time *at* home. He proudly explains, "I had four hundred twenty-nine networking meetings between March eleventh and December first."[11] Jim averaged more than one networking meeting a day. On the day that I first met Jim, after meeting me for several hours, he went on to a networking meeting as well as another appointment later. He would get home shortly before Amelia would arrive back home from her job. Jim's pride in his networking capacity is blunted by Amelia's dismissal of it. He says, "She has no idea that I'm now perceived as an expert on networking and have been asked to speak seven different times on the topic."

But Amelia actually does have a good sense of how Jim spends his days—she just interprets his extensive networking differently. Amelia says, "So, he does a ton of networking. I mean, I've never seen anybody go to more breakfasts, lunches, and dinners, and networking meetings and events." When Jim and Amelia discuss his career, Amelia counsels him, pointing out that "There's gotta be a different avenue." She is quite skeptical of the industry around job searching—including networking. In this, Amelia's skepticism mirrors that of scholars who have described the emphasis on networking as leading unemployed Americans to see themselves as morally flawed because they do not find new jobs quickly. The focus on the self obscures the focus on the broader economic context which produces unemployment in the first place. These scholars describe the industries around job searching that have cropped up as profoundly exploitative.[12] Since Jim has been unemployed for a while, Amelia thinks the advice to increase how much he networks is incorrect, saying "You know, the definition of insanity, right, is doing the same thing over and over and expecting a different result." For Amelia, Jim's networking is busy-work. It is unproductive because it has not yielded the desired outcome: a job for Jim. Amelia and Jim also point to the well-documented issue of age discrimination. Both are aware that Jim's age, as he nears fifty, makes him an expensive hire from an employer's perspective, and they are worried that the longer he is unemployed—and the older he gets—the less likely it becomes for him to find a job. In this, the Radziks echoed the concerns of other couples in this sample, where the unemployed individual was aged over forty.[13]

Amelia is aware that while unemployed, Jim actually doesn't spend much time *at* home—certainly not enough to warrant a Problem of Jim at Home. Yet, the time that Jim does spend at home is problematized, especially by Amelia, in explicitly gendered terms. One of the things that bothers Amelia about Jim's unemployment is her perception of his eagerness in waiting for her to return home from work each day. Amelia says, "Sometimes I feel like he's a puppy dog waiting at the front door 'til I come home going, 'OK, she's home! *Now!*' I'm like, 'Leave me alone.'" Amelia compares Jim's behavior with that of wives in the oft-invoked ideal of a post–World War II, White, suburban, 1950s family. In this ideal, wives planned their days around their husbands, often greeting them with a cocktail as soon as they arrived home from a long and difficult day at their job. This was often not an ideal for the housewives themselves.[14]

In her classic book *The Feminine Mystique*, Betty Friedan described the phenomenon of educated, White women staying at home and focusing on the domestic as "the problem that has no name"—a deep existential problem of meaning, ennui, and belonging that plagued the same White, suburban housewives who were supposed to relish the domestic.[15] Amelia somewhat similarly interprets Jim's staying at home as a disconcerting experience for him because he does not know how to occupy his time. But it is also uneasy for her, since she perceives Jim to depend on her for social interactions.

Most of the families in this sample, like the Radziks, live in affluent, largely White neighborhoods. The Radziks live in a three-bedroom, two-and-a-half-bath, suburban home. It is smaller than the grand four-thousand-square-foot house on an acre of land they had owned over a decade ago and sold as Jim's employment fluctuated, but it's still a big house. The spacious homes of the families in this study are often surrounded by an equally spacious yard. The streets of the neighborhoods they live in are pristine, lined with leafy trees. The calm and serenity of their neighborhoods is punctuated by the bustle of its residents only at set times during the day: when the school bus drops off children and when professionals return to their homes starting around six o'clock in the evening, filling up the driveways that had previously been empty. These neighborhoods are designed to allow space between neighbors, rather than familiar proximity. The contact the unemployed men in this study had with their neighbors was generally limited to a wave or a quick nod if they saw each other in the street.

The isolation in American society may mean that Americans "bowl alone," but this isolation is not evenly spread: women still talk with and confide in more friends on a daily basis than do American men.[16] American men often identify their wife as their closest friend, while wives tend to have several friends they lean on.[17] Sighing deeply, Amelia tells me, "It's like, I come home at night and he's like, 'OK, so, how was your day?' And I'm just, like, I just want to be by myself for ten minutes!" As is common in professional jobs, Amelia works extremely long hours and is exhausted by the time she gets home.[18] Her role also includes constant interaction with people; she craves some time by herself when the evening comes around. Jim has far more free time, and despite his networking, he does not interact with people as much as Amelia does in the course of a day. This contrast in their situations means that Amelia is frequently frustrated at her husband's dependence on her for companionship. She pits her own independent interests against his dependence: "I'm involved with a couple of organizations, and I've got a big crocheting event this weekend. And I was working on it last night, and he's like, 'Come sit with me.' And I'm like, "I'm working on my crocheting.' And he's like, 'Come sit with me.'. . . So, there's that definite need for understanding that I need my space and my time." Tellingly, Amelia's description of Jim's lack of occupation—not just of paid work, but of what to do at home—echoes the ennui of the White suburban housewife. To underscore this, Amelia adds, "So, it's almost like the stay-at-home mom but now it's the stay-at-home dad and the mom's out working." Understood in this manner, Jim's staying at home becomes an unenviable, and stigmatized, reality.

Amelia talks in terms of Jim as an additional child for whom she now bears responsibility. Jokingly, she explains that when their son was making a list of colleges to apply to she told him, "Don't go away to school, because I can't be Jim's friend, 24/7." Jim's unemployment has been emotionally difficult for the Radziks. For both Jim and Amelia, this is partially due to the fact that they are uncertain about what Jim should do while he is unemployed and at home; it is ambiguous territory for them. Amelia's response during this bout of unemployment is to deadpan her way through it. For the Radziks, this is just one period of unemployment in a professional career where Amelia has seen Jim being carelessly tossed about by an unkind and unpredictable labor market that is slowly, but surely, corroding his sense of self. Jokingly, Amelia explains that she often calls her daughter, who is away at graduate school. "There's times when I'll call my daughter and I'll be like, 'Your child is driving me nuts.'" Amelia has decided to turn this emotionally challenging time, one that many would view as tragic, into a more lighthearted one. She continues, "That's what I call him: 'her child.' Right?" Laughing, she continues, "And she's like, 'He's driving me nuts, too.' I say, 'Well, it's your turn to babysit. I can't babysit anymore. Like, can I send him to you for the weekend?'" Venting in this way to her daughter, the Problem of Jim At Home becomes, at least temporarily, a shared concern, somewhat stripped of its darker undertones.

Despite these attempts at breeziness toward their situation, there is a disconnect between Amelia and Jim as they try to reconcile the demands of her paid work and his enduring unemployment. This limits their intimacy too. Speaking about their sex life, Amelia refers to her busy schedule, saying that she defiantly tells Jim, "If I don't want to be intimate with you, guess what? I'm not going to be.'" She explains that "we cuddle at night . . . but [sex] we've put on the backburner." For Amelia, part of their differences in sexual desire are directly linked to her perception that Jim has far more time than she does.[19] She says, "You've been waiting. . . . I'm tired. I've had a long day." Jim's staying at home looms over the Radziks, mediating the minute and intimate aspects of their lives.

Often, Amelia has direct conversations with Jim in which she tells him some variation of, "'You have to do something. . . . I don't even care if you go to Lowe's and do spring cleaning for them. I don't care what. You need something now.'" As we will see later, Amelia's response is also motivated by concerns for Jim's mental health. To encourage him to find a way to occupy his time, besides networking, Amelia took a drastic step: she recently gave Jim an ultimatum to get out of the house: "I said to him, I said, 'I don't care what you do, but you've got to do something by July first. I'm done. I'm done being the nice one. . . . You have 'til July first to figure it out; otherwise you're gonna work at McDonalds. Because I'm done. Like, I don't want to hear it's gonna cost you more to go work at McDonalds. No, I'm done. You're getting out of the house.'" Jim's presence at home, for a web of reasons, is discomfiting for Amelia. To address this, she suggests that he take up any available job, including one far below his professional credentials.

Jim finds Amelia's ultimatum troubling and counterproductive to his goal of looking for a professional position:

> Oh, that was hard to hear. And it was always a point of contention because I would say to her, "Alright, so let's say I get a job at Home Depot or Lowe's or whatever and I'm making ten dollars an hour. Is my time better spent at Home Depot making ten bucks an hour or looking for a job with a base salary of a hundred sixty [thousand dollars]? Am I better off working on my résumé or working at Home Depot? Am I better off taking a nap to get rested up for all my networking than making ten bucks an hour?'

His cheeks flushed red, Jim pauses for a breath. Jim has a clear idea about the kind of job he deserves. He expects his expertise to be acknowledged and rewarded in the labor market. But Jim's sense of an appropriate job for himself is specific to his race, class, and gender location. The labor market does not mete out rewards equally for paid work. Factors like race, social class, gender, and sexual orientation matter tremendously for who gets rewarded in the labor market. Research repeatedly shows that equally qualified women earn less than men, even in comparable jobs, but also that equally, or more highly, qualified women are often passed over in favor of men for prestigious jobs.[20] Both Jim and Amelia assume that Jim can get a well-paying job; they may not have had this assumption if it were Amelia who was unemployed. Their home has become an especially feminized space, both in how Jim and Amelia organize the space and how they think about who belongs in it. In many ways, Amelia and Jim are now working hard to create a family form that has not been their own reality for the past decade. This preoccupation with Jim needing to be out of the house is unusual for several reasons, including the fact that he doesn't actually spend that much time there. Equally puzzling is Amelia's insistence that their family needs his income.

Fears of Downward Mobility Push Men Out of the House

Amelia's income and her health and retirement benefits from her high-level managerial position form the financial backbone of the Radziks' lifestyle. Women from the professional and managerial social classes, like Amelia, are more likely than other women to maintain continuity in their careers. That being said, wives earn more than their husbands in a little over a quarter of heterosexual, married families.[21] Demographically speaking, Jim and Amelia's earning dynamics are more egalitarian than typically found in American marriages, including within their social class. Yet Jim and Amelie imbue with meaning his unemployment and staying at home belies the realities of their financial set-up. Their interactions are guided by their understanding that Jim's not providing economically to his family is highly unusual. In their specific context, where White men accrue greater rewards for their educational credentials and tend to earn more than women; staying at home is an anomalous behavior that requires some appropriate explanation.

Amelia's income, Jim explains, "doesn't support our lifestyle, but it provides a baseline." This statement might seem perplexing, as Amelia's sole income is almost four times the median US income of a household of four.[22] But Jim is not comparing his family to the millions of Americans who have a lower household income. Instead, he is comparing his family's financial situation to people in their social circle. For them, the "baseline" of their lifestyle includes a home in a wealthy suburban area, paying for two children's college education, planning on helping at least one out with graduate school expenses, and annual domestic and international vacations. They also have considerable other assets, such as a beach house, stock options, and retirement savings. Jim and Amelia see potential income from Jim as important to maintaining these aspects of their life, including ensuring that their children, too, maintain their class position.[23]

Although Jim's income has seesawed for the past decade, he continues to emphasize that his erstwhile income was essential, as it was often higher than Amelia's during the period he was employed. This "norm" did not hold with any consistency for the last decade. But Jim focuses on a time, now elusive, when he earned more than Amelia. Jim and Amelia compare what once was—even if for a brief period of time—to what now is. Jim suspects that Amelia is especially focused on this, "I'm sure she thinks that when I get my job that our lifestyle will return to what it was." Jim and Amelia are engaging in what sociologist Viviana Zelizer terms "earmarking"—or "creating distinctions among the uses and meanings of existing currencies."[24] Jim earmarks his income, not Amelia's, as providing the rightful financial backbone for their family. Amelia's considerably more stable income is downplayed as being insufficient for the lifestyle that the Radziks *ought* to have.

Their fears of downward mobility, that they will have to compromise significantly on their lifestyle, is based on this comparison to what they once thought they could afford and what others around them seem to be able to easily afford. Fully aware that what is a necessity for them is a luxury for most, Jim thoughtfully says, "You know, it's funny what you consider to be necessities in life. For us, a necessity has always been somebody to come in and clean the house." Amelia echoes this sentiment saying that what she needs to feel financially secure are what she categorizes as small luxuries: "As long as I can have my cleaning lady come, I can go get my nails done, I can get my hair done, I can go shopping, I'm OK." For most people these are unaffordable luxuries even at the best of times. In Jim's and Amelia's social world, these are some of the standards of life. But being able to maintain your standard of living is a powerful psychological requirement: in terms of mental health and overall well-being, fears of downward mobility matter. Research shows that financial downfalls, such as experienced during unemployment, have adverse impacts on physical and mental health when they also lead to a loss of social class status, or downward mobility. In terms of well-being, especially mental health, these impacts are, counterintuitively, worse for more affluent individuals and families because external shocks— such as the loss of a job—are a more anomalous experience. The disadvantaged, ironically, can weather such events with somewhat more alacrity since they tend to experience such shocks as a part and parcel of their life.[25]

Amelia and Jim have combined all of their finances and bank accounts. As Amelia describes it, "It's all one big happy pot." She adds that the financial management is Jim's responsibility, "I let him manage the money. He's better at it than me." Historically, middle-class White couples have treated women's money as "pin money" or the "cream" to the main income brought in by the husband.[26] Couples have different ways of managing money; but in one study almost 70 percent of respondents agree that couples should integrate at least some of their resources. A dominant belief is that individuals within a couple should pool some resources, but maintain some independently.[27] During times of crisis, such as declaring bankruptcy, the work of money management often falls to women as men cite being too disturbed and worried by the state of their financial affairs to make smart decisions.[28] On the whole, the management of money burdens women and provides power to men.[29] In the Radzik home, Jim and Amelia pool their funds and Jim both manages and controls their money.

In practice, this means that Amelia has less knowledge than Jim of how his unemployment impacts their finances. She continuously expresses her worries about their finances to Jim. Jim says, "If you ask my wife if we've cut back, she would say, 'Absolutely.' And I say, 'That's a farce.'" Although dissatisfied with their primary reliance on Amelia's income, Jim is adamant that his management of their assets means that they have not had to suffer lifestyle changes. He prides himself on being financially savvy and on having mitigated the worst financial impacts of his unemployment through his careful investing.[30] Jim explains, "We've been using stock options [for the past three years] to supplement her income. I've done different financial tricks to supplement the money that we need while the kids are in college." Taking a deep breath, he recounts, "Last year we went to Mexico. The year before we went to Mexico. This year we're going to Mexico. We're going to New Orleans in May. In June we're taking the kids to Europe for two weeks." Shaking his head, as though responding to Amelia's worries, he adds for emphasis, "I've been out of work a year!"

Despite Jim's assurances that financially they are still fine, Amelia can't help but worry. She says, "Jim will say, 'You think our lifestyle's changed by me not working, but it really hasn't. Like, we still go on a vacation; we're going on a vacation over the summer with the kids.'" Pursing her lips and reflecting for a few seconds she says softly, "But, there's still that voice. You know, like, I just got an award at work that came with four thousand dollars. And I'm like, 'Oh, maybe I'll buy myself something.'" In line with scripts that have historically framed gendered roles in couples as "Mr. Breadwinner" and "Mrs. Consumer," Amelia explains how Jim, who manages their finances, responded: "And Jim's like, 'No, we're gonna use that to pay for our vacation.'[31] And I'm like, 'But we were paying for the vacation before we knew about this, so why would we have to use that? Let's put that aside for something special.'" These may seem like small worries, but for Jim and Amelia whether they can support their children through college and take an international vacation are the very essence of what it means to belong in the social class in which they've raised their family. A recent incident is fresh in Amelia's mind as proof of their lifestyle change, "We have a couple friends and they're very successful. And they want to go do lavish things. Like, they're all turning fifty; they want to go do a 'guys' weekend somewhere. Then they changed it to a couples' weekend, and our friend says, 'We found this comedian and we found this really good package deal at this hotel.'" Jim and Amelia own a beach home eight miles from the hotel in question. Amelia told Jim, "'I'm staying at my own house for free. They have the money. I'm not spending three hundred dollars a night when I have a house eight miles away—just ain't happening.'" Although adamant that this particular weekend would have been far out of their budget, Amelia softens, adding, "From a man's perspective, he wants to be able to do that stuff." For the Radziks, there is a quiet ache in giving up some markers of their affluence.

Fears of being unable to afford what makes their life *their* life have consequences for Amelia. At a restaurant near their home, after ordering a small salad with dressing on the side, Amelia turns to me, explaining her choice of meal, "I've gained a ton of weight since he's been unemployed." When I ask why, she is forthright, "Stress. That's it. I mean, I work out. I try to watch what I eat. They always say stress increases your weight, and I truly believe it." It is in this context of the Radziks' financial expectations and aspirations that Jim's unemployment and Amelia's insistence on pushing him out of the house and toward paid employment are best understood.

Income inequality in the United States is high and deeply linked to racialized processes. The families at the top of the income distribution tend to disproportionately be White. Indeed, White Americans often start out with an initial wealth advantage that widens over the life course.[32] The families in this sample, like the Radziks, have been the beneficiaries of this inequality. Yet objective realities and subjective fears often don't align. In a study of insecurity, sociologist Marianne Cooper finds that it was the wealthiest of families, worth in the millions of dollars, who experienced the greatest sense of emotional insecurity, or, as Cooper put it, whose fears about financial security were "scaled up." These fears may be vested in a hidden sense of entitlement that the world is shifting to remove privileges that had been a given. These fears and concerns form the backdrop for how the Radziks and others like them make sense of men's unemployment. By continually emphasizing downward mobility, couples frame unemployed men's income as indispensable. Consequently, men's staying at home becomes an entirely undesirable anomaly. Rather than producing new cultural scripts about men's relation to the home, couples reproduce scripts about the peculiarity of men at home, even in cases such as the Radziks' where this reproduction of gender norms is at odds with the enduring financial setup of the household.

What Will the Neighbors Think?

But of course, this production of a gendered home is drawing on cultural scripts in a specific social context. Despite Jim's unemployment, his family's affluent lifestyle is a far cry from how Jim grew up in a Jewish, blue-collar family, where his father, a salesman with an unsteady income, was the sole provider. He grew up, as he says, "very, very poor." Money was always a source of conflict between his parents. Jim recalls a jarring tension between his mother's persistent desire to "live an upper-middle-class lifestyle" with the reality of their lives. For the last three years of his parents' marriage, when Jim was in his early teens, "the electricity was being shut off, the telephone was being shut off. On-and-off food stamps. We had nothing. It was a very difficult time financially."

Professionally and socioeconomically, Jim has moved far away from his childhood experiences: he was the only member of his family to attend college, and then got a full ride to graduate school for an MBA. According to Jim, he experienced early success by being sought out for a large conglomerate's Marketing and Research department and being rapidly promoted. Jim perceives his unemployment in this context of upward mobility, material achievement, and ostensible financial security. He says, "It was hard for me to admit that I felt like I was not a success."

Amelia, too, thinks that unemployment and staying at home deeply impact Jim because, "He probably wonders what our kids think of him not working, because he had a dad that didn't work." Success for Jim means being able to support his family in a way that his own father was unable to. Depending entirely on Amelia's income damages Jim's sense of self. Amelia adds, "I think he wants to support his kids. I think he feels bad that he can't do more for the kids because he's not working." Implicit in this ideal of success—as a worker and as a father—are realities that have primarily been the arena of the affluent, where parents expect to provide children with a plethora of educational, enrichment, and other experiences.

Jim would much rather be employed, not just to contribute to his family, but also because paid work accrues social status. He frankly says, "Who I was professionally became a big part of my persona. You know, being able to tell people I was the marketing director or the global marketing director—that really played into my ego, the fact that we lived in this prestigious neighborhood." Jim still compares his upward mobility to his childhood. While he is proud of the distance he has come, he fears that he may soon not be so different, after all, from his father. Jim sees his father as failing to provide a certain lifestyle for his mother. Here Jim is invoking the notion of men as breadwinners, a label that references the experiences of White, middle-class American families as the touchstone for "normal."

In turn, Amelia's insistence that Jim's staying at home is highly unusual is driven in part by how others perceive Jim's unemployment. Amelia explains, "Friends of mine say, 'I give you a lot of credit.' They say, 'I couldn't have done what you do. There's no way. I would have left him, I would have, you know, kicked him out.'" Amelia continues, "And I go, 'Don't get me wrong. I've thought about it all.' But then I go, 'What's that proving?'" Jim, too, is quite upset by how he thinks his family situation is being discussed by friends. Rolling his eyes, he says, "Gossip is not a positive thing. It's talking about others behind their back. 'Oh, the Radziks have to move. Jim lost his job; they can't afford the house so they're moving.'"

Given the long duration of Jim's unemployment, it has become difficult for the couple to ward off questions about whether Jim actually is trying to find a job. Jim himself recognizes how his attempts at securing employment are often invisible. He voices what he guesses their friends may be saying to Amelia: "'I can't believe that he's been in a job search for ten months and he hasn't found anything. Is he really looking for a job?'" Sighing, shoulders drooping, Jim continues, "They don't know the detail of what I'm doing. What they see is a blurrier picture of 'he's out of work, why are you putting up with that' type of thing." He looks up at me for reassurance, a sliver of a crack in his demeanor of bravado, visibly troubled at the thought of how others in his social circles might be perceiving him.

The Problem of Jim at Home is a problem of how to make Jim seem to be "morally unemployed"—that is, trying hard to find paid work and deserving to be employed. The solution, particularly from Amelia's perspective, is that Jim should take "a job, any job" as Jim dismissively paraphrases Amelia's ultimatum. The Problem of Jim at Home can only be solved if Jim is very visibly *not* at home and is, instead, in a recognizable workplace.

Is Jim Depressed?

A final and important thread shaping Jim and Amelia's negotiation around how Jim should relate to the space of the home is Amelia's concern about his well-being. She says, "So, I don't care what the profession is. . . . It's his well-being, and that's what I'm the most concerned with—is his well-being—because he does get very depressed." Amelia is not wrong in wondering about the implications of unemployment for Jim's mental state. Unemployment is associated with poor mental health outcomes, particularly for men.[33] Amelia adds that she gets worried when she sees Jim napping at home, because to her that is a sign of his depression. "He goes through like these really, really depressed days. And that's why I think he naps a lot."

Jim, who has had frequent interaction with therapists even prior to his unemployment, concurs with Amelia's assessment that when he takes naps, it is usually a sign of depression for him. He says, "I mean, I've had days where I'll take a nap at two in the afternoon and I'll go to bed for three hours. I don't mean lie down on the couch and put a blanket on. I mean, I take my clothes off, I put on pajamas. I go to bed! That's not healthy." Research finds that men often do not seek treatment for mental health issues, but it was quite common in my sample for men to be cautious about their own mental health. Many were seeing therapists or taking medication for their specific condition.[34] These resources are available because these families continue to have access to health insurance, often through their wives.

For Amelia, the solution to the problem is not necessarily therapy or medication, which Jim has been doing anyway. Rather, she sees his depression as partly rooted in Jim's inability to exercise control and authority over his life. Managerial and professional workers like the Radziks typically exercise authority in their workplace.[35] This is especially true for White men of this social class, who are seen as experts and authorities. Men of other races, particularly Black men, and women of any race often struggle to be seen as legitimately occupying spaces of authority in similar occupations.[36] For White men, then, the loss of workplace authority may be particularly disorienting.

In this study, many men, including Jim, sought to balance the loss of their authority at paid work by trying to exercise authority at home. Amelia sees this connection clearly, telling me, "He was in a mood, and he started taking it out on our daughter. Like making directives towards her about things. Like, she's twenty-two years old—she's gonna make her own decisions." Mimicking Jim, Amelia adds, "'Well, I'm telling you this as your father. You're gonna do . . . .'" For Amelia this is a clear substitute for the authority that Jim no longer exercises in a workplace context, because he is unemployed. She noticed it because it was particularly out of character for Jim, "Because he doesn't ever ask to control." Jim's children, Tim, a high school senior ready to head to college, and Sarah, who is about to start law school, also noticed this. I interviewed the two of them individually. Tim, for example said, "Like he was always on my case about the smallest things, because he had nothing else to occupy his time. So that put a lot of stress on me. . . . Like he would focus on like taking out the trash. Something small like anybody could do it, but he would get upset with me if I didn't do it right away . . . just like these smallest things would occupy his mind 'cause he had nothing else to worry about." Sarah, too, explained that Jim would have uncharacteristic outbursts of anger at small things as a way of getting control. Cupping her palms to her right, she explained that this was an area of his life where her father felt "he doesn't have control." She slid the cupped palms over to the left saying, "So this is where he tries to get control." Like Amelia and Tim, Sarah concurred that because Jim does not have control over his work, he tries to get it by trying to exert authority over his family members.

Amelia insists that Jim needs to get out of the house. Their daily conversations affirm this. It is a message that Jim understands loud and clear, although at times he disagrees with Amelia's assessment. It is in this complex context, where Amelia and Jim have fears of downward mobility and concerns of what others think of them, as well as worries about Jim's overall well-being, that Amelia is trying to get Jim out of the house as quickly as possible.

Revisiting the Radziks

I stayed in touch with Jim Radzik on and off for the greater part of the next year. Deeply embedded in networks of white-collar job-seekers, Jim remained a strong supporter of my research. He marshaled his networking expertise and experience and put me in touch with leaders in various peer-led networking groups as well as unemployed acquaintances. Although most of them did not ultimately participate in my project for myriad reasons, Jim was an invaluable "informant." I also often ran into Jim in many of the job searching events that I frequented in the course of my research.

I scheduled formal, separate interviews with Jim and Amelia about seven months after the original interview, when the "ultimatum" deadline that Amelia had given Jim had passed. I wanted to see how things had unfolded for both of them in the aftermath of this deadline. I met Jim in the same Starbucks close to his home in a charming "downtown" area of a small town. With Amelia's support, Jim was able to realize a dream of having his own business. He had opened a window installation company. As Jim told it, the signs that this is the way his career should now proceed had been there all along. He took the Myers-Briggs test—a disputed, but popular, tool to gauge where an individual's skill set lies. "The result," he said, "was I was borderline president/CEO of a company." To Jim, the decision to become self-employed seemed at once serendipitous and foreordained, but serendipity was probably not so much a factor. As scholars have noted, in the transformation of the labor market white-collar workers are being advised—for example through job clubs—to develop "personal brands" and to consider themselves as "companies of one."[37] The entrepreneurial self has become a commodity on the labor market. Even in standard employer-employee relationships, workers are cautioned to think of themselves as self-employed entrepreneurs, and ostensible entrepreneurial activities—even when exploitative of workers—are promulgated through various avenues, including dominant ideologies in job search clubs, through career coaches and career advice books, and the liberating promises of platform economies.[38]

Amelia, on the other hand, was more circumspect about this outcome. "I probably would've preferred something else. I probably would've preferred something that was . . ." raising her eyebrows dramatically, she continued, "Like, where did windows come from? Like, you know what I mean? Like, all of a sudden that's like the business model." She says, "He's good with measurements, so yes, the measuring you're fine." Shaking her head, she explains that Jim may not have the entire set of skills to flourish in this endeavor. "But, like, creatively looking at something and how to use the space and design it—not his key competency." Sighing, she adds that because she is "risk averse" she would have preferred "something more suited toward some of his skills."

Jim attributes Amelia's ultimatum as being a catalyst, saying, "It was Amelia who would say, and she had to say this a number of times, "'You know, you've really been in transition [unemployed] a lot longer than you think.'" He elaborates, "Now, I don't know if it was coincidental that things unfolded so that on June thirtieth I literally could say to her, 'Well I've made my decision, this is what I'm gonna do.' I don't know if it was coincidental or how much of it was her saying to me, 'You need to figure something out by June thirtieth.' But it worked out that way. I think it was June twenty-ninth I said to her, 'Well, it's figured out, I beat your deadline by a day.'"

Amelia, too, worries about her role in spurring Jim to become gainfully employed. Uncertain about the result that her ultimatum seems to have

led to, she second-guesses whether her ultimatum was a productive strategy, saying that she hopes Jim won't "just make a decision because I gave
you a timeline; make it the *right* decision." The ultimatum, as Amelia
implicitly points out, had several layers: gainful employment for Jim, yes,
but ideally employment that would be long term and not a financial liabil-
ity, as a business in an unchartered area might be. She adds, "So I think he
honored [the ultimatum], I just hope he honored it in the right aspect."
Amelia's ultimatum had been driven by several concerns, including Jim's
self-esteem and mental health. She says, "I think he's been happier because
he's got a purpose, where before he didn't. So I think it's good to see him
happy.

The decision to open up his own company, in an area with which Jim
was entirely unfamiliar, was a huge one. It required a substantial investment from the Radziks, of several hundred thousand dollars from the
get-go—including a significant portion of their savings. Of course, not
everyone has access to such an option, including the ability to acquire
these savings in the first place.[39]

The Radziks' decision to spend a significant proportion of their wealth
by investing in this risky venture illuminates the importance of complying with imagined, but idealized, images of how to perform a "family" in
America. It means getting Jim out of the house and reemployed.
Establishing his company will require long work hours. With a twinkle in
his eye, Jim describes his feelings, "I'm very excited. I'm confident. I ran
my first advertising two weeks ago, and I generated terrific response, so
I'm very encouraged." With his self-deprecating humor, Jim adds, "But
they do say a fool and his money are soon parted."

A ROOM OF TERRY'S OWN

Terry Clarke, a White unemployed engineer in his late fifties has been
married to Sandy, a White paralegal, for over twenty-five years. They have
two sons in their early twenties, their older son is employed and lives at
home in order to save on rent, while their younger son is at college.[40] Terry
spends a lot of his time at home, saying, "I have the house to myself during
the day." The Clarkes view Terry's unemployment as a temporary state that

can be amended by enabling Terry to job search from their home. The Clarkes' experience of Terry's unemployment is shaped by the idea of A Room of Terry's Own. The Clarkes have focused on upgrading their old home office so that Terry has a place to call his own. Instead of pushing Terry out of the home, Terry and Sandy direct their efforts toward making Terry comfortable. Why do the Radziks and the Clarkes have such different responses when it comes to unemployed men staying at home? What does the difference in their divergent responses reveal about how these White families in the professional middle-class expect unemployed men to relate to the space of the home?

Faith, a Tested Marriage, and Greater Togetherness

Terry has been the primary earner during the course of his marriage to Sandy. Terry has a master's degree and Sandy has a bachelor's degree. Until his most recent layoff six months ago, Terry earned a base salary $105,000 a year, plus bonuses, in comparison to Sandy's base salary of $72,000 a year (though she frequently earned more through overtime hours). Devout Christians, the couple met through a church group. Their faith has been especially important during the rougher periods of life, like the one they are currently experiencing. Sandy ranks Terry's job loss as one of the toughest things they have had to face, saying, "We've been fortunate where we haven't had a lot of personal tragedy."

This is not the first time that they have experienced work- or finance-related setbacks. The Clarkes lost a substantial amount of their retirement savings in the stock market downturn that occurred after the tragic September 11 attacks. They set to work on building up their lost investments, but the Great Recession wiped out a significant portion of the savings they had built up. Since then, the Clarkes have been consulting a financial advisor to better protect themselves from events beyond their control. Because the horizon for retirement is also approaching, they are trying to pay off their house, currently valued at over half a million dollars. The Clarkes are not seriously considering downsizing to a smaller house at this stage. Terry says, "I don't mind selling my house, but it would be a huge amount of work. I mean, I've lived in the house for twenty-three years, so there's a lot of stuff in the house." Chuckling, he adds, "I joke it's a ten-pound house with fifteen pounds worth of stuff in it." Just a couple of years ago, when Terry was still employed, the Clarkes invested in their house by putting on a new roof and renovating two of their bathrooms. Their financial situation currently is not dire enough to warrant, as Terry puts it, "shrinking my financial footprint." Aside from the mortgage on their house and some loans to currently support their younger son through college, the Clarkes do not have outstanding debt.

In the midst of recovering from these national and international financial events, several years ago Terry had to transition from one role in his organization to another. The process of this transition was messy and ambiguous. The Clarkes became concerned about Terry's future in this company, where he had worked for the major part of his professional life. Sandy explains, "During that time it was such stress. It was very difficult for him to deal with that. This time it's been much better." Their older son, Cody, who met me for an interview, recalls the time similarly, saying, "I think that was a lot, *lot* harder than it is now. . . . I think having gone through it once he feels more relaxed. I think it's like this is not the end of the world." In this earlier transition, Terry did not technically lose his job, and Sandy says, "He never quote unquote really lost it because it was just like another transition to another job." But Terry felt he had been demoted and sidelined. This had hit Terry as being shameful, and he described it as the most "emotionally difficult" experience in his career. They compare his current unemployment to this process of changing roles a few years ago.

Sandy and Terry understand this current experience of Terry's job loss through constant comparison with this earlier experience. Sandy says, "He has been able to verbalize it. [Before] he didn't even tell his parents for a long time. He didn't want them to know. . . . But this time around he has made the conscious effort to explain to people: 'I'm out of work.'" Sandy attributes this change to Terry's faith, saying, "I think his faith has carried him through a great deal." But she also attributes it to a larger personal development, "I think it's that he is growing as a person and he recognizes it's not a weakness to say that you're without a job. There are a lot of people who are without a job right now. I think it was a huge fear of his that he kind of had to grapple with." Although Sandy does not mention this, during Terry's earlier experience of role transitions, unemployment was more stigmatized; the Great Recession was crucial in normalizing unemployment for white-collar job-seekers. Terry's no longer viewing job loss as a "weakness" is likely a response to changing norms about employment.[41] As Sandy explains it, earlier the prospect of unemployment shook Terry's worldview. For Terry, his role as a man, a husband and father, had been profoundly vested in his job.

Sandy attributes the present experience of unemployment as being more positive, as it has brought them closer. She says, "And I think it's because he's been able to talk about it and we've been able to share ideas." Pausing, Sandy softly differentiates this from prior experiences: "He would always view anything that I would say to him as a criticism. And I'd say to him 'I'm not criticizing you. I'm just trying to understand.' But it was such a sensitive issue or . . . sensitive part of who he was, his job was so consuming to him, that it was very threatening." I will examine how couples come to view similar statements and gestures as supportive or critical in chapter 3. For now, it's important to note that this difference in interpretation shaped how the Clarkes understood and framed Terry's unemployment—as an obstacle that they could overcome together.

Terry emphasizes the role of religion in helping both him and Sandy weather this rough phase: "The bottom line is that sometimes God lets His children go through crap, you know, or difficult circumstances. Very, very bad circumstances sometimes. . . . So it's a matter of me seeking God praying, spending time in prayer, asking Him to work on my behalf to speak to me." He explains how Sandy has been present for him when it comes to his faith, leading them to both be more in sync with the other: "This is why faith is required. Things can happen and God doesn't automatically show up with a cape on to say 'I'm going to make it better for you.' You've got to go through the fire, so to speak. And so that's where I'm at. And my wife is good in encouraging me in that way." Sandy agrees about the importance of faith in bringing them together. She says, "I think in part it's our faith, God. I really believe that. It's the anchor for us in our lives. And trying to work together and, and build consensus and, you know, that we're attacking this together and we . . . pray about it." But this sense of togetherness is something they have developed in the course of their marriage, particularly by learning from prior experiences with uncertainty at the workplace. They consciously apply these lessons for a stronger marriage now. The Clarkes approach Terry's unemployment as an opportunity for the two of them to help Terry find a job *together*. Their older son, Cody, too, describes his parents' relationship as now being "a bit closer. I mean I know they care about each other."

Organizing the Home to Facilitate Job Searching

Job searching is a serious endeavor for families of unemployed men. To facilitate men's job searching, these couples often create an in-home office for unemployed men. The homes of these affluent, professional families frequently already include a home office. Families who adopt the Clarkes' approach typically upgrade the home office, buy new computer hardware, software, and furniture to create a pleasant space from which men can job search.

Terry explains how he upgraded his home office, "I just bought [Microsoft's] Visio to learn. Visio is a tool, so I might read the book [for it]. And it's not that hard to learn fortunately."[42] Couples here direct their efforts to making men more marketable and employable. The space of the home is reconfigured to bolster this. Terry has a single-minded focus: to find an appropriate job and to do so as quickly as possible. He does this by prioritizing a mixture of job applications and skills development. Assessing Terry's job searching activities, Sandy says: "I think he's actually enjoyed being home. Not having to be accountable to somebody else in terms of their timeline. . . . He's usually up by seven. And he has a focus: he'll clear the decks, get ready. He'll start to look for jobs. He's spent a lot of time enhancing his résumé and talking to recruiters . . . and whatnot. . . . But he likes having to be the master of [his schedule]. Likes to control that." In this context, the home takes on a new meaning for the Clarkes. For both Sandy and Terry, the home becomes a site where Terry proves to outsiders that he is an ideal job-seeker who is *morally unemployed*. He is not squandering his time. He is doing his utmost to get reemployed in an appropriate, new position.

Sandy contrasts Terry's behavior with an acquaintance of hers who lost a job. She describes her acquaintance as being so dejected as to be unable to job search. For him, staying at home, which Sandy clearly associates with a fruitful approach to job searching, was unbearable. Sandy explains, "One attorney that I worked very closely with has been out of job since January. And he and his wife have parted ways. He's now living with his mother. He's in his forties and it's been just horrendous. Horrendous. It's been very, very painful for him. What he did was he started doing all these triathlons and all kinds of stuff like that. And it's like he didn't even want to deal with looking for a job."

Terry, too, sees his own presence at home as signifying his determination to find a new job, resolutely saying, "I'm home to find a job." The Clarkes have a strong ideal of a family and the role each member plays in it. Terry's role is clear: to be out of the house and employed. But to reach this, they deem it acceptable for Terry to stay at home. Demarcating space helps demarcate time for job searching for these unemployed men.

Even families with greater financial constraints than the Clarkes spent money, time, and effort to create spaces conducive to men's job searching. Examples of families who experienced this, from the broader study, include the Baron and the Easton families. Whereas Sandy earned a significant portion of the household income, in the Baron and Easton families, Todd and Doug, respectively, had been the primary earners, and their wives earned considerably less. They were, consequently experiencing more financial constraints, but they responded in similar ways. Todd Baron, a marketing professional, is an unemployed father of three sons under the age of ten. His wife, Kimmie, works part time at their sons' elementary school. But it is Todd's $110,000-a-year income that supports the Barons' lifestyle. Todd has been unemployed and looking for employment for the past ten months. He and Kimmie decided, after some discussion, to wall off a section of their living room so that Todd could have an office space where he could job search. He could be at home without the distractions of being at home. Todd explains the importance of setting up this office space:

> The fact that I have a little home office and I could shut the door is good. . . . So it was probably the best thing we ever did. . . . If we didn't have that, that would suck because I'd probably be sitting at the dining room table with papers and spread out my laptop. . . . But the fact that I could just shut the door, and even if the door's open, I'm in there, you know, it's walled off. Nobody sees me unless they come to the door. It's a big piece of solid wall, you know, in our living room.

This space of his own is important to Todd, as it is for Kimmie. Todd adds, "I think she likes some of her space, too."

These couples assume that having an office space will help unemployed men look for employment. But it also serves an important emotional function: it provides space between the two spouses during a time when emotions can be volatile. Todd Baron explains how the office is necessary to give both him and Kimmie space from each other. "I'll shut the door and I'll be on the phone. . . . After she gets back from work, she'll pop in and say hello." Seeing her unemployed husband can be frustrating for Kimmie, especially if she thinks he is not focusing on job searching. Shutting himself off in his office can shield both of them: "I think she just psychologically is like you're sitting at home again, what are you doing? 'You're in your shorts and a T-shirt,' so I think it's just hard for her." The imagined ideal of a male-breadwinner family imposes a burden on the men in this sample: they are being asked to fulfil a family role that is becoming structurally obsolete, even for White professional men. At the same time, this ideal also carries with it privileges, in this case, access to dedicated space in the home.

Alice Easton's husband, Doug, once the primary earner in their family, has been unemployed for two years. Alice agrees with Todd's speculation that wives like to have some physical space in the home between husband and themselves. In Alice's case it's important because she works from home: "It can put a strain on the relationship: because I was able to see what he was or wasn't doing, and that can be frustrating at times." The office space serves an important emotional function for these families, visually separating men's unemployment even while they are at home. Spatially demarcating a space for unemployed men and for their job search activities is important simply because men's unemployment looms so large over their families.

Although unemployed men's families are preoccupied with fears of downward mobility, they also simultaneously spend considerable money on items that help men reorganize the space of their home to better suit their job searching needs. How can we explain this apparent discrepancy? A potential answer may lie in the fact that these families see men's unemployment as temporary, no matter how long it's been since the man held a job. These men and their wives do not see men's unemployment as signaling men's retreat from the labor market. They justify spending money on upgrading or creating home offices as an instance of spending money to make money.

Revisiting the Clarkes

Close to a year after my first interviews with Sandy and Terry, I reached out to both of them to see how they had fared in the intervening year. During a hot and humid summer in the American Northeast, I met each of them individually. The year had been filled with personal losses for them. A few months before I met Terry again, he had lost his mother.

I met Terry at an upscale café near his new, downtown workplace. In a freshly pressed powder blue Oxford shirt and khakis suitable for the summer weather, Terry is noticeably cheerful, although he had never been particularly glum. He has a new job that pays him an hourly rate of about $50 per hour, with no compensation for sick leave or other benefits. He still has health and retirement benefits from the job he had lost the previous year—where he had had a long tenure. He says, "I don't need the medical. There's no vacation, it's all hourly. But that's alright."

I was surprised by Terry's equanimity; as an hourly job, this is very well-paying. But it pays considerably less than what Terry had earned previously. Moreover, Terry now reports to a man who is twenty-five years his junior in age. Terry is excited about his work, adding enthusiastically, "Right now, I'm kind of in a learning mode, a pretty intense learning mode. . . . My sense is there's a fair amount of opportunity here, so I would love to be able to work here. We'll see what happens." Although visibly animated about his new job, Terry has taken two key lessons from his unemployment to heart: he has active networks for job leads should he lose his job again, and he is keeping his credentials and certifications up-to-date. These projects, which he started during unemployment, remain a part of his professional vision.

Sandy is happy that this period of uncertainty and rejection is over for the time being. Two weeks before meeting me again, Sandy lost her father. The last few months until his death had been filled with travels to his home, in another state in the Northeast. Despite a busy and trying time, Sandy explained that she felt she could not leave me "in a lurch," overwhelming me with her kindness at discussing her personal experiences in the midst of such devasting losses. Sandy's soft-spoken, supportive demeanor, even toward me, a relative stranger, echoed Terry's appreciation of Sandy's care and support of his job searching activity during his unemployment.[43]

CONCLUSION

A home is both a space and an idea. In The Problem of Jim at Home and A Room of Terry's Own, the idea of home pivots on what it means to be a family and the different roles that a husband and a wife *should* occupy in it. As such, this is an idea that is informed by gender norms that themselves vary by race and class. Unsurprisingly, as White families, the Radziks and the Clarkes evoke fuzzy, nostalgic imagery of a bygone era when men provided and women supported them.

The couples in this chapter are aspiring to a hegemonic vision of home and family. It is symbolically powerful, even as the reality has been eroding over time. Both Jim and Terry have a complicated relationship to the home, albeit in different ways. At the crux is a concern with what the home says about how men relate to paid work. At stake is the combination of space and task. By pushing men out of the home—although through different types of interactions—both families in this chapter are upholding symbolic visions of an ideal family. In so doing, these families are aligning themselves with powerful, easily recognizable, and valued social positions.

While there are many ways of being a man and demonstrating masculinity, hegemonic masculinity refers to the most dominant and powerful form of masculinity in a given context, where some men dominate other groups of men and women.[44] In the American context, fulfilling the demands of hegemonic masculinity is usually contingent on employment. But typically, this expectation is one that White, affluent men have been most able to meet. For decades, working-class men have encountered far more inconsistent employment histories. Men of color, including those with advanced degrees, are much more likely than White men to experience unemployment, and for longer times.[45] The findings in this chapter show families seeking to adhere to conceptions of hegemonic American masculinity—this masculinity is not always available to, nor always prized by, those who are not White and/or privileged.

No two marriages are alike. The Radziks' and the Clarkes' marriages carry the distinctive stamp of their own individual journeys and disparate upheavals, including a miscarriage, multiple job losses, deaths of parents and in-laws, and sibling feuds. In this study, these two families are on the more privileged and older end of the spectrum. Even as their experiences diverged both from each other and the other families in the sample, they enacted two of the main themes of how the home is gendered during men's unemployment. Both approaches do the same work of reaffirming the gender system by earmarking men's income from paid work as essential for their respective families. These families could have turned the gender system on its head by being more accepting of men's time at home. Instead, they are willing to go to great lengths—and in some cases spend a considerable amount of money—to maintain the gender system.

The space of the home is inscribed as a feminine space through the everyday interactions and understandings of these couples, and men are often seen as trespassers.

2 Idealizing the Home and Spurning the Workplace?

She actually enjoys not being at her job because she gets to be a mom.

—Larry Bach, husband of unemployed woman

I feel like I'm just a mom right now. I'm not anything else.

—Nicole Lenoir, unemployed woman

Most of the families in this study naturalize the presence of unemployed women in the home. Women and their husbands frame women's unemployment as enabling women to *correct* an imbalance in their work-family life that has resulted directly from the woman's employment. The American imaginary idealizes the home as a space of comfort, a haven, and women's rightful place. But this long-standing image has emerged from the particularities of White, middle-class families. Here, genteel women were expected to embody the domestic. Black women in America have always been working outside the home—either through coercion, as in slavery, or due to the structurally weak marginalized positions of Black families. Historically, a male-breadwinner Black family has been more economically fragile than a male-breadwinner White family. White and Black women's relationships to paid and unpaid work hinge on specific axes of raced and classed experiences that these unemployed women encounter.[1]

These different histories and contemporary realities play out in the unemployed families in my study. For unemployed White women, the space of the home often becomes a site of respite and security during the emotionally turbulent time of unemployment. Some of them rush to embrace activities traditionally associated with the norms of White womanhood. They relish cooking and cleaning. Rather than viewing themselves as unemployed, they emphasize their motherhood. Other women in the study, however, resist the idea that unemployment means a sense of ease at home.

This chapter follows the experiences of two families, the Bachs and the Forresters. In the first instance, Darlene Bach, a White woman, encouraged by her husband, claims the space of the home as rightfully hers. She discusses how her employment had previously prevented her from spending much time in this, her natural habitat. She takes pride in the domestic. This is the dominant experience of unemployed women in this study. In contrast, Gina Forrester, a Black woman, does not see immersing herself into the domestic as a source of respite. She asserts that she is engaging in a meaningful—if unpaid—activity in the form of establishing her own nonprofit organization. Rather than conforming to the norms of White domesticity, Gina worries that unemployment will force her to abide by the norms of the stay-at-home mother.

Darlene and Gina start off with widely divergent understandings of the home while unemployed. But this changes over time. The better part of the year into her unemployment, Darlene finds that domesticity and the home no longer offer her solace. She is itching to get back to paid work, irritable toward the constant and unending demands of the home. Over time, Gina, too, shifts her focus. Switching from a focus on establishing her nonprofit, she aims to obtain a more standard and lucrative position in the corporate world.

FEELING AT HOME, AT HOME

On a cool April morning, I sit with Darlene Bach at her kitchen table. The square kitchen has a skylight where sunlight streams in, falling in shafts on the birch table and tiled kitchen floor. The kitchen is directly at the end of the short hallway that leads from the main entrance. To the left of the hallway is a living room with a couch, couple of armchairs angled artistically, and a piano. One side of the living room has a wide entrance into the small dining room, which has a table seating six and a sideboard. From the other side, the dining room leads into the kitchen as well. Above this main floor, there are three modest-sized bedrooms, each large enough to fit a queen-sized bed and other furniture—a narrow dresser, a desk. Below the living room there is a laundry area and a large family room (mostly used by Darlene's husband, Larry, to watch "his YouTube videos or whatever," as Darlene explains). This family room has bookshelves and a comfortable couch with a rectangular ottoman in front of it. It opens out onto their backyard.

Today, as Darlene and I sit at her kitchen table, Darlene's slim, leather-bound planner is spread open in front of her. There is a spacious block of time for every hour in the planner. Days are densely covered in color-coded dots. Noted in it are brunches and dinners with friends and moms' groups; talks and theatrical productions at the high school her fifteen-year-old son, Parker, attends; and pickup and drop-off times for Parker's extracurricular activities. Darlene holds a pen poised above the planner as she consults it while we discuss when I can visit her family during the next week. "I have a dinner on Tuesday with a friend at six in the evening, but Larry and Parker will be home. On Wednesday," she turns to look at the wall calendar next to her where there is a note in her handwriting, "Larry has a dinner out, but I'll be here and so will Parker. My Thursday's pretty open. I might make something to take over to my brother-in-law, something they can keep in the fridge, but you're welcome to be there. On Friday, I have squash with some women at the club at seven-forty-five a.m., and then a talk after that." She taps the pen against her lips and adds, "But the talk is for something you have to pay for, and you have to be a member first in any case, so you wouldn't be able to come there."

As we continue discussing the days I can visit her family, Darlene concentrates on her planner. She opens her iPad and swipes at it a couple of times. After a minute or two she looks up at me and says, "Parker has a track meet, but it's at home. So that's good." She pauses for a few seconds considering the scheduling further, "So if you come at three-thirty that's perfect, because we can just go over to the school soon after and watch a bit of the meet." She pauses, and resumes talking, more to herself than to me, "I hope the meet finishes at four-thirty because otherwise we might not be able to make Parker's squash lesson at five at the club." She pauses again, unable to resolve this potential conflict in Parker's schedule before continuing, "And after the lesson we'll be home for dinner, although Larry won't be here for dinner."

Now in her early fifties, Darlene grew up in a blue-collar family and had been the primary earner in her family. She enjoyed a long career as a marketing executive in a variety of industries. She is five feet, six inches with wavy, strawberry blond hair curling just above her shoulders. Her eyes are a clear hazel, and her resolute mouth has a slick of frosted pink lipstick. Darlene exudes an air of primness, keeping her mouth pursed at times and her face stoic. She has been married to her husband, Larry, an administrator at a local public university, for twenty years, and they have a teenage son, Parker. Larry, a clean-shaven man with neatly brushed dark brown hair sprinkled with silver, is in his late fifties. He has a thin, wide mouth and expressive brown eyes, which he frequently rolls and uses to exaggeratedly express disbelief and astonishment. Lurking underneath his expression is a playful smile as though he is constantly amused by the world, and never more so than by Darlene and Parker.

Prior to losing her job, Darlene had usually earned almost $150,000 as her base salary, topped off by generous bonuses; Larry has been bringing home a steady paycheck, but in a more modest amount of about $50,000 per year. Four months ago, Darlene was let go from the family-owned corporation where she had been employed for two years. The process of being let go was painful, and Darlene sobbed as she recounted it to me in our interview. Now, though, Darlene is buzzing with enthusiasm at her ability to stay at home, even if involuntarily. Her days are busy with a myriad of activities, and the home provides a sense of respite—a welcome change from a workplace that had turned increasingly negative before eventually letting her go. In this initial period of unemployment, Darlene is excited about submerging herself in domesticity. Staying at home has provided Darlene with an alternative, and meaningful, way of recalibrating her identity: from a rejected worker to an involved wife and mother.[2]

The unemployed women in my study—largely White and from the professional middle-class—reference powerful, idealized, but unequal, visions of the healing power of the domestic. They feel comfortable at home, slipping into domestic surroundings with ease. These women invoke long-standing scripts available in their particularized social milieu. Most salient are the expansive demands of motherhood encapsulated in the term "intensive motherhood."[3] This ideology frames motherhood as women's highest calling, measured in terms of emotional investment and time spent with their children. It is a hegemonic ideology, aligned with White, middle-class expectations. Unemployed women in this study frequently associated the ability to be present *at home* as key to motherhood. Although losing a job is difficult, staying at home often tempered this for many of them. They reported feeling that staying at home enabled them to center their lives on their children. This was enormously important; most had always been extremely involved in monitoring their children's lives by keeping close tabs on education, extracurricular activities and social development. The exacting—and unreal—standards of intensive motherhood mean that mothers in this sample nonetheless felt that their careers detracted from their time as mothers. With prodding by their husbands, most of these unemployed women deeply embraced the culturally available cult of domesticity, where the space of the home—and the motherhood it represents—becomes a source of validation, at least for a time.

Intensive Motherhood and Staying at Home for Children

Darlene had enjoyed her work, despite the brutal ninety-minute commute each way that she had for her most recent job, the business travel she was required to do that kept her away from her family, and other extensive demands that have become normative among professionals.[4] During lunch with a friend who has taken early retirement, over bowls of steaming soup, Darlene wistfully explains what losing her job means to her. Leaning back in her wooden chair and tilting it, she rests her head against the wall and says, "The sad thing is I loved my work. I liked the people. I liked the job. So, to have that taken away . . ." she trails off, as her friend glances over and nods sympathetically. Despite her pain at her job loss, Darlene acutely felt that her job had kept her from her home. This, she became convinced, was adversely affecting her teenage son, Parker. Darlene recounts an incident to me that underscored to her how she needed to spend more time at home for Parker's sake, "And in fact, I came back from one of the trips and that was the one time he said to me, and he's never said that before, 'Promise me you'll never go on another business trip.'" Shaking her head as though reliving the distress it caused her to hear her son plead in this manner, she added, "And I was like 'Whoa!'"

Darlene's experiences align with the experiences of other mothers like her—White mothers from the professional middle-class. These mothers recount feeling pulled apart in two demanding directions. On the one hand, the institution of paid work, particularly for highly educated and skilled professionals, is taxing. Cultural norms around the workplace privilege "ideal workers,"[5] who can work long hours, are contactable around the clock, are willing and able to travel for extended time periods, and will put in after-hours appearances at work-related social events. These expectations can be difficult to reconcile with the demands of intensive motherhood, which assumes that mothers do not have responsibilities of paid work and are able to focus exclusively on mothering.

This demographic of mothers is the most likely to harbor expectations of continuous and uninterrupted careers and the most likely group to meet these expectations.[6] This poses an ideological tension as they simultaneously wrestle with the demands of intensive motherhood.[7] They often feel guilty, thinking that they are cutting corners at home and work.[8] Darlene was taken aback at Parker's sense of insecurity about her physical absence from home. From Darlene's perspective, her absences from home due to work responsibilities took a toll on Parker. "I was working in the bedroom upstairs, and he would come up and he would say 'Hello' to me. He was checking to make sure I was there. And then he would go downstairs and he would do his thing. So it's like he didn't even need to interact with me." Pausing, Darlene reflected before adding, "He just needed to know I was there." The home is not a neutral space, particularly not for Darlene. It is charged with reminders about where she should be—at home, rather than at work. Her unemployment offers her the ability to fulfill these demands, which she, like many working mothers, felt she had often failed. Being at home affirms a culturally valued identity as a mother.

Darlene transfers this sense of being able to be a more available mother to feminized spaces outside the home as well. Although saddened by her job loss, Darlene also feels like a "superwoman." Being unemployed means she can spend more time at home and on Parker. She explains what unemployment means for her: "It was great to be able to do the things that I didn't have time to do before. Like participate more in school things. I felt happy. I felt really happy about it, 'cause it's like this is a taste of what it's to be a stay-at-home mom. That you can show up at school and hang out there for three hours, working on a fund-raiser and selling donuts and Swedish fish to kids to make money for the school."

Darlene feels at home in feminized spaces such as her son's school. She elaborates on how her ease in these spaces populated by other mothers enables her to focus on Parker and his development. She sees herself as being better able to emulate the behavior expected in intensive mother-hood: "And I was able to actually learn a lot of things. The other mothers would be telling if a teacher walked by, 'Don't get that teacher. If you get that teacher for math, immediately transfer out. They're horrible.' And I'd be taking notes [chuckles] 'OK, what was that person's name again?' So there's like a whole other network. They're very welcoming. So that part I felt good about."

Darlene feels a sense of belonging and camaraderie with other mothers she encounters, and she actively seeks them out in these spaces. But this is accessible to her because of her particular location in the race-class-gender nexus. Instead of being an unemployed professional, Darlene can be a *stay-at-home mom*—a culturally legitimate, alternative identity. This identity is not available for most men, but neither is it available for all women. Sociologist Dawn Dow explains that Black professional middle-class women do not see being a stay-at-home mom as culturally feasible for themselves. They worry about being perceived through an unflattering prism and being labeled a Welfare Queen. The disparaging imagery is one from which Black women from the professional middle-class actively distance themselves.[9] Darlene's joy and comfort at seeing herself as a stay-at-home mom, even if temporarily, is shaped by her position in this inter-section of social hierarchies.

Darlene's husband, Larry, says, "She actually enjoys not being at her job because she gets to be a mom. You know, she gets to go meet the other ladies at the squash club, mothers of the squash team, and sell donuts at breakfast for the squash team." The squash club that Larry references is an exclusive country club to which the Bachs belong. It is over a century old, frequently hosting international athletic coaches who have competed in the Olympics for their countries. The club is an importance space and institution for women in the American upper classes.[10] The club helps maintain elite networks and traditions, historically among White families. The club also gives Darlene access to another space that celebrates her status as a stay-at-home mom, and buttresses her privileged position in the American social hierarchy.

Larry is actively encouraging Darlene to make the most of this time at home. He says that he would "be perfectly happy to have her just sort of hang out and enjoy life." Larry's encouragement of Darlene's time at home is not limited to the duration of her unemployment. Instead, his message to her is that she can take this involuntary unemployment and turn it into opting out of paid work altogether. This would enable her to spend even more time at home. This is a surprising piece of advice offered by Larry. Although Larry has been employed for over twenty-five years at the same place, Darlene' substantially greater income has made possible their lifestyle, replete with annual international holidays; domestic vacations; a home in one of the nation's most affluent suburbs; and Parker's aspirations to attend not just any Ivy League university, but Harvard, Princeton, or Yale. Despite the empirical erosion of the male-breadwinner family structure, cultural norms around the male-breadwinner ideology continue to reign.[11] Larry frames his suggestion that Darlene could even stop job searching altogether as a function of financial feasibility. Like Jim Radzik in chapter 1, Larry, too, is engaging in a process of earmarking, where he frames his income as sufficient for their family's needs. This belies their financial reality, as their lifestyle is predicated first and foremost on Darlene's earning power.

Couples such as the Bachs in this study deploy a gender strategy that normalizes women's presence at home. A gender strategy is "a plan of action through which a person tries to solve problems at hand, given the cultural notions of gender at play."[12] The problem these couples encounter is how to understand and resolve the woman's unemployment. Should it be treated as a devastating experience, a mundane reality given a shifting economic context, or perhaps an opportunity? Couples overwhelmingly tend toward understanding women's unemployment as an opportunity.[13] This response illuminates the gendered ideals that are powerful for them. Couples activate race- and class-based gendered ideals, framing women as guardians of domesticity. Staying at home becomes glorified rather than a source of shame or unease. The women in this study, as predominantly

White, unemployed women, have access to spaces aside from their home that also affirm the value of staying at home and that identify them as part of a privileged group in so doing.

Feminizing the Home

Although Darlene is unemployed, her days are busy and filled with activities, many of them revolving around her son. During her unemployment, Darlene embodies the look of a quintessential, White suburban mom with an SUV. Instead of business outfits, such as the sheath dresses with a statement necklace and two-inch heels she used to wear for work, Darlene now dresses in athleisure: black yoga pants, comfortable sneakers, and soft fleece sweatshirts in colors like baby blue and hot pink. Athleisure worn by Darlene denotes a high social status.[14] Her nails are well manicured, and she has swiped on a layer of pink lipstick and a touch of rouge on her cheeks. She is perfectly at home being at home during the work week.

Mornings, Darlene often meets a friend for a coffee or participates in workshops geared toward unemployed job-seekers held in different suburban locations. These events usually take place from nine to eleven on weekdays. This timing is deliberate, in order to provide structure to unemployed job-seekers' days. Workshops take place in spaces rented by career coaches running the workshop and peer-led networking events take place in a coffee shop or restaurant like Panera. In peer-led groups, unemployed professionals network with each other, share tips about job leads, and function as an outlet for disappointments and frustrations in the job search process.[15] After these meetings, Darlene either grabs a soup and sandwich from the restaurant or goes home to fix herself a light lunch. These meetings occur every weekday, but Darlene only goes once or twice a week because, as she explains, "really what you have to do to find a job is to do one-on-one kind of individual meetings."

Darlene's weekday afternoons are spent in any number of ways. She has taken this involuntary time off as a sign to get different aspects of her home organized, such as filing old papers and discarding clothes. One day when I visited the Bachs, several large plastic trash bags were piled near the front door. Waving them off, Darlene turned to me saying "those are old clothes that we need to send to Goodwill." Another day, I came to find several cardboard boxes filled to the brim with photographs, placed near the piano in a corner of their living room. One box teetered on top of the piano stool. Darlene is organizing a backlog of photographs from their family vacations, including a two-week vacation to Japan a couple of years ago.

Some of her time is also taken up in volunteer work as an alumni mentor for the sorority she had been in during college, which she started after she lost her job. This volunteer position requires her to participate in and organize social events, such as a recent meeting for which she ducked out one afternoon to purchase gold foil paper, photo frames, and streamers from a nearby crafts store. The Bachs' kitchen table has become a crafts area, as Darlene often spreads out her wares there. If she needs even more space, she moves to their dining room table. These days, she is often clipping photographs from sorority reunions to fit into photo frames to decorate local chapters of sorority houses, or gluing glitter to banners for upcoming events at the sorority. Thus, even when activities take Darlene out of her home, it is to other feminized spaces where her newly adopted identity as a stay-at-home mother is welcomed.

Darlene's knick-knacks from her various home projects and volunteering activities, as well as her job search, have oozed into different parts of the house. Although Parker had wanted his mother to be at home more, now he is less pleased with what this has meant for his own space. He sulkily told me one of the things he dislikes about his mother's unemployment: "My mom's home all the time now and she doesn't bother getting her own desk. She just, like, comes into my room and just takes all this stuff off of my desk and just shoves it somewhere and then just uses it as her work desk. And that's really annoying."

In unemployed women's families, their unemployment is not seen as a grave problem, as it is in the families of unemployed men in this study. There is usually no space separately demarcated from where women are expected to job search. Neither do these families with unemployed women feel a need to regulate their interactions around women's job searching, as we saw with Todd and Kimmie Baron in chapter 1. This should be surprising: these women have held high-paying jobs. Their income is often a substantial portion of the overall household income. The way that women and husbands here make sense of women staying at home emphasizes that women's inherent responsibilities are at home. Paid work, even for these highly accomplished women, is viewed as optional. The professional workplace, as scholars have pointed out, is merely a gender-neutral term for a highly gendered, and masculine, space where men continue to be more readily accepted. Similarly, the home is not a gender-neutral space either. For professional unemployed White women like Darlene, the home serves as a haven that may blunt the sorrow of losing their job. These women, as Darlene's example illustrates, do not have to explain away their presence at home; it is expected.

The ideal of contributing to their family through domesticity is alluring for unemployed White women in the professional middle-class. They can activate a valorized identity as a stay-at-home mom. Their networks and the social spaces they frequent affirm this. This gender strategy in these couples is an understandable response, since it socially props up both unemployed wives and husbands in their particular social context. In this time of uncertainty, when the economic basis of the Bachs' lifestyle—Darlene's job—has been wrenched, the Bachs could have highlighted the importance of Darlene's paid work. Instead, both Larry and Darlene activate cultural understandings about Darlene's role at home, which is based on a male-breadwinner family structure—this has never been a reality of their lives

THE HOME IS NOT ENOUGH

Other women in this study did not share Darlene's experience of ease at home. In this section, I delve into the case of Gina Forrester, a Black woman in her late forties. Although the workplace is hardly any kinder to Black women than to White women—it is, in fact, usually even more hostile—Gina does not idealize the home while unemployed. Gina's experiences echo those of a minority of women in this sample. Through mundane interactions with their spouses and children, and through their own meaning making, these women actively distance themselves from the space of the home and the arena of the domestic. They hold on to their identity as workers.

Gina lost her executive-level corporate job a year and a half ago. Tall and slender, Gina dresses stylishly. When we meet, she has on heels, silk joggers, a button-down silk blouse, paired with a slim paisley scarf. Gina, whose family is from the Caribbean, emigrated to the United States as a child, along with her parents and five siblings. A naturalized US citizen, she was educated primarily at elite, private universities on the East Coast. She has advanced degrees from two Ivy League schools, including an MBA. While Gina's annual salary was $150,000, her husband of over twenty years, Mark, a Black policeman who also emigrated from the Caribbean in his childhood, commands an annual income of about $100,000. Chuckling, Gina describes how Mark reaches this income level: "He actually works a lot of overtime."[16]

To explain why despite her higher earning capacity in terms of overall wealth there is not as extensive a gap between her and Mark as one might expect, she says, "I think the other thing is I've taken some breaks, so I haven't had a steady progression. So when I look at articles about what an Ivy League MBA should be making—I'm clearly not on that trajectory." Gina invokes individual choices to explain her uneven career history and her constrained wealth accumulation. She does not highlight factors such as structural racism and outright discrimination that continue to keep Black women out of the most lucrative and prestigious positions, even when women have the kind of elite credentials Gina possesses. As an example, although Black and Latina women in the corporate sector ask for raises and promotions at the same rate as White women, they get worse results, and are paid less than their White counterparts for similar work.[17]

Among college-educated women, Black women are the most likely to have continuous career trajectories, making Gina's splintered path somewhat unusual. Gina describes herself as "kind of a little on mommy track." For example, after her fifteen-year-old daughter was born, Gina proudly says, "I *negotiated* a package that allowed me to take a year off." This too is unusual, because rather than intensive motherhood being a guiding principle for Black professional women, the concept of "integrated motherhood"—working outside the home, being financially self-reliant, and assuming kin and community help with child-rearing—is usually more powerful.[18] Black professional women sometimes do prefer the "mommy track," as Gina here says, with this decision being vested in a racial logic. In a study of Black women who modify their careers, Riché Barnes explains that by curtailing paid work, Black women emphasize their investment in their marriage and children, framing this decision as being squarely in the service of family *and* community.[19] In a context where Black women have historically worked outside the home (whether that work was paid or not), opting out of paid work outside the home becomes a radical decision.

Gina's larger salary equates to her being the primary earner in her family, but neither she nor Mark see her as a primary earner. This has a lot to do with how Gina and Mark organize their finances. Gina says, "So one thing we never did was to pool our funds. Some people open up a joint account. We've always had separate accounts." Couples with a higher education level are more likely to have both a joint account *and* separate accounts for each spouse; usually pooling a majority of their resources but keeping some separate. Black couples, however, are less likely than White couples to have joint bank accounts.[20] For the most part, this separation meant that the Forresters did not have arguments over allocating money, and Gina explains that "there were never questions around, 'Well, where are those funds going to and what are these funds going to?'" The Forresters also had clarity on the financial obligations of each partner to the family. Gina adds, "We had this understanding that we would kind of split the bills. We knew what we were responsible for." These obligations were not agnostic to the difference in income. Gina recounts, "What we did is we really kind of split the household bills, according to income roughly. So I ended up paying more of the bills than he did." The way Gina and Mark managed their bills was that "he had the mortgage and the telephone, but then I had most of the other bills." These other bills include items such as utilities, insurance payments, and taxes and bills pertaining to a couple of apartments that they own jointly and that they rent out. Gina manages the logistics of this investment in private property.

The biggest expense for them has been sending their two daughters to private school. This was more important to Gina than to her husband, "I say 'we,' but it was *me* taking the lead to send them to private schools. So we've been paying the tuition from preschool. And I took that on." During times of economic uncertainty, affluent parents actually increase how much they spend on their children's education. They often see the expense of prestigious—and expensive—private education as a necessary armament against a continually shifting economic reality where the rules of jobs and careers are shifting.[21] Education becomes an important line of defense as families are left to devise their own, individualized solutions to weather growing economic uncertainties. Families such as the ones in this study are best able to do so, despite experiencing unemployment that can last a long time and occurs frequently. Gina adds "I don't know that Mark always agreed with that. But he sort of let me have the say in it." Shrugging her shoulders Gina adds, "But then I also paid for it." Gina's description of the financial division in her household, especially her financial independence, aligns with prior findings about the value of financial independence as a key characteristic of identity and expectation among Black professional mothers.

Fighting "Housewife Mode"

Gina does not see her unemployment as a time to reignite a domestic sense in her, but neither is she in a rush to get out of the house. She has a firm stance, similar to Terry Clarke's, that she has the right to be at home as she figures out her next professional steps. This confidence comes from her understanding that through her savings she is continuing to meet her financial obligations to her husband and children. She says that she has often reminded Mark that, "I'm still paying my portion of the bills." The first year of her unemployment, Gina covered her expenses through the severance package she received from her former employer, and then from government unemployment benefits. For the last six months, she has been dipping into her savings. She describes herself as "frugal" and her family as having "lived below" their means. She believes in having "multiple streams of income." For the Forresters, this has typically come from both their incomes and the joint returns from rental income, as well as other assets such as stocks. In addition, both Gina and Mark have retirement accounts; Gina's contains around half a million dollars.

As Gina explains it, what bothers Mark is this period of limbo. From Gina's description, Mark wants one of either two things: for Gina to be employed, or for Gina to be more clearly caring for the home. It bothers him that Gina is not doing either. Instead, like some of the unemployed men, Gina is marking out her home as a space suited for job searching.

But further motivating Mark's concern is his belief that Gina is squandering her potential. Gina describes how Mark views her, "as an MBA, right, I have all of these opportunities in front of me and I'm not taking advantage of the opportunities." Shaking her head wistfully, she adds that Mark believes "I could find a position tomorrow and that I'm not taking advantage of that." Gina, too, believes in her employability, but she thinks this time to carefully evaluate her career steps is necessary. She is tired from the rat race of the corporate sector. Gina is taking her unemployment as a time to think about moving toward a financially viable *and* meaningful career for her. She is specifically interested in establishing a health nonprofit. But, because this is a new area for her, she is taking her unemployment as a time to do due diligence before making any decisions.

Mark, in contrast, assumes that Gina's being at home means she can take over the housework. Lowering her voice, Gina says, "The other conversation we'll have is, I'm on the computer. And he'll say, 'You're on the computer?' I say, 'Well, the kind of work I do. If I'm putting together strategy [for my nonprofit], it's gonna mean that I need to be at the computer for four hours.' He doesn't acknowledge . . ." Her voice trails off. She struggles to articulate Mark's response to her treating the home as an office, "If I'm doing something, he'll say, 'Can you take care of that?'" waving her hand as though pointing to an unfinished chore. Gina continues, "And I'm like, 'Well, I'm actually doing something.'" Gina fights to maintain the home as her office. Sadly, quietly, Gina explains that "even in this space where I'm trying to figure out what my next vocation is going to be, I feel like what I'm doing is not valued."

Gina is convinced that she needs to take the time to chart out a future career that she can be reasonably satisfied in. This desire is not news to Mark. Gina acknowledges that Mark has usually been a supportive husband. He has encouraged her to take the space she needs. Gina explains, "He said, 'So, you really need to pursue what it is that you're passionate about.'" For Gina, this explicit encouragement from Mark is crucial, shaping how she approaches staying at home while unemployed. "And so I really felt like I got the OK, and that was important. That was very important to me, that I had his support. And he really made all the difference, because I probably wouldn't have stayed at home to pursue other career options if there was a different message coming from him."

Mark's words support Gina taking the time she needs, but his actions are not always congruent with this. The Forresters are experiencing ambivalence about how to respond to Gina's unemployment. Their individual responses vary. This ambiguity is vested in the absence of cultural scripts for unemployment in contemporary dual-earner families. At times, Mark veers toward treating Gina as a stay-at-home mom on whom the responsibility of the household falls. Resolutely, Gina says, "I've kind of railed against, this idea that I'm home and so I'm responsible for the management of the household. We've had some conversations around that, and where I've said, 'OK, well, I won't be able to cook and do all of these things.'"

For Gina, just because she is at home does not mean that she should bear the entire responsibility for the upkeep of the household. She does not want "to be defined by those things, right?" She continues explaining how staying at home but not immersing herself in the domestic means an ongoing resistance toward Mark, who harbors, as Gina says, an "undercurrent" of the expectation that the home would be Gina's responsibility. She explains that Mark has "kind of the expectation that I'm in the housewife mode." Shaking her head firmly, she says, "And I'm fighting this: 'Well, I'm not a housewife!'" She elaborates, "I think there's a raised expectation for certain things." Here, Gina refers to the responsibility of keeping the home organized and clean. She continues, "But I still tend to be the one who's trying to keep the house looking halfway clean. And he'll come in and throw things down, and I end up cleaning it up." Gina feels she is doing more than Mark to keep the house clean, and, like Terry Clarke, she does not see this as a suitable use of her time. Yet, from Mark's perspective, Gina has reneged on their understanding that they are a two-income family; since he feels pushed into being a breadwinner, he may feel that Gina should take over the responsibility for the home. For Gina, though, the situation is not as clear cut, and she envisions herself back at work—but at her own pace. Her home does not become a source of validation.

Embracing Carework at Home

While Gina rejects the idea that housework should naturally fall on her shoulders while she is unemployed, she embraces another kind of feminized domestic activity: carework. Here, I use *carework* to refer to the unpaid work, most often done by women, for family members.[22] Daughters tend to do more carework for parents. They organize and keep track of parents' medical appointments. Daughters provide emotional care and comfort. In Black families, adult children tend to help elderly parents, while in White families, adult children are more likely to receive help from parents. White families, especially affluent ones, provide significant financial support to adult children. In contrast, Black families exchange more in-kind help, such as help with childcare, housework, and transportation. One study showed that Black and White men are surprisingly alike when it comes to providing carework; race differences in carework exchanges are driven by Black and White women.[23]

Gina experiences her unemployment within this context of dense carework among Black families. A while before Gina lost her job, her elderly mother had been diagnosed with Alzheimer's. At that time, her mother lived in a duplex home in a city about a two-hour drive from Gina. Gina's mother lived on the first floor and another daughter lived on the floor above. Gina and her mother are close, and during this time Gina's mother "had really kind of come to me and asked me for help in a way that she hadn't really approached my other siblings." Wondering about this to herself as she recounted this to me, Gina adds, "She raised six children. . . . I think she has a different relationship with everyone. So I'm not sure what it was." Regardless of why her mother asked her and not her other siblings, Gina wanted to help: "I think I was in a place where in terms of the things that were important to me, she certainly was one of those things. So, she actually moved in with me. . . . So there was a point where I didn't want to go back to work because she was here. And I thought, well, this is what I need to be doing now while I can do it." Having her mother move in was temporary, lasting for six months. During this period, Gina set up her mother's own home with services and equipment that would allow her mother to live independently, at least during the early stages of her Alzheimer's.

Most of the participants in this study are in their forties and fifties and have elderly parents, many of whom need intermittent help. For unemployed White women in my sample, carework for elderly parents and in-laws also featured as another feminized space that affirmed their staying at home. The few Black women in this sample had qualitatively different relationships with their own parents. Another unemployed Black woman's mother lived with her full-time. A wife of an unemployed Black man was concerned about their finances because she wanted to install a stair-lift costing about $10,000 in her father's home so he could move around his own house with ease. Gina became a full-time caregiver for her mother for a portion of her unemployment. Yet, this deep act of caregiving did not translate into an affirmation of staying at home or relishing the domestic.

"We're a Two-Income Family"

Despite Mark's promise to support Gina as she figures out her next career move, Gina says that he intermittently emphasizes the need for her to be employed. Occasionally Mark reminds Gina that, "You know, we're a two-income family." From her perspective he clearly points out that a male-breadwinner, female-homemaker family structure is not what either of them signed up for. Gina thinks that her unemployment is worrying for Mark, saying, "He sort of had the weight of being the one that was employed and really kind of carrying the load from that standpoint." Mark started putting in even more overtime hours than he had before. According to Gina, Mark feels that he has to "work more" because he is the only one employed. Although Gina and Mark maintain separate bank accounts, the constraints in Gina's income flow means that unanticipated expenditures fall more on Mark now. Gina explains, "If there's an emergency that comes up, I look to him to handle that emergency." Recently, one of their payments from a rental property was considerably delayed. They had to pull from Mark's income to pay bills that Gina's income would normally cover. Gina explains that they both feel they no longer have "financial freedoms." Managing financial blips that would have been minor when Gina was employed have become a source of strain.

Gina acknowledges Mark's worries, but she is adamant that being unemployed has not meant that she has forsaken her financial obligations to her family. She deems these important. She sees herself as a having a "bit of a cushion" financially that allows her to feel more relaxed. But her financial comfort has been waning as her unemployment has endured.

Mark's concern, too, may be coming from a feeling that they no longer have as much leeway to comfortably deal with unanticipated payments. In an uncertain economy, where losing a job is fast becoming a universal experience, the Forresters also wonder what would happen if Mark's job was jeopardized. They rely on his job for benefits such as health insurance. They see his job as an important line of defense in an economy where basics of life—such as access to affordable and high-quality healthcare— continue to be linked to a bygone model of employment. No wonder the Forresters, and especially Mark, feel vulnerable. Revving up the number of hours he works is Mark's response to Gina's unemployment; he does not want her to get too comfortable at home.

Her ability to meet her financial obligations means that Gina does not fully agree with Mark's assertion that they have become a one-income family. For Gina, providing for her family is—at this juncture in her life— neither tied deeply to a job nor to doing more housework. Mark is more averse than she is to a sole earner or male-breadwinner family. Rather than seeing it as a valuable and "normal" family form as in other families in this study, it induces anxiety for Mark. Gina says, "he's taken on more of a stress around kind of being the breadwinner, where he didn't have that before." As the Forresters contend with Gina's unemployment, their gen- der strategy is to hold on to the idea of themselves as a two-income family. But Mark and Gina have different ideas about the responsibilities this entails. So, every now and then, Mark gently reminds Gina of what he thinks a two-income family means.

Gina and Mark display considerably more ambivalence toward an unemployed woman's presence in the home than do the White couples in my study. At times Gina expresses a sense of ownership at staying at home—not in order to cultivate the domestic, but rather as a space from which to map out her career path or care for her mother. Being at home is also not the predominant way in which Gina thinks about motherhood. For Gina, motherhood is vested in how to be a role model for her daugh- ters. She says, "I've always tried to have my own life outside of what my children are doing. So that's been important." She further adds, "but I cer- tainly was a role model for my daughters, you know, in terms of my career." Mark usually supports her values, which are outward looking rather than based on activities centered on the home. At other times, though, Mark underscores their implicit marital contract in which they imagined and planned for a dual-earner family.

While Gina, a Black woman, resisted the tropes of White motherhood the most forcibly in my sample, she was not the only one to do so. Although this manner of relating to the home was not dominant in my sample, other unemployed women in this study also articulated a similar resistance. In this study, unemployed women with this approach did not neatly map on to age categories, race, or gender beliefs, likely because the group of women in this sample itself was limited.

WHEN IDEALS BECOME DISAPPOINTING REALITIES

In the initial few weeks, even months, of their unemployment, women in this study overwhelmingly framed it as an opportunity to revel in the realm of the domestic. They expressed excitement about more quality time with children. But this allure of the domestic was ephemeral; idealized visions of the domestic gave way to a yearning for stimulation from paid work. These highly educated and well-paid women, after being at home for a while, often longed to return to the labor force as active participants.

But this is not always easy for women. When it comes to hiring, especially in elite occupations, employers continue to discriminate against women, especially mothers. One experimental study found that among applicants to elite jobs—for example in top law firms—a high social status helped men receive more favorable evaluations from employers. Researchers call this the "class advantage." Women from the same social class received no such boost in evaluations. Instead, they were perceived to be less committed, going against the workplace expectations in these occupations.[24] This "commitment penalty" that women face is one aspect of the US policy landscape where caregiving needs are expected to be met through privatized, usually expensive, solutions.[25] Unemployed women's responses to their unemployment evolves over time, shaped variously by their experiences in trying to find appropriate jobs for their skill levels, their prior experiences with jobs, and the age of their children.

In this study, Padma Swaminathan, an Indian American woman in her forties with two elementary school–aged sons was pleased that she had more time at home and with her sons. In her job search she focused on jobs that would allow her to have "mommy hours," as she puts it. Yet, two years after her job in the health care industry ended, she is now back at work full-time. She explains that even though she has a full-time job, which is not what she had anticipated, "it's very conducive to flexibility; it kind of works around your schedule. That's just the way that this role is set up." She explains, "If I need to do something with the kids for a couple of hours, I might just log off, go take care of that, come back, log back in." Padma is particularly conscious of how jobs in her field of health care are insensitive to the caregiving responsibilities of their workers. But she also recognizes that well-paying jobs tend to be full-time ones. When she encountered a full-time job that she saw as respecting her motherhood, she accepted it. "Our boss is very, very supportive of insuring that people that have families have a nice balance in the summertime so that the kids get equal attention." But she remains cautious, "So, far so good; we'll have to see how it works."

Unemployed women are searching for jobs in a backdrop far more variable than unemployed men. Unemployed women are often conscious of looking for jobs that will enable them to meet their responsibilities for unpaid work. Their status as mothers is particularly salient for this, and, of course, they are searching for jobs in workplace contexts that continue to be visibly and invisibly discriminating toward women and mothers in particular.

Revisiting the Bachs

Six months after I observed and interviewed the Bachs, Darlene is still unemployed. She is getting antsy now because she has been unemployed for ten months—exceeding the amount of time she had allotted for finding a new job. She has started volunteering at a veterinary school nearby. Although Darlene terms this "volunteering," this position provides $20 per hour, which is considerably more than what many jobs pay. This position also allows her to feel part of a workplace community, which she has been missing. She says, "You know, it's just a very positive atmosphere there. There are young people there. You know, there's dogs. Everybody's happy to be there. They know what their work is. Like, they really don't grumble about, 'Gosh, I really don't want to be here.'"

Nearing a year out of a job, Darlene is far less sanguine about feeling at home in her home. This is exacerbated by another big change in their lives: Larry also lost his job several months ago. I spent several hours over a few weeks observing the Bachs again, ten months into Darlene's unemployment. Both Larry and Darlene are quicker to express anger and irritation than before. In a follow-up visit to their home, Larry interrupts a conversation I was having with Darlene. He has returned from a lunch with friends. He is wearing a knee-length raincoat, since it had been raining steadily outside. Motioning outside to the bags of leaves they had raked and placed in large garbage bags which were lined up at the edge of their front yard, Larry says, "So they said the bags weigh more than fifty pounds and they won't take them away?" Darlene's lips are shut tight, and her arms tightly crossed against her chest. She nods. Larry continues, "I guess we'll have to take the bags away ourselves." Darlene does not lift her face, but rolls her eyes to the top, like she is trying to put minimal effort into looking at him. In a quiet voice she turns to Larry and looking at him steadily, says, "You mean I'll have to take them." Larry tilts his head to the side and in a cajoling tone says, "Don't be like that!" He points his index finger at her and wags it, mock-castigating her. Darlene does not reply, but continues looking at him. Because of the rain, the bags have patches of dark brown where the rain has seeped in deeper, making them heavier, as the leaves have soaked up the rain water.

Larry speculates that Darlene doesn't like having to share the space of the home with him now that he is unemployed, "One of the things that she doesn't like is the fact that I'm not away from her. I don't care, but she doesn't like it. And I think one of the reasons she went and did the volunteering was just to get out of the house." Darlene is urging Larry to find a job and get out of the house. Larry has a severance package, which lasts him until the end of the year—still several months away. Darlene's approach is similar to Amelia Radzik's; she talks about a Problem of Larry at Home. She is alarmed that Larry seems perfectly content staying at home, "I'm trying to push him to do something, even, like, aside from the money issue. I'm trying to point out to him: 'Hey, if you're only sixty now, and you live 'til you're eighty or eighty-five, that's twenty years. You cannot spend twenty years in this house reading the *New York Times* every day and just puttering around. Like, you need to get out. You need to be interacting with people and doing things.'"

Unlike Darlene, Larry does not feel any urgency to find a job. In fact, were it up to him, he would take this layoff as his shift into early retirement. He is fascinated that my own father whom he has asked me about several times, would retire from his job at the age of sixty. Larry broaches this subject with me each time we meet, often in front of Darlene, saying wistfully, "Retire at sixty! Can you imagine that!" His own dreams of an early retirement, he explains, are not a possibility given Darlene's expectations. "I've been subjected to some anger about several things that were sort of a constellation: not being morally uneasy about my place in the universe because I'm not working. . . . A couple of weeks ago, she just finally had an explosion and essentially demanded that . . . I needed to find a job. Right now. So last week I signed myself up at a temporary staffing firm and she basically said, 'OK. Good first start. Keep looking.' She wants me to get a job immediately."

Darlene is far more worried about his lack of a job than she was at a similar time about her own lack of a job. Ironically, one of the ways that Darlene had reconciled herself with her unemployment in the earlier months was to emphasize her usefulness for Parker. But she is dismissive of similar reasoning from Larry. Rolling her eyes she says, "Oh, he always has some excuse. Now the current excuse is, 'Well, I have to be around,' he says, 'to shuttle Parker back and forth for his sports things.' Like, 'You don't really have to! You know, we'll work it out.'" Now, close to a year into her own unemployment, Darlene also has a sense of urgency to be reemployed herself. She is downright irritated by things that had brought her joy in the earlier months of unemployment. Furrowing her eyebrows and frowning she describes how she feels about doing things for Parker: "I have kind of mixed feelings. I mean, I'm happy that I do it for him, I *can* do it for him. I am sometimes wondering if he doesn't have to be self-sufficient. So I have been thinking, like, 'Oh, he's gonna go to college in a couple of years.' And so there are things I should be teaching him, so now he hasn't had to organize his stuff—you know, get himself together, get breakfast." For Darlene, immersing herself in the home had been about embracing a specific kind of motherhood. It provided a sense of legitimacy to Darlene. Unlike men such as Jim Radzik and Terry Clarke, Darlene did not have to worry about being morally unemployed. She could simply be a stay-at-home mom. Over time, though, this vision lost its dazzle for her.

Fifteen months after she lost her job, and half a year after Larry lost his, things have changed for the Bachs yet again. I visit their home and Darlene, Larry, Parker, and I catch up over a home-cooked dinner. Darlene has prepared a beautiful kale salad with cranberries dotting it like jewels. We also have baked salmon, fresh rolls hot from the oven, and roasted vegetables. After over a year of unemployment, Darlene has started a new position in a large multinational corporation, earning a similar salary as the one in the job she had lost. Larry, too, has fulfilled his promise to Darlene to find paid work. He has started working as a gardener. This is wildly different from the sedentary administrative position in a squarely white-collar job that Larry had held for the majority of his career. Working at all appears to be a decision in response to Darlene's insistence that he cannot just stay at home, that to be a moral man he must work. Larry sees his current work as a curious experiment in response to Darlene's entreaty; it has not changed his social class position, since their ample assets and Darlene's job means that they continue to live in an affluent neighborhood and harbor hopes of sending Parker to an elite college. As a gardener, Larry's days start early, at four in the morning, and end late in the evening. At six this evening, just returning from a gardening job, Larry looks exhausted. There's a bandana tied around his neck and his denim overalls have patches of mud and dirt from kneeling in flower-beds. Most of his work, Larry explains to me, occurs as part of a landscaping crew, usually in affluent residential areas. Rainy days are annoying because of the inordinate amount of mess, but he enjoys this strikingly different job. He goes to sleep each night, he says, like a baby because of the physical exhaustion.

Revisiting the Forresters

When I meet Gina, another year later, it has been two and half years since she has been unemployed. Gina is impatient to get back into the paid labor force. She says, "I'm sort of anxious to be working, and to kind of have more of a routine." While exploring potential career pathways had been important earlier, she says, "I believe that I was sort of doing what I needed to be doing, and now I'm kind of in a different place, and I need to move on." But, she adds, "I really think that everything has a season," and the season for her now is to be in a full-time paid job.

Despite her conviction in her employability and credentials, she has faced a series of disappointments with promising job opportunities that have fizzled out. She says, "I would have anticipated that I would have had something by now." Most recently she was in the final rounds of a series of competitive interviews. But a new CEO was appointed. He decided to change the organizational restructuring, eliminating the position for which Gina had been interviewing. She says, "that was very disappointing." Not getting jobs has been a dejecting experience. Shaken, Gina asks, "Why has it taken so long?" Like many unemployed people, Gina internalizes her unemployment, wondering out loud, "So what's wrong with me? Why can't I get a job?" This leads her to pick at flaws she perceives herself as having, "Is it because I'm getting old, or is it this, or is it that?" These question become a quagmire, reeling her in to endless circles of speculation. The corporate workplace does not fairly reward skills or experience, penalizing women for being women, especially in elite occupations, and being especially unforgiving for workplace interruptions such as periods of unemployment, or leaving the workforce due to caregiving responsibilities.[26]

A year ago, Gina emphasized the importance of getting her nonprofit established. Although the nonprofit continues to exist, it is far less of a focus for her now. She explains, "I have settled on the fact that, well, the nonprofit will be there; it's not gonna be my main focus, but I want to look at how I can use that to sort of leverage into my next position." Gina's attention is now fixed on something "more conventional." Her enduring unemployment is causing her deeper financial concerns. She is getting increasingly uncomfortable with having to dig into her savings, "I think in my own mind, I have my thresholds, you know, and then you get a little bit more anxious with each threshold." Recently, Mark has suffered an injury which prevents him from doing more overtime work as well.

There have been other changes at home too, for which Gina is thankful. In the early stages of her mother's Alzheimer's, her mother had moved to live with Gina for several months. The end-goal, as Gina explains, was always to have her mother set up with the appropriate equipment in her own home in a metropolitan city about two hours' drive from Gina. Gina says of her mother, "She's doing better. That whole journey that I was on to set her up so that she had services in her home. We've kind of finalized that." She continues, "I do feel like that, for the most part, has been concluded, and so I can sort of move on from that. And I have a little bit more space to kind of close that chapter and focus again about getting a position."

CONCLUSION

In the American imaginary, the home has varied meanings. A powerful one is persistently that of the home as haven—women's appropriate domicile. But the home has never been uniformly regarded as a sanctuary or deeply coupled with femininity for all women. The home-as-haven image is one that enmeshes White middle-class women specifically. This image can sometimes be a source of respite. In the Bach family, we see how Darlene and Larry activate gendered traditional tropes—although these have never quite captured the realities of their lives—as they contend with Darlene's unemployment.

The domestic offers Darlene respite during an emotionally difficult time. Unemployment is difficult, but working, too, can be rife with stress. One study shows that workplace stress can be more harmful than unemployment.[27] For women, especially those in higher-level positions such as Darlene, the corporate workplace has historically been unkind. Women face daily reminders about their status as outsiders in the workplace, have their authority questioned more often, and are frequently the "only" in a workplace, for example the only woman in a C-suite position.[28] Workplaces not designed to take account of women's lives, leave, as one of my women respondents put it, a "bad taste." Women's unemployment does not occur in a contextual vacuum; unemployment is often just one more painful experience in a long history of workplace slights and rejections. The domestic, framed as a source of joy, can be a foil to the workplace, which itself is sometimes a source of deep, although often invisible, sorrow.

During unemployment, affluent White women like Darlene activate a domestically vested and culturally valued identity. Unlike her male counterparts, Darlene is less obligated to prove herself as being morally unemployed; instead, she can become a stay-at-home mother. Doing so bolsters Darlene's privileged class and race status, especially as she navigates the spaces of her social milieu. She finds camaraderie among the mothers at her son's school and with the women at her country club. Interactions in these affluent White spaces, alongside Larry's affirmation, invigorate her understanding that adopting a stay-at-home mom identity, rather than being an ideal job-seeker, is an appropriate response to her unemployment. Intensive motherhood depends on these social institutions that prop it up, naturalizing a socially constructed mode of behavior.

The passing of time, however, reveals the fragility of the ostensible naturalness of intensive motherhood. Over the long term, Darlene yearns to reenter the paid labor force. The appeal of the domestic sours. This was not the case for all the women in this sample. For some, like Padma Swaminathan, the domestic remained as important as ever, but also unattainable as they took stock of the landscape of available jobs.

For other women, such as Gina Forrester, the home is less intertwined with ideals of culturally prized womanhood. For Black women from the professional middle-class, staying at home does not quite offer the respite it does for White women. Instead, for these women staying at home runs contrary to their expectations of financial independence. These women also do not navigate social spaces that unequivocally bolster staying at home. Neither do their interactions with others, especially their husbands, affirm staying at home as an appropriate choice. Instead, unemployment throws up ambiguity about how to interact, especially with their husbands, becoming more acute with the passing of time.

Unemployment is par for the course in the contemporary American economy. The experiences of Darlene Bach and Gina Forrester illuminate how powerful conventional images of home and paid work, as well as experiences with these institutions and spaces, shape unemployed women's responses to their unemployment. The particular images that women and their husbands find compelling, and that they attempt to comply with, shape their gender strategies. These vary based on the specifically raced and classed experiences of these women and their families.

PART II

Gendered Time in
Job Searching

3 Dinner Table Diaries

INTERACTIONAL QUANDARIES AND THE IDEAL
JOB-SEEKER NORM IN FAMILIES OF UNEMPLOYED MEN

A devoted focus on job searching is an obvious way for unemployed people to comply with the ideal job-seeker norm. Men and women experience the ideal job-seeker norm in different ways; men are particularly subjected to pressures to seek employment. The case studies in this chapter explain two main variations in how couples seek to help men comply with the ideal job-seeker norm. Job searching is a delicate and difficult topic, especially if it continues for a lengthy period of time. Searching for a job means braving one rejection after another. Talking about it, especially daily, is not easy. Some couples manage to navigate the treacherous terrain of these painful, but important, conversations with aplomb, but others struggle.

The first couple I discuss, the Goldbergs, adopt a "warhorse anchoring" approach, in which they recall previous marital challenges that they have overcome. This allows Tamara and Kevin to collectively produce a unified definition of what Kevin's unemployment means. They establish a set of "feeling rules" for how to interact around Kevin's unemployment. Feeling rules are a "form of pre-action" that function as a powerful guide for shaping behavior; these rules establish a "sense of entitlement or obligation that governs emotional exchanges."[1] Feeling rules shape interactions within social institutions, such as families. In contrast, the Janssons do not agree on how to define Robert's unemployment. Nor do their feeling rules quite align. Their interactions around Robert's job search are often frustrating for both Robert and Laura, draining them of energy rather than revitalizing their sense of togetherness.

Taken together, these case studies explain how the varied ways couples define men's unemployment, and the different feeling rules they establish to talk about it, produce divergent marital experiences in professional middle-class couples experiencing unemployment.

TWO WARHORSES IN BATTLE TOGETHER

Kevin Goldberg, a senior project manager in his early fifties who previously worked in the health care industry, lost his job about a year after he and his wife of almost eighteen years, Tamara, nearly divorced. Tamara and Kevin, a White couple, met over two decades ago at a singles event that Tamara had organized. After dating for a few years and being engaged for a few more, they got married. They have two children, a six-year-old daughter and a thirteen-year-old son. Kevin and Tamara both have full-time careers; Tamara is a tenured associate professor at a large state university. She has one of the most secure jobs possible, earning $72,000 a year in addition to a bonus, typically $2,500, that her university gives for Christmas. When she teaches in the summer, she earns additional pay. In recent years, Kevin's annual income had approached close to $200,000, not including benefits and bonuses. In most high-earning American couples, men earn more than their wives, and Kevin too has been the primary earner for most of their marriage.[2]

For Kevin, who admits to traditional ideas about gender roles, providing for his family has been a big part of his identity. He says, "Well, as you might guess, just being from the culture that I am, the . . . American way is for the man to take care of the family. So, you know, it wasn't unreasonable for me to see myself in that role, and that's what I wanted to do." Kevin's views are not particularly uncommon among American men of his background—White, professional, and middle-class—who see their ability to provide economically for their family as key to their participation in married family life. While this aspect of masculinity is culturally dominant, it is nonetheless often rejected by men who are not structurally positioned to support their families financially—for example, by working-class men who work in low-wage, unstable jobs, without benefits. These men often emphasize their ability to provide for their family by doing work around the home and providing affection to children.[3]

Tamara, who identifies as a feminist, explains that her own ideas of gender equality are at odds with Kevin's. She says, "I think one of his thoughts was always 'Well, I make more money. I'm the breadwinner.' Although he felt guilt about this because he knows that I don't believe in that. I don't believe that men should have more of a say than women or whatever. But I think he always felt like, and it was an underlying sort of theme, 'Well I make more money so I should get to decide how things are and things should work for me.'" The loss of his role as a provider hit Kevin hard, and he would often seek reassurance from Tamara: "He said to me 'Well, I've always made a good income, haven't I?'" Tamara would respond to these comments by telling Kevin that he was not reducible to the income he provided. As she reported to me, "And I said 'Well, yeah but I don't care about that.'"

Now that he isn't working, Tamara believes Kevin appreciates her career more. She says, "I think that being in the situation where he wasn't making most of the money made him understand the value of the fact that I had a career." Kevin explains that although the financial consequences of his job loss have been considerable to their family—by dint of how high his income had been—Tamara's job has shielded them from the most severe impacts: "In most cases it would have been catastrophic you know, for most families. And it was for several of the other families. For example, a lot of high-level executives were let go too, who were of the mind-set that they were the money earners and their wives didn't need to work. It was those people probably who had a lot of trouble."

Even so, Kevin's job loss has been emotionally devastating for him; Tamara terms it a "trauma." The Goldbergs are convinced that the company Kevin had worked for acted in bad faith when it came to letting Kevin go. They are currently embroiled in a lawsuit with the company. The months leading to Kevin's layoff were long and deeply unpleasant, as the company sought one unsuccessful reason after another to terminate Kevin for cause, eventually fabricating a resignation from him that ended his employment. Tamara had started guiding and supporting Kevin through the layoff process. Since then, she has been similarly involved in his job search and in supporting Kevin as he strives to find his footing as an unemployed man.

"Warhorse" Anchoring

Tamara is enmeshed in Kevin's job search, playing an active role in helping him strategize his next career moves. They had learned the skills they needed to weather Kevin's unemployment without damaging their marriage by overcoming past challenges. Tamara explains, "He and I, we've been through a lot. But we came very close to divorce the year before this happened, and we had worked through all of our issues." The Goldbergs perceive their relationship as a warhorse—a strong, fierce, and battle-ready beast that has faced impossible challenges in the past and is now ready to support them in any challenge that life throws their way.

Many of the Goldbergs' past challenges relate to disagreements over their children, specifically their thirteen-year-old son, Josh. Josh has been diagnosed with bipolar disorder and consequently often experiences mental health issues, including severe depression, which has led to several suicide attempts. Tamara explains, "Kevin could not accept that there was really a biological issue with our son. He wanted it all to be, you know, about behavior or that he was spoiled or things like this." Sighing deeply, she continues, "So that really put a lot of stress on the marriage." Selecting her words carefully, Tamara adds, "It put a lot of stress on me because I felt like I had to choose between the marriage and my child. That's not a choice I wanted to make necessarily."

The disagreement between Tamara and Kevin over how to deal with their son ran deep. It troubled Tamara, because she thought Kevin's behavior toward Josh might be harmful to Josh. She explains, "At the point where I almost left, that was one of the things I said, 'You have really got to change how you look at the kids, and particularly your son, or I'm leaving.' Because I felt like it was doing tremendous damage to my son at that point. I said to him, 'You need to understand that your son has an illness. That this is not his fault and that we need to be a little understanding and help him work through these things rather than getting mad at him for the way that he is.'"

To work through their issues, in the year prior to Kevin's job loss, Tamara and Kevin started regularly seeing a family counselor. The therapist encouraged them to focus on what had drawn them to each other in the first place. Tamara explains, "She made us think about what it is that threw you together in the first place. That you're attracted to this person because they offer you something that you feel like you want but you may not have yourself." Kevin and Tamara credit counseling with having taught them to better appreciate and enjoy each other. Tamara continues, "We like each other and we have a lot of respect for one another. It was just sort of getting to a point where we could put aside all of the external nonsense and get back to that. That the other person in the marriage had value and was important, was a good person, and that we feel like our lives were enriched by being with the other person." This also meant putting aside their "workaholic" tendencies to take out time each week for each other, without the children present. They consciously made time for a walk around the neighborhood, a dinner out with friends, or a night out dancing. Sometimes Kevin's mother, who lives nearby, will take the kids for a night on the weekend so that Kevin and Tamara can have some quality time together.

Kevin's unemployment entered the Goldbergs' lives just after they had implemented these practices. Tamara explains, "So we actually were in a pretty good place to deal with it. We had strengthened our communication skills and things." Tamara says, "When you come to the brink of divorce, there's bad blood. It doesn't get to that point unless there's bad blood. And I think over a lot of the years we built up a distrust of one another and one another's motives. When you feel that that person is almost like an enemy, that they're undermining you." Because being a provider was so integral to Kevin's identity, losing his job left him feeling bereft. He became nervous about how Tamara saw him. He wondered if Tamara, who had pushed for a divorce earlier, would see his unemployment as a failure, and would go through with a divorce. Tamara says, "I think he did wonder if that was going to make everything blow up and make me want to leave." Kevin strongly credited his job and income as the major things that he brought to their marriage, "In his mind I think one of the contributions that he makes is financial." Shaking her head resolutely, Tamara clarifies, "But for me that was not a question. . . . We had already come to the point where we had the option of saying 'No,' and we had decided that that wasn't what we were going to do. We were going to stay together. And so this never entered into that equation for me. That was a decision that was already made." Instead, the only question for Tamara was how to get through Kevin's unemployment unscathed, together. "It was, 'OK, how do we get through this? How do we get him back on track? How do we recover from this?'"

For the Goldbergs, getting through this unemployment means working as a team, with Kevin as the lead, on his job search. It means communicating frequently, and with depth, about his job search efforts. Kevin and Tamara both perform roles for each other, *and* for themselves. As the "ideal job-seeker," Kevin is doing his utmost to get reemployed, and Tamara is supporting him in this.

Working as a Team

Tamara and Kevin faced the process of Kevin's job loss as a team. When rumblings of downsizing started making the rounds six months before Kevin was finally ousted, Tamara sought to reassure him. She explains, "So he kept saying to me 'I'm afraid that I'm going to lose my job.' And the only thing I would say to him is 'I don't understand it. If they wanted to eliminate your position, why wouldn't they have eliminated it in the summer when they let go of everybody else?'" This was Tamara's way of cautiously trying to reassure Kevin. She encouraged him to start preemptively job searching. "He was looking for jobs and I said, 'By all means look. And let's be very careful and let's document things and let's watch what happens.'"

A few months later, Kevin received a poor performance review. This came, ironically, the same year that he had received a company-wide award for excellent performance. This honor was complicated by the fact that Kevin had been nominated by a former vice president, who had then been let go. Kevin shared the details of his performance review with Tamara— they have made it a point to discuss their professional matters openly and frequently with each other. Tamara explains her understanding of the situation, "And then there were some other strange things that went on. In his annual review they tried to make him responsible for a failure to report an adverse event that really was not his job to report." Kevin again turned to Tamara for support and advice: "And he talked to me about that. He said, 'I think I should challenge that in my annual review.'" Tamara had supported him unequivocally, saying, "Absolutely. It's not right. You challenge it.'" Kevin and Tamara established a pattern during this process in which

Kevin updated Tamara with each development. Given that Kevin was in the process of losing his job, it seemed natural to them that they would focus more on Kevin's workplace issues.[4] This pattern continued to hold after Kevin lost his job and turned his attention toward finding a new one.

When Kevin was finally let go, the Goldbergs were aligned in their perception that Kevin had been treated atrociously by his former company. They saw any attempts by Kevin's former company to fault his performance as baseless. Kevin himself is a bit more downcast than Tamara on this point—his understanding that his performance was not a real issue and his feeling of failure don't align well. He says, "I think one can't help feeling like you've failed. At a baseline level, the unconscious level." He acknowledges, "But consciously I knew better, you know." Tamara has played a crucial role in consoling Kevin that his job loss was not his fault, "And my wife was looking in from the outside and said the same thing. That it's clear, you know, that these are engineered situations to get people out. Nobody, none of them, did anything wrong, it's just that the company is trying to find ways to cut their losses and save themselves."

In her classic study of unemployment, *Falling from Grace*, anthropologist Katherine Newman explains that the question of *fault* for job loss matters greatly in terms of how wives either do or do not support their husbands. In families where wives blame their husbands for losing their jobs, the marriages were much more strained than in those cases where the wives see the job loss as undeserved, even if the material impacts on these families were the same. Newman wrote her book in the 1980s, when being laid off was still a relatively rare experience. Today, downsizing, rightsizing, and layoffs have become familiar parts of the American, indeed the global, experience. How you lost your job is no longer as important as how long it takes you to find a new one.[5] The couples in my study were more concerned with how men behave *after* their job loss, rather than the reason for their unemployment. Given the ubiquity of employment insecurity, this shift in couples' focus makes sense.

Constructing the Ideal Job-Seeker and Reproducing Masculinity

The fact of being unemployed is not as stigmatizing as it once was. The duration of unemployment matters more. Unemployed men and their wives thus often seek to mold unemployed men into ideal job-seekers to ward off this stigma. The ideal job-seeker is an unemployed person who focuses intensely on regaining employment, protecting time solely for activities that facilitate reemployment. Kevin has been entirely occupied with his job search, describing his days and activities in the following manner: "During the day, I would devote that to looking for work. Networking, making contacts. You know, anything I could think of." Kevin rattles off a long list of activities that took up his time, "I've always kept lists of contacts that I've made over the years. I contacted them. LinkedIn was really good. I asked other people who they were working with, career consultant-wise. I joined local networks, for other people who are unemployed, to help them find work." As many of my men and women respondents put it, "searching for a job is a full-time job!"

Kevin did another thing that many men, but not women, reported doing: he established a consulting firm.[6] This is a particular artifact of the class position of these men. Mid- and late-career professionals often turn to consulting only after losing their jobs. The consulting firm usually only has one consultant—the unemployed job-seeker—and usually no clients. Consulting—even if only on paper—is a way of managing impressions and defraying stigma from unemployment. The purpose of the "firm" is to provide unemployed men with a more legitimate calling card when applying for jobs. Instead of an unemployed job-seeker, these men became "consultants."[7] When newly unemployed men establish these firms, they are generally doing so to access standard jobs with benefits. Kevin says, "I actually established it right after I lost my job." He continues, "So I set up the consultancy immediately. But in parallel I was looking for full-time employment too."

Tamara proudly describes the time and effort that Kevin puts in to finding employment, "He was spending as much time as he used to work, trying to find something." She elaborates, "So he applied for *everything*, even things that were not really remotely the right thing for him." Continuing, she says, "We got him his project management certification, so he had to do a training course. That took some time to study for that and amass a certain number of hours of credits for that." Beyond this, "He spent a lot of time networking. He did a startup with the ex–vice president [of the company, who had nominated Kevin for the outstanding performance award]." Tamara is very much looped into Kevin's job searching activities. Nodding approvingly, she says, "But he was always busy. He was extremely busy just doing different things and trying to find ways to get himself back on track career-wise."

Tamara could have resented the time Kevin invested in job searching. She could have expected, for example, that his unemployment, meant that he could now spend more time on housework.[8] But Tamara encourages Kevin to be the ideal job-seeker by focusing on job search-related activities, "I said to him, 'You haven't had to go out and look for a job in twenty years. You had no reason to expect to." She prods him to spend time polishing his job searching skills, telling Kevin that, "You have to get your interview skills back up to par. You have to understand what the ethos is out there now. You have to fine-tune your CV. You have to figure out what's the best path for you." More importantly, she legitimated job searching as a time-consuming process by telling Kevin, "All of these things take time." It has been important for Tamara to help Kevin get accustomed to the slowness of the reemployment process, saying that she was "Trying to help him understand incremental progress so he didn't feel like he was spending all this time and not getting there."

Kevin and Tamara have aligned understandings of the time and effort it takes to be an ideal job-seeker. But these ideas are not gender-, class-, and race-neutral concerns. The ideal job-seeker, like his counterpart the ideal worker, has access to support from a specifically imagined home and family. This is a two-spouse family. The employed spouse, usually the wife, continues to manage housework, often outsourcing it to domestic help. The division of housework, as we will see in chapter 5, may not shift substantially, but continues to be organized in alignment with anachronistic but powerful ideals about the home and marriage. These aspects combine to guide the interactions of these couples.

The Feeling Rules of "How Was Your Day?"

A very important question for Kevin and Tamara these days is asking each other "How was your day?" The question itself is a shorthand for daily check-ins to keep Tamara involved in the job search. Tamara takes the lead in asking this question, as she has done since before Kevin lost his job. As Kevin searched for flaws in his performance or himself, Tamara reassured him. She says, "We spent a *long* time working through that." Tamara was a consistent "cheerleader," as she says, and a counselor to Kevin, "I just *very* gently, had to work through that with him."

Tamara is describing what sociologists call "emotion work." Arlie Hochschild describes this as "the management of feeling to create a publicly observable facial and bodily display."[9] For Tamara, counseling Kevin with the face of optimism comes at the cost of concealing her own worries about his unemployment. Emotion work matters because it is the kind of micro-interactional work that upholds unequal, normative expectations for gender. The emotion work that Tamara is doing is shaped by specific norms that are powerful for the Goldbergs, even as they go counter to Tamara's feminist sensibilities. In this particular case, one of the most important gendered norms is that Kevin's sense of self-worth is inextricably linked to his ability to provide a privileged level of lifestyle for his family. Tamara focuses on replacing Kevin's own interpretation—that his job loss was his fault—with her own, kinder one. Tamara saw it as important to "persuade him that they were getting rid of a lot of the more highly paid people—people with health care issues or people in their family with health care issues, people over fifty." Kevin received his wife's concern for him as Tamara intended—as helpful, "It was a two-way street. It's *always* a two-way street. I couldn't have gotten through it without her support. Her very positive input all the time."

Even before Kevin lost his job, the Goldbergs established a pattern of interacting where the simple, four-word question "How was your day?" served to signal a space of comfort. The Goldbergs have instated feeling rules that make possible such communication.[10] "Feeling rules," as a part of emotional work, involve the social set of understandings that govern how and when we express our emotions. Tamara has identified and explicated these feeling rules surrounding Kevin's unemployment in the context of their marriage. Their feeling rules stem from an understanding that Kevin's job loss is, as Tamara names it, a "trauma," with Kevin consequently being in a "traumatic mind-set." Defining his unemployment as such means allowing Kevin time to process this trauma. "I felt like he needed to feel that he was the one that worked this out and he was the one that found a resolution."

One practical consequence of this approach has been that Tamara has not revealed to Kevin that she thinks full-time, standard employment may no longer be a possibility for him. She wonders whether he will ever find full-time work again, or whether consulting—well-paid and prestigious, but non-standard—will be the best kind of work he can hope to get. Tamara explains, "So I did not up-front say to him I think this is going to probably take eighteen months. I sort of tried to ease him into that and let him come to it on his own because him specifically, but I think men in general, this is a big assault on the ego and the sense of self."

Defining the situation of Kevin's unemployment as a trauma shapes the Goldbergs' feeling rules for interacting around his unemployment. The resolution to this trauma will be reemployment in a position similar to the one Kevin lost. The jobs that Kevin and Tamara have in mind for him are well-remunerated and prestigious positions available only to the top echelons of workers. Like Jim Radzik in an earlier chapter, Kevin and Tamara are relatively choosy about the jobs for which Kevin is suitable. While Kevin harbors hopes for a standard job of the kind he lost, Tamara has relaxed that particular criterion. Tamara refrains from hurrying Kevin up to the realization that standard employment has probably slipped forever out of his grasp.

Tamara is very deliberate in her interactions with Kevin, strategically performing and articulating her support as he strives to find a job. The first feeling rule is that Kevin should understand her intention is only to help him. As she explains, "I really felt like it was sort of key to getting him through this and getting him to understand everything that I was doing was to get him back to work." Clarity about her intentions, that she wants to prop him up, not tear him down, is buttressed by the remaining feeling rules.

The second feeling rule is to give Kevin the space to understand the situation on his own terms. She explains, "I had to play a supporting role in that, and I could advise kind of gently." She elaborates, "But I felt that there would be very negative consequences if he felt pushed in any way, or he felt like I wasn't supportive, or he felt like I was negative." Raising her eyebrows and pursing her lips, Tamara adds, "I had to be very careful."

The third feeling rule dictates that Tamara should offer a positive spin on Kevin's job searching experiences, even if those primarily consist of rejection. She does this by emphasizing piecemeal progress in the job search process. Kevin's job applications frequently result in callbacks but have yet to produce an offer of a job. Kevin became worried, and it became Tamara's job to encourage him. She explains, "I would say to him, 'All these people applied for things for months and months and months and months and they don't even get a callback. So clearly, you're doing something right. . . . It's just you haven't found the right thing yet.'" Tamara puts great faith into how her verbal interactions with Kevin will motivate him. She describes how else she would seek to restore his self-confidence, by telling him, "'It's just really competitive. Think of all the people you know that are out of work.'" Tamara's aim was to "help him see that, that there was progress being made that wasn't necessarily a full-time position or a paycheck. But that he was making progress."

The fourth feeling rule for the Goldbergs pertains to suspending the *economy of gratitude*.[11] By framing Kevin's job loss as a trauma, and his consequent job search as taking place within a toxic residual haze of that trauma, Tamara emphasizes that this has not been a normal time in their life. Emotional reciprocity could not be expected. While she focuses on supporting Kevin, she also accepts that he might not be in a position to fully acknowledge or appreciate this. "I don't think he sort of had the emotional wherewithal to say, 'Thank you very much for doing this or this.' And sometimes he would get upset and he would blame me. But I think that's part of working through the trauma." Kevin, in his retrospective interview with me, acknowledged her support, saying, "She has offered a great deal of positive support. Unfailing positive support—I think that's really what's gotten me through." He credits her tremendously, adding that Tamara "shared my plans what I was doing and planning to do, to, you know, navigate through this thing. And it was just sort of a team effort, and we managed it together." He also recognizes that while this was a difficult process for him, it was also challenging for Tamara, "I know it was very hard for *her*. I know sometimes she must have been discouraged." Suspending the economy of gratitude means affirming that Kevin is the spouse more in need, and so he can, if necessary, make demands that may not be quite so acceptable during other times.

"How was your day?" is a simple question, but for Kevin and Tamara it is a hopeful one. It cultivates togetherness and reifies their trust in each other. This four-word question underlines that Kevin's job loss and job search is not Kevin's problem alone—it's *their* problem.

Tamara as a Helpmeet

In their interactions with each other, both Kevin and Tamara are following specific scripts that they have produced for this unstable time in their lives.[12] Kevin, like the other unemployed men in this study, seeks to fulfill the role of the ideal job-seeker. Tamara, too, is following a gender-specific script: that of the helpmeet. A quaint term, *helpmeet* captures the idea of a set of traditional, normative, and gendered behaviors expected of wives in White, professional, middle-class America. It is worth pausing for a moment to consider how Tamara, a profoundly self-reflective person who desires gender equality in her marriage, understands her own role in the couple's interactions.

Tamara situates herself in the broader context of women's role in heterosexual marriages, saying, "If you're going to be married and you're a woman, you just better be prepared to be the one that is the linchpin. Because, fair or not, that's most women that I know—that's the way it is." Tamara further explains: "I just think that in realistic terms that marriage places a greater burden on the woman in terms of keeping the family together. So, I think the emotional linchpin of a family, if it's functioning properly, is in most cases the wife or the mother."

Tamara acknowledges the social expectation for wives to fulfill the affective role within marriages. She describes wives as being the "emotional barometer of the couple." She sees herself fulfilling this gendered role, "So I sort of knew that things were going to fall apart if I didn't hold them together." Kevin strongly agrees that Tamara has been critical to ensuring that they weather his job search as a team. He says, "She never, she *never* makes me feel any less of a person than I was." While Tamara has taken on a decidedly gendered role as helpmeet, this role is ironically due to her own career—where she brings her knowledge of the labor market into her interactions as a partner with Kevin regarding his job search.

These feeling rules have nevertheless put an enormous burden on Tamara, particularly since Kevin's transition period to contract-based labor has been ongoing for almost two years. She adds, "So it was very stressful for me." Speaking directly to the issue of how she is doing emotion work for Kevin's benefit, and thus upholding a particular set of ideas of marriage and family, she explains how she has redefined her thoughts about equality: "What I had to come to realize is that a partnership doesn't mean that he has to give me the same things that I give him or perform the same roles that I perform. We can still have a kind of equality." The process of marriage counseling was crucial in changing Tamara's perspective on marriage, largely by encouraging her to see marriage—and the role of the wife—as something that she has actively chosen to accept. For Tamara, this acceptance means "If I choose to be married, if I prefer to have him in my life than not have him in my life, this is just one of my roles and I'm just going to have to accept that." From Tamara's perspective, the institution of marriage, in which both she and Kevin are playing their gendered parts, is immutable. Rather than presenting a moment to innovate on the institution of marriage, Kevin's unemployment has crystallized their respective, gendered roles.

Almost a year after losing his job, Kevin works as a consultant—that is, a consultant with clients. He has gotten comfortable with the idea that he will likely never have a standard form of employment. He does not find this as painful a prospect as he once did. From Tamara's perspective, Kevin needed time to contend with the trauma of his job loss, "He probably would have found something much, much quicker. But I think it took him a while to come to sort of accept that" he could not expect full-time employment of the sort he was used to. This was a struggle that Tamara felt was important for Kevin to go through.

Kevin's current consulting project is in a different state, and he commutes home for the weekend. He feels ambivalent about being a consultant: pride that he has work, but reluctance with the *type* of employment he has. Shrugging his shoulders, he says, "This isn't ideal at *all*. It's work, and it's good work. And it's even interesting work. It's been very difficult to find though." But while Kevin deems his situation less than ideal, he does not find it particularly unusual. He sees himself as experiencing a very common side effect of contemporary working life. Nodding slowly, he says, "Like I said, it's kind of the America of today."

A MEETING OF THE MINDS . . . EXCEPT FOR ROBERT'S JOB SEARCH

Robert Jansson, a White forty-nine-year-old who had held jobs with titles like communications director for large companies, lost his job seven months ago. He had been at his most recent position for just about a year, but neither he nor the company found it to be a good fit. Robert and his wife of five years, Laura Jansson, who is also White, live with their four-year-old daughter, Tessa, and two-year-old son, Taylor, on a quiet, clean street. It's easy to discern that this is a wealthy, predominantly White neighborhood when you spot the individuals who get off the train in the evenings: tired men in suits holding briefcases and iPads. Their jackets are folded and slung on their arms. Women wear silk shells over pencil skirts or with pantsuits. Their heels are glossy, hair immaculately arranged. Their hands often show the flashing wink of a discreet diamond. A group of high-end shops catering to this neighborhood's clientele clusters around the train station: a Lilly Pulitzer store, a specialty stationery store, and a luxury makeup and beauty products store. It is picturesque, even idyllic.

The Jansson's three-bedroom home is halfway down a tidy street bordered with quaint, but sturdy, stone houses. The home is on the smaller side, overflowing with Taylor's and Tessa's clothes and toys. It was not meant to be a family home for them; Robert bought it when he was still single. There are no picket fences here; instead, the front yard of each house ends at the pavement, creating a buffer between the private gardens and the road.

In some ways, Robert and Laura are a study in contrasts: Laura has a brisk, take-charge manner and alert eyes. When she first meets people, she examines their face as though sizing them up. She left New York City and moved in with Robert several months before they married, but she retains her New York demeanor—energetic even at the end of long workdays, animated at the thought of spending a few hours with Robert and their kids together. Robert has large, soft blue eyes that seem dreamy as he takes in his surroundings. He has a wide, easy smile. For the several weeks that I observed the Janssons in their home, it was usually Robert who opened the door to let me in, greeting me with a warm smile that instantly put me at ease about being in their home during a time that is clearly stressful for them.

For Robert and Laura, inviting me into their house to understand their lives during Robert's unemployment is a way to support and appreciate intellectual life. Robert and Laura's relationship can be succinctly described as a "meeting of the minds"—where this refers to the joy and satisfaction they get from sharing their interest in political and social current events. They deeply enjoy substantive discussions on a range of topics, particularly politics. Even in the midst of Robert's unemployment, parenting two young children, and Laura's busy career, they make the time to take pleasure in each other's company. They make room for little moments of togetherness, sharing thoughts, jokes, and laughter and finding delight in each other.

Despite his work history in the lucrative corporate sector, Robert continues toying with pursuing a PhD in the humanities, envisioning a life of the mind where he gets grants, publishes, and attends conferences on arcane and inaccessible philosophical topics. He resolutely describes himself as a "writer" who just happens to work for corporations. This is an important aspect of his identity. Laura has a much more practical bent when it comes to life in academia. She nonetheless agrees with Robert that it is important for their experience to be recorded and shared broadly so that people can understand what contemporary unemployment in professional families looks like.

But while they have a meeting of the minds in most aspects of their life, they are not in agreement when it comes to Robert's career. The same question that Kevin and Tamara use to anchor their marriage—"How was your day?"—is instead a fraught site for conflict about how Robert's career should unfold. Both Robert and Laura quietly tussle to realize their vision of his career.

Striving to Be "Grown-ups"

Laura and Robert have been no strangers to "transitions," as Laura terms it, over the course of their marriage. Laura elaborates on the flurry of life changes that the Janssons have already experienced in the course of their marriage, "It's funny, we've gone through transition more than anybody should in the time that we've been married. So, he's had three jobs, we've had two kids, and lost two parents in about five years' time. So, a lot of transition." Right before their wedding, Laura lost her job. For a few months, she ran her own public relations company. This was her full-time occupation for about a year and a half. She has extensive experience in this area, typically working within large media companies. The arrangement suited both Laura and Robert, since the couple had Tessa during this time—the flexibility of self-employment allowed Laura to combine having a new baby with paid work. The second period of unemployment—although voluntary—occurred when Robert left a job that dissatisfied him. He was confident that his skill set and experience would allow him to find a comparable job quickly. Instead, Robert ended up being unemployed for a year, which, as Laura explains, was unsettling for him. "He was surprised that it took him as long as it did to find a job.

For Laura, more than for Robert, these transitions are emblematic of a life together that is still somewhat embryonic. These transitions have left Laura feeling as if they have not yet begun to live "grown-up" lives. The Janssons are fortunate in many ways, having escaped the worst financial repercussions that unemployment can bring. The financial implications of Robert's unemployment, however, impact their lifestyle. The Janssons can neither upgrade their car nor buy a larger home, both of which had once seemed probable. Their vacations have been limited. Like many other parents in the professional middle-class, the Janssons consider it their responsibility to raise their children with awareness of the world outside the United States. Being able to travel internationally with their children is a goal for them.[13] But they are not yet able to comfortably meet these goals.

Even so, the Janssons still retain many of the key lifestyle characteristics of the professional middle-class. Given a landscape of limited policies to support American parents with children, families in this social class often depend on privatized—and expensive—solutions to childcare. This is particularly true for dual-earner parents. The Janssons, for example, continue to employ a full-time nanny for their two children. Of the ten families in this study with an unemployed man and at least one child who was not yet old enough for kindergarten, seven continued their existing childcare arrangements. Childcare can be prohibitively expensive, even for affluent families in the United States. But the Janssons see paid childcare as an essential investment to allow Robert to focus on his job search. The Jansson's decision is also driven by a second consideration. Laura is afraid that they would forever lose their nanny, whom she and the kids love, if they let her go now.

The Janssons have instead made smaller financial changes. They spend less on dates and are more mindful of where they eat out. They try to minimize costly social outings with friends. Their biggest financial worries do not concern their present lifestyle, but rather their inability to build up financial reserves for their future.[14] Affluent families—who are over-whelmingly White in the United States—actively seek to advantage their children through such expensive measures as participating in extracur-ricular activities, providing access to prestigious educational institutions from kindergarten to college, and injecting financial transfers into chil-dren's adulthood. They also often receive significant financial help from their own parents to secure their children's class positions. Not being able to build up wealth deflects from these aims, which are characteristic of what being from this advantaged social class entails.

Having to let go, temporarily at least, of this vision of an upper-middle-class life has been hard for Laura. She explains, "I think the hardest thing has been putting many life plans on hold. I really want to move into a new house. I really would like to plan great vacations. I drive a car that's four-teen years old." Laura acknowledges that these concerns may, on the face of it, appear to be shallow. For her, though, these material accoutrements are intrinsically linked to how she defines life for an upper-middle-class family, "I think that while they sound very material, I think they kind of represent a life experience that I was hoping that we would be able to enjoy as a family." Laura's desire for a large house is tied to her vision of family life: "One of the things I wanted to do was be able to have Thanksgiving. I'm forty-three years old and I've never been able to do that." Biting her lip, in a softer voice, she adds, "I had to go to my little sister's house 'cause she had the room. So, I kind of feel like being the old-est sibling in my family it's kind of my responsibility to do that." Laura's vision of family life is embedded in the imagery of affluence, where she expects that both her and Robert's jobs should provide a relatively high standard of living. She is restless to get back on track toward realizing this vision.

Robert, too, feels like life is on hold, especially in terms of his aspira-tions, but Robert is less concerned with the symbolic value imbued in physical things. Instead, Robert yearns to go back to graduate school, earn a PhD, and embark on an academic career. He feels as if his true vocation has been put on hold. Robert explains how this pull toward academia has been "a constant tension in our marriage." He adds, "I want to go back to school." Robert is clearly concerned with the financial consequences for his family if he goes to graduate school, to the point that he notes that he could choose to pursue a degree in a program more closely related to the corporate sector. He explains, "And I could even do something that was more business oriented if I needed to. Like there's an organizational dynamics program that's interesting." But Robert is fully aware of Laura's deep reservations about being unable to afford the lifestyle she thinks they ought to have at this stage of their lives, "But she's going to have none of that, because like I'm going to pay money and not be bringing in money. We have two young children. That's not the lifestyle she signed up for, right?"

Laura has communicated her expectations for her lifestyle—given that they are a professional, dual-earner couple—clearly to Robert. He pinpoints these: "So she expects that we're going to travel to Europe and do what we did when we were first married, you know. Like she's expecting we're going to have a second house somewhere. She wants a different lifestyle." Robert, too, has become accustomed to a handsome salary. He acknowledges that it's not just Laura who has such desires. He continues, "And I appreciate that. I like that, too. I like traveling. I'd like to have a house at the beach." Still, the fact that for the past twenty years he has been in a career that is not his preferred choice continues to be a source of regret for Robert. He feels as though he is missing out on the life he is meant to be leading professionally: "But at the same time, I want my dream. My dream job, as it were, I'd be a history professor somewhere, you know. Or teaching social theory somewhere." Robert explains that he has tried to address the topic of a career change for himself toward a more academic one, but Laura has not received those overtures enthusiastically. "I've tried to broach it a few times. That's not going to happen. I know that's not on the table for discussion, so that's why I'm still looking at corporate jobs."

This tension in Robert and Laura's marriage manifests in different understandings of what the feeling rules should be during this critical time. The Janssons do not define the nature of Robert's unemployment and job search in the same way. Robert sees ambiguity in his career path, whereas Laura is certain that Robert needs to be pursuing his current career with zeal. In one of our interviews, she told me, "I think in his heart of hearts, he's not going to get the job that he wants because the job that he wants is *your* job, Aliya. He wants to be a college professor and an academician and he started on that path, and that ship kind of sailed." Rather than hanging on to dreams that are difficult to realize, Laura's characteristic go-get-'em attitude means that she thinks Robert needs to move on. "I look at it, you know, you either need to create new dreams or figure out what you can do to kind of meet that need, that desire, that passion that you have. Because at the end of the day, you have a family with two kids and that is where the focus should be."

The absence of a unified definition of the situation, however, means that the feeling rules under which Robert and Laura continue to operate are frequently misaligned. The two implicitly disagree on the feeling rules. For Laura the first rule is that Robert should want to continue on the path of the career he has had so far. Robert is less convinced. He is using his unemployment to consider—even if just hypothetically—other options. When Robert and Laura discuss and interact around his job search and his career, they do so in a context where each has specific visions about how their life together should look. This vision mostly overlaps—they both want travel, comfort, and to raise their children as individuals who are knowledgeable about the world outside America. Yet Robert is more ready, at this point, to make some material sacrifices to pursue another career. His heart is not entirely in his job search. This context informs how Robert and Laura discuss and interact when it comes to Robert's job search.

Divergent Feeling Rules for "How Was Your Day?"

Robert and Laura lead busy lives. Any given evening after Laura comes back from her job, the nanny leaves, and Robert and Laura prepare dinner, the atmosphere in their home is frenzied. Weekday evenings it is usually just the four of them in the house. Like many White families in the professional middle-class, neither of them have family members who live particularly close by. Most of Robert's and Laura's siblings live either a flight or at least a few hours' drive away.[15] Their children have play dates rather than casual drop-ins. Their home is a private space, and they do a significant part of their socializing outside it.

On weekday evenings, the house is bustling, with pots, pans, utensils, and crockery being taken out of cupboards and drawers. Paper and plastic bags rustle, the loud exhaust fan whistles, and vegetables sizzle on the stove. Taylor keeps up a nonsensical chatter, as two-year-olds do, making sounds with toy cars and trains. Sometimes, Laura stops what she is doing in the kitchen to strike a chord or two on the piano in the dining room to please Taylor. Taylor, who is fascinated by the piano, rewards her with a grin. It is in the midst of this noise and these small acts of family intimacy that Robert and Laura carry on conversations. Sometimes one is in the kitchen and the other in the living room; they call out to each other over the cacophony.

The question "How was your day?" is code to prompt Robert to provide updates on his job search. It is asked and discussed in this buzzing context. Laura is usually the driver behind these daily conversations, although Robert sometimes offers updates on his job search unprompted. One evening, for example, Robert and Laura keep up a friendly conversation while setting the table. Laura starts off by saying, "So how was your day?" Before Robert can answer, she energetically adds: "Did you read the list of jobs I sent you?" Robert turns away from her and picks up something from the kitchen counter. In a softer, tired voice, he says, "I actually only skimmed it at the end of the day, so I didn't have a chance to look in detail." Laura checks out job boards, emailing Robert jobs she thinks he may be interested in or suited for. Laura's behavior was not particularly unusual in the couples I spent time with; the wives of unemployed men reported checking job postings, reading cover letters, and providing advice on their husband's résumés. Laura resolutely pursues the question. As soon as everyone is seated at the table, Laura turns toward Robert and says: "Well, I looked it over and there were three jobs that would be great for you, Communications Pro . . ." Robert interrupts her, saying, "Communications Pro? Like in the Midwest?" Laura shakes her head and says, "No, it's in the Northeast."

At this, Robert shrugs his shoulders and goes to fetch a glass of water he had left in the kitchen. He appears disengaged from this conversation, responding halfheartedly. He enters and exits the room, seemingly in an attempt to avoid the conversation. When he enters the dining room again, Laura persists, mentioning another position: "I thought the Chemico one would be good?" Glancing at her, Robert responds with a noncommittal shrug, "Yeah, but you need to know someone to get in." Laura keeps going.

She sits up straight, smiles, and says, "I know someone at Chemico!" In a more subdued voice than Laura's, Robert responds with "So do I. Not that they've ever helped me." Turning away from Laura, he walks to sit down in his chair. Tonight, the conversation about job searching had ended.

This somewhat tense exchange reflects the fundamentally different feeling rules that Laura and Robert have about how the interactions should proceed. Robert believes that he should not share all the emotional ups and downs that he experiences as he searches for a job, in part so that he can protect Laura from these emotional upheavals. Robert says, "You don't want your job search to become so overwhelming." He explains: "Let's say you're having personal problems; you have personal depression or personal whatever. You don't want to use your wife as a therapist and dump on her constantly. Because then your whole relationship will become based on this experience and this kind of conversation." He elaborates, "I don't like to use my friends and marriage relationship as my sounding board for all my painful whatever. So I don't dump on her." He continues by explaining that were he to constantly share his grief, Laura— or anyone, really—would become annoyed, "And so she's ultimately not going to want to stay in that situation." Robert's individualized perspective is stoic. His preference for containing the pain of his unemployment within himself echoes research findings that show that men are less likely to seek help for emotional and mental well-being.[16] Women, in contrast, may be more able to rely on friends, usually other women, for such support. Robert seeks to protect Laura from his sorrow.

In terms of his job search, Robert explains that Laura "knows 20 percent of what I'm going through, maybe 25 percent. Maybe I'm not as honest as I could be. So some relationships may be a little more open. Maybe they're 50 percent." Robert's reasons for not disclosing the details of his job search with Laura are based in consideration for her, but Laura rejects the premise. She feels she ought to be deeply involved.

In a chat with me later about Laura's general approach to his job search, Robert described it as being more active and involved than he was comfortable with. He feels sensitive and vulnerable, saying: "One of the things you feel when you're unemployed is you're hypersensitive to disrespect much more because you're feeling like you're not appreciated, you're not respected because clearly nobody wants you on the market, right, you're unemployed. You're constantly struggling with self-respect, identity issues on a daily basis." Unlike the Goldbergs, who have decided that normal feeling rules can be suspended during this time, Robert simultaneously expects Laura to give him space and act as if everything is normal.

For her part, Laura is trying to be supportive toward Robert, even as she too worries about his job search. But trying to be supportive, Laura says while laughing hesitantly, "takes a lot of hard work!" She adds, "But I know that I have a tendency to come off with a tone that sounds like 'What are you, an idiot?' And I need to temper that. That's not just with Robert, that's a personal weakness that I often have to temper. Especially in this situation with Robert I have to work really hard to temper that because he's not an idiot. He's a really smart guy and he deserves to be employed and he deserves to have a great job that he's happy with." Although Robert wants to separate Laura from what he sees as his individual concern, Laura yearns to be involved. Laura strategically regulates her tone and words when she speaks with Robert, all in hopes of being supportive, but Robert sometimes reads her attempts to be helpful as vexing. The feeling rules associated with the topic are further complicated by the fact that Laura is far keener on Robert continuing to work in the corporate sector than he is. These interactions serve to continually emphasize the importance of Robert's job search in their relationship, but they can be draining for both spouses.

The Challenges of Being an Ideal Job-Seeker

Both Laura and Robert expect Robert to follow the norms of the ideal job-seeker. For Robert, though, his ambivalence toward his career makes it difficult to apply himself toward the process of looking for employment. He describes himself as "INTJ" (Introvert, Intuition, Thinking, Judgment), using the common parlance of the popular Myers-Briggs personality test used in corporate workplaces. He explains that, because he is an introvert, the networking aspect of job searching is particularly difficult for him. He says, "But I kick myself in the job search. I know I'm not doing things in the job search that I could be doing more effectively. Like networking . . . I feel like it is an imposition any time I reach out to my contacts. I don't want to feel like a drain on them." Robert moreover blames himself for forgetting the cardinal rule of job searching: that you never stop searching for a job until you get a job.[17] He explains, "When I was having deep conversations with this one company, I let other things kind of whittle away. You can't do that. You've got to stay active—*whoosh, whoosh, whoosh*—on multiple fronts. And you've just got to, you *got* to keep at it. Even if you think you got a job offer imminent, you gotta keep going out on interviews and talking to people and, and I think I probably wasn't as aggressive." Robert is hard on himself for having let up on intensive job searching when talks with one company seemed to get serious, although they did not ultimately work out. Robert also has neglected the "skills improvement" aspect of being a job-seeker, as he believes that his existing skills and experience should be enough. That they haven't been continues to surprise him.

Watching all of this, Laura characterizes Robert as being out of sync with the current job search process. Laura is keenly aware of when Robert's job search slackens. She explains, "He was most recently interviewing for a position and he thought he'd gotten up to the last round of interviews. Because he was meeting with some pretty high people and then he didn't hear anything. During that process, that third round, he found out that there were more people still in contention than he thought." Shaking her head in annoyance, Laura continues, "He didn't say specifically that he stopped looking, but he kind of stopped looking, because he thought this was an almost sure thing." That Robert stopped searching for other potential jobs was exasperating to Laura: "To me that kills me, because it's like, 'You don't have a job!' There is no guarantee. There is no offer letter. My own perspective would be like you are pounding the pavement until there is an offer letter in your hand." Laura expressed her discomfort at Robert's approach to the process. She continued, "And he said he screwed up. Those were his words. I said, 'You don't have an offer, so why would you stop looking?' He said, 'I screwed up.' . . . You have to remember that even in the best of times, there's definitely more than one person applying for the same job. That to me was frustrating." The Janssons' different responses to this episode demonstrate another disjuncture in their feeling rules: Laura expects that Robert should be humble and striving until he gets a job, whereas Robert remains confident in his professional value.[18]

Besides his unease with networking, and his certainty that he would get a job that he ultimately did not, Robert also found himself getting distracted by his academic inclinations. He would often pause his job search to spend time reading new books in his academic interest—books unrelated to his professional career. Robert has an academic friend who loops him into ongoing academic conferences and presentations. Once, for example, Robert describes, "So I found out he was delivering a paper at this conference [near me] and I'm like, 'Are you doing anything for lunch? I'll meet you. I'll come, hear your presentation and come to the conference, for instance. And we'll have lunch and whatever.'" Robert, who lives in a suburb in the northeastern United States, is conveniently located to major hubs for academic networking, including cities such as New York, D.C., and Philadelphia. He describes how his unemployment afforded him the ability to indulge in academic pursuits from time to time: "It's nice to be able to live where we live. I can go to New York in the course of the day while the nanny is there. . . . But normally I wouldn't have that kind of luxury and be able to go to a conference in the middle of the day and hear a presentation." Wistfully, Robert adds, "I'm an academic by nature, so it feels good for me. Here I am at [Ivy League University], hanging out at a conference. I would love that lifestyle, you know?" Shaking his head as though willing himself back to reality, he says, "Well, I could get to indulge that." Robert finds it difficult to enact the expectations of an ideal job-seeker when he is not entirely convinced he should be working in the corporate sector.

Laura wants to disabuse Robert of what she sees as his overly romantic notions of the academic life. "I tell him this: he thinks of a professor as what a sixty-year-old professor is. A sixty-year-old philosophy professor, a guy who is sitting in a room—his office has the walls lined with books and he sits there and thinks and then writes a little bit, thinks some more and then writes a book." Shrugging her shoulders, Laura continues, "The fact of the matter is that doesn't happen. My sister happens to be a professor in science, so I have a little bit of firsthand information, plus I do know other professors. It's not all like sitting and thinking and ruminating and writing books. One of the things I love about him is he has romanticized views of things, but they're not necessarily realistic."

Robert and Laura's interactions are shaped by a context in which they lack a unified vision for his career. Their conversations around his job search amplify these long-standing differences. In the absence of a mutually agreed-upon vision, they have not been able to transform "How was your day?" from a charged question to one that pulls them together.

CONCLUSION

A simple question—"How was your day?"—can offer remarkable insights into a couple's vision of their class standing, ideal family structure, and marriage. The mostly White, professional middle-class families profiled in this study operate under assumptions that both partners will be gainfully employed in high-status, standard, and stable positions commensurate with their credentials. Their bar for "acceptable" jobs is particularly high for unemployed men.

Couples mostly agree that an appropriate job should be standard, full-time, and well paid. In the case of the Goldbergs, however, we see that Tamara is initially more receptive to a nonstandard job for Kevin—consulting—than Kevin himself is. This is largely because of Tamara's own understanding of the changing nature of paid work, namely, that standard jobs are eroding and even high-status occupations are subject to instability. She also recognizes that her own career as a tenured faculty member ensures the family's access to important benefits, such as health care and college tuition waivers for her family. Kevin has a harder time reconciling this with his internalized identity as the primary earner for the family. For the Janssons, the expectations of maintaining a specific lifestyle are more salient than those of social roles. As Robert wistfully contemplates life as a professor, Laura wonders when they'll be able to buy a new car. While an academic position meets the social expectations of middle-class life, Laura understands that Robert's earning prospects would be significantly less than in the corporate sector—and that is assuming he completed his degree and obtained a job.

Tamara is right: job stability is eroding in the United States. And yet the families in my study hold some of the most privileged occupations in America. Prior to their unemployment, they had achieved the American dream. For families like the Goldbergs and the Janssons, male unemployment is an aberration in their professional middle-class status, an aberration that must be eliminated as soon as possible. Interactions over the nature of the husband's job search therefore make up an inordinate amount of these couples' marriages. But incongruent definitions of the situation and varied feeling rules produce divergent interactions. For some couples, the stress of unemployment drives them closer together, while, for others, it highlights existing tensions.

In my larger sample, I found that those couples with longer marriages (those exceeding fifteen years) typically used some sort of warhorse anchoring to weather the storm. They could draw on shared marital memories of previous challenges. Even marriages that neither party described as especially strong often came together over the course of the unemployment. In contrast, those couples with shorter marriages (especially those less than ten years), experienced men's unemployment as one of the main challenges that their family had encountered. Caring, loving, and strong marriages appeared to tread a shaky ground, as couples strove to define the situation and establish feeling rules, with varied levels of success.

4 Can Women Be Ideal Job-Seekers?

In contrast to unemployed men, unemployed women, are gently nudged *away* from the behaviors associated with the ideal job-seeker norm. The couples in this study adopt a neo-traditional approach to how unemployed women should go about finding a job. They justify the woman's presence in the home—and out of the workforce—by emphasizing the appeal of domestic roles.

In this chapter, I delve into three case studies. In the first case study, featuring Eileen Boyle, I highlight how, rather than organizing their days around job searching, many women in this study fit job searching into other responsibilities, typically centered around childcare and housework. The ideal job-seeker norm retains only faint power over these families. Instead, with the encouragement of their husbands, unemployed women often use gendered language to emphasize the importance and meaning of their unpaid work over their paid work.

In the second case study, of Caroline and Ben Anderson, I show the marital tensions that arise in the (rarer) cases when unemployed women *do* adhere to the ideal job-seeker norm. Both women and their husbands view this compliance as aberrant. As an exception, this case study illuminates the often unstated, but quite prevalent, norm that unemployed women should dive into domestic activities.

Finally, I present a third case study of Rebecca and Chuck Mason. Instead of cajoling Rebecca to embrace the pleasures of domestic life, Chuck expresses disappointment that Rebecca lacks professional motivation. While both Chuck and Rebecca express preferring a situation where Rebecca is employed, they do not invest time or money to facilitate her reemployment. The case of the Masons reveals the gap between expressed beliefs and actual behaviors.

These three case studies shed light on the subtle and mundane challenges that the unemployed women in this sample experience as they search for paid work. These couples' interactions around women's approach to job searching divert women from the strict expectations of the ideal job-seeker norm.

SQUEEZING A JOB SEARCH INTO DAILY LIFE

Eileen Boyle is a friendly and candid White woman nearing fifty. Thickset, with curly, shoulder-length, dark blonde hair, Eileen's blue eyes take in her surroundings with sharp curiosity. This may be a remnant of her twenty-seven-year career as a field investigator in the insurance industry. Eileen lost her job three months ago, after being accused of using confidential insurance information for personal gain—in her case, checking that the car her sixteen-year-old daughter had purchased was not stolen. Eileen is hurt, and angry at the manner in which her long career with the company ended.[1]

Now, her days are primarily filled with home-related tasks. Eileen is job searching, but she fits this around her domestic activities, which usually center on her two children, a daughter and a fourteen-year-old son. Eileen's job search is fragmented. Even though she spends a considerable amount of time on her search, especially right before any interviews, the hours she spends tend to be patched together. Eileen's case, in which her job search is secondary to other, mostly household tasks, is typical for the majority of women in my sample. Their approach to minimizing the urgency of women's reemployment is at odds with the material reality in these families, in which the wives had contributed a significant part of the household income. In about half of the cases, the women earned as much or *more* than their husbands.

Eileen is one of the women who had earned significantly more than her husband. She has a college degree and earned close to $100,000 a year. In contrast, her husband, Danny, dropped out of high school. His job—as a custodial staff member at a nearby school—is anomalous. Most college-educated individuals tend to be married to others who are college-educated, including those in this study, making Eileen and Danny somewhat unusual in this respect.[2] Additionally, Danny comes from a wealthy family—his father was an executive at a pharmaceutical company, who in turn inherited a vast amount of money from his own father. Children of college-educated individuals, like Danny, are highly likely to obtain college-degrees.[3] The considerable wealth that Danny's octogenarian parents have, Eileen says, will eventually come to Danny and his siblings. Enough, Danny's father has told him, that "none of them will have to worry about working again." Affluent White parents, like Danny's, are the most likely to provide financial gifts to their adult children throughout the life course. This includes help with key purchases, such as a home, as well as intermittent financial injections. Initial race-based disparities in wealth are exacerbated over the life course, advantaging Whites in America over other racial groups.[4] Despite Eileen's unemployment and Danny's low-status work, Eileen and Danny are more protected than most other American families.

Danny's siblings all went to college. He has a brother who is a vice president at a multinational organization. Danny, though, just wasn't cut out for anything beyond high school. Chuckling, Eileen explains, "Very bright, but just wasn't a student, let's say. Genius-level IQ, actually. Like reflecting back, he probably was dyslexic, but it wasn't diagnosed when he went to school." Consequently, Eileen has been the breadwinner throughout their marriage, since her husband earns, at best, a third of her income. Danny's parents help out at times, providing gifts of money or small loans—something they have been doing more of since Eileen lost her job. But most of the time, the Boyles live off of Eileen and Danny's income. They have accumulated about $100,000 in Eileen's 401(k) and have a separate pension account. They've established college accounts for their two children. Currently, Eileen says, the accounts cover two years of college for both the children. In part because they expect a considerable inheritance, the Boyles are relaxed about how much they save.[5]

Given that Eileen and Danny primarily rely on Eileen's income, you would think that there would be excessive pressure on Eileen to find a new position. Yet Eileen describes her own job search as more fragmented than do most unemployed men in this study. When I ask Eileen to tell me more about how she searches for a job, she instead rattles off a list of errands that occupy her day and center on her kids, "Now I get up, take [the kids] to school because neither of them likes the bus in the morning time, and that's just something we fell into doing." After that, Eileen mostly has the morning and afternoon to herself. She spends this doing "the normal stuff around the house that I did anyway," such as household chores or sometimes preparing for upcoming job interviews.[6] She continues, "I pick my daughter up from school. My son has football. So, if my husband can't get him, as horrible as it sounds, it has been really convenient because their schedules this fall have been so horrendous." Chuckling at the irony that her unemployment eases their family life, Eileen shakes her head and says, "I don't know what I'd be doing if I was working. So, get him from football. He has Scouts one night a week, so I get him to that."

The extracurricular activities that Eileen describes are a mainstay of middle-class American family life. Parents in this study see these activities as investments in their children's educational and occupational future. As job insecurity becomes the norm, parents seem to be emphasizing extracurricular activities even more, often as a way to help children develop "passions." Parents often express a belief that this will advantage children in unstable job markets, where hiring often turns on personal characteristics.[7] Children from working-class and poor families are less likely to be enrolled in as many organized activities, often due to their costs. This type of errand, which occupies much of Eileen's time, is specifically middle-class.

In between all this business of daily life, Eileen stitches together a few moments, and when she is lucky, hours, for her job search. She often ends up job searching while she waits to take either her son or daughter home from their extracurricular activities. When her sixteen-year-old has her after-school shifts at a café near their home, Eileen says, "Depending on what shifts she's working, there are times I'll just bring my laptop and hang out in the café and do job searches, send out résumés, send out applications, that sort of thing." Only when she has a concrete goalpost, like an upcoming job interview, does Eileen spring into job mode.[8] "So if I get an interview, I'll spend, I don't know, eight, ten hours preparing for the interview. So that's pretty much how I spend my day." For unemployed women, like Eileen, job searching takes priority at key moments—like before an interview. Otherwise, they slip into a domestic routine, often with the support of their husbands.

In these families, the wife's unemployment becomes a moment to shift economic accountability squarely to the husband's shoulders.[9] Eileen reminds her husband, "Now it's time for you to pick up the pieces and time for you to man up and do what you need to do.'" This is a defensive strategy—to thwart any criticism that her husband may make about her job loss. Practically, there is not much more that Danny can do in terms of increasing their household income. Eileen and Danny are both well aware that Eileen's earning potential is higher than Danny's. But Eileen's comments pointedly foreground Danny's gendered obligation to provide—not hers. Even though Eileen has worked and out-earned Danny throughout their marriage, she invokes what is for her an ideal: of the homemaker wife with a provider husband. Nor was Eileen the only woman to do so. Other women in this study consistently draw on culturally shared scripts that place the responsibility for providing for their families on men. Their unemployment becomes an opportunity to re-create traditionally gendered ideals of the family.

While Eileen is trying hard to find another job, she is not doing so in a way that adheres to the ideal job-seeker norm—namely, that job searching should be her sole, narrow focus, requiring a specially demarcated space in the home and the majority of her time. Nor, unlike most unemployed men in this study, does Eileen feel the need to demonstrate to Danny or to others that she is adhering to the ideal job-seeker norm. Eileen is forthright with Danny and does not try to protect him from any emotional repercussions of unemployment (unlike Robert Jansson, for example). Eileen turns the tables by pointedly invoking notions of a male-breadwinner as normative and desirable. Of the twenty-three unemployed women in my sample, nineteen reported a fragmented job search experience similar to Eileen's.

Women's job searching, by and large, is fragmented, and thus starkly different from most of these unemployed men's experiences. But the less common experiences of job searching—women who job search like men and women who *don't* job search like men but whose husbands wish they did—also reveal ruptures in beliefs, behaviors, and economic realities.

CAROLINE'S "OBSESSION"

Caroline Anderson is a tall and athletic woman in her late forties. She is dressed casually in jeans and a zip-up hoodie for the sunny, but slightly nippy, fall day when we meet. Caroline, whose work was in the health industry, has been unemployed for eleven months. She is laser focused on regaining employment; that is a priority for her. Her husband, Ben, though, wishes that she were less focused on her job search. He encourages her to see her unemployment as a time to delve into the domestic (something that has never quite appealed to Caroline) and relish time with their two sons, aged twelve and fourteen.

Caroline and Ben have been married for over seventeen years. They met during a class they were taking at night school in the early 1990s. After taking a few years off after high school, Caroline attended college as a night school student in her twenties. Ben, on the other hand, started his own college journey back in 1985, finally graduating with a bachelor's degree almost two decades later, in 2004. Ben is a slight, clean-shaven man, with a close-cropped head of blond hair and dark brown eyes. He has an easygoing manner. Dressed casually in jeans and a button-down checked shirt, we meet at a local bar where he often gets together with friends after work. Ben explains why it took him so long to get a college degree: "I only had about four or five classes left and I would have gotten my degree right after she did. But I quit school and focused on saving money so we could get married, buy a house, all that stuff. The degree was secondary to me, because I was already in the industry of my choice, my career." Ben, a religious Catholic and a professional in the insurance industry, presents a specific image of his family informed by gender norms: of a household where he bears the economic responsibility, to the point of postponing his educational aspirations.

Although, as we will shortly see, Caroline is intently focused on her job search, in some ways she agrees with Ben's ideals of a family life, saying: "If I didn't have the stress of looking for a job, I think I would be a typical stay-at-home mom and be even more involved in school and do even more things with my kids. But it's not that way. I really do need to work. I thought about maybe working part-time, but we do have debts that we want to pay off." Caroline frames her employment as necessary to their household and obstructing her from realizing a more traditional family ideal of a male-breadwinner family. Elaborating on this she adds, "Now would be a good time for me to be home, or working part-time because my kids are young. When they're off in college, I wouldn't want to be working part-time, I would want to be working full-time. But now is when we have all the debt. So it's kind of like life works almost backwards."

Although Caroline expresses finding the prospect of being a stay-at-home mom alluring, from her perspective it does not jive with the family's financial situation. Both Ben and Caroline idealize a one-and-a-half-earner model, where men provide the main income for the family and women are the primary caregivers. In practice, however, Caroline's and Ben's incomes have been equally important to the life they have built together. In the past five years, before she lost her job, Caroline's income had been the mainstay of their family's financial well-being, since Ben encountered one bout after another of unemployment and underemployment. Things had stabilized a few months before Caroline lost her job because Ben had received one. Both were employed for a few overlapping months, and each contributed about half to their annual $150,000 income.

Ben self-consciously brings up the fact that Caroline's income has usually been higher than his, "I was never emasculated by my wife making more money than me. I thought, 'Oh, that's great!' I look at the whole house income. I didn't care. I was in a job that I loved. She didn't care either."[10] Although Ben dismisses this disparity in their earnings as meaningless, he thinks Caroline finds it unsettling to no longer be earning at all. With the hint of a smile, Ben raises his hand to just above his head saying, "She wants to be back up there with me. I think she has a little bit of competitiveness with that." Ben hasn't asked Caroline directly about this, "I haven't brought that up with her to ask her, 'Is that affecting you?' Because I know she would immediately deny it: 'No, no, I don't care.' But I know there might be a little bit of jealousy." In her own interview, Caroline did not mention feelings of competitiveness with Ben over their respective earnings. Instead, she praised Ben's job as allowing them to weather her unemployment relatively unscathed financially. Comparing her own unemployment to Ben's earlier, she describes Ben's job loss as being financially harder on them than hers has been, saying, "So I just feel like if we got through that, we can get through this, because now my husband's doing much, much better. If it weren't for his good job, we would not be in the position that we're in." As such, Caroline is like Amelia Radzik in chapter 1 in terms of emphasizing Ben's employment as necessary for the household—even though usually she earned much more than him. She did agree, though, that her paid work is extremely important to her, and so she focuses on finding a job.

Caroline was one of four women in my sample who adhered strongly to the ideal job-seeker norm. She was intensely focused on her goal of quick reemployment and structured her days accordingly. Caroline describes how she spends her days: "Usually I'm at the computer. . . . I contacted this person; I contacted that person. I spoke to this person on the phone. Really trying to 'work my network,' because I saw a job here or there or whatever it was. And so I got a phone number of someone I had been trying to get in touch with and I was on the phone with that person for a while, so I feel like I was working a full day. It was all job search related." Caroline's home is now her office, as it was for Terry Clarke in chapter 1. Her approach to job searching and her emphasis on obtaining paid work aligns more with that of the unemployed men in my study than other unemployed women.

Ben recognizes that Caroline's paid work matters tremendously for how she thinks of herself. He explains to me that Caroline is focusing on finding a job because she feels the stigma of unemployment: "I think she likes working. I think she misses it. She hasn't said to me, 'There's a social aspect,' but when she gets into conversations with people, 'What do you do for a living?' and she can't come back with a, 'Oh, I do this.' She has to say, 'Well, I used to be in this. I'm unemployed right now.'" Caroline has never discussed the sense of social stigma with him, but Ben believes that it may play a bigger role than Caroline lets on. Ben finds this mystifying. He compares Caroline to his brother, who is also unemployed. He understands his brother's sense of shame, because he is a man. He explains, "Now my brother, on the other hand, it [social stigma] is a big issue. But I think that's because he is a guy. He's got the ego. He doesn't want to talk about it. So I haven't talked to him about his job situation in over a year because he gets upset about it." Ben points to both social as well as what he considers intrinsically masculine reasons—the "ego"—that his brother experiences over his unemployment. But, as Ben sees it, these reasons do not apply to Caroline.

Caroline and Ben disagree over Caroline's intense focus on finding a new job. Caroline complies with the ideal job-seeker norm, but Ben does not think she should. During Ben's own bouts of layoffs in recent years—two in the past five years, one lasting four months and the other nine months—he spent the period frantically looking for paid work: "When you're out of work, and especially, I guess as a father and a husband and quote-unquote, 'head of the household,' right—if I want to be old fashioned—you feel that pressure of being out of work and feeling like you need to produce and bring some income into the household." Despite having felt the pressure to job search himself, he counsels Caroline to view her unemployment as an opportunity to spend time with her sons. Ben is more traditional than Caroline, which he attributes in part to his faith. Their experience illuminates how husbands coax their wives to comply with gendered expectations that emphasize women's participation in unpaid work.

Pathologizing Caroline's Intense Focus on Her Job Search

Caroline's experience departs sharply from unemployed men's, though, when it comes to how her husband responds to it. While wives of unemployed men encouraged their husbands and expected that men's job searching would take priority over domestic chores, Ben is disappointed with Caroline's tunnel vision. Mimicking Caroline, Ben hunches his back, and mimes typing furiously on a keyboard. Pausing, he looks at me and explains, "She's on her computer morning, noon, and night. It's a big distraction to me, to my kids, and to the house, and to our way of life."

Throughout their marriage, the domestic realm has never been particularly alluring for Caroline. Although she has usually done the majority of the cooking in their family, planning elaborate meals for the family, for example, or immersing herself in chores such as picking up and dropping off her sons from their extracurricular activities is not Caroline's way of showing care for her sons and family. Now that she is unemployed, Ben has been hoping that Caroline might be nudged into following these more traditional patterns of demonstrating affection to her family. He is frustrated that this hasn't been the case. He continues, "She's kind of obsessed. *Obsessed* is a strong word, but I don't know how else to say it other than if you can be strongly determined, she's like ten blocks beyond that. To me, she's obsessed with trying to get a job, any kind of training that will better her. She looks for anything all day and trying to make connections with everybody."

Caroline's behavior does not align with Ben's cultural expectations about femininity and motherhood. Ben pathologizes Caroline's focus on her job search, saying: "It's almost like my mother, who has dementia. My father lives with her twenty-four-seven. He wants her to be his lifelong partner, wife, and be there in conversation. It doesn't happen. He can't help her and it frustrates him. Sometimes he's able to catch himself and realize it. Other times he gets frustrated and probably angry with God or whatever, and he'll reach his boiling point and not realize that he's not talking to somebody that can rationalize with him." Ben continues by extending the analogy between Caroline's job search and his mother's dementia. "I apply that situation with my wife, because I can't change her, I know that." Instead of confronting her directly, Ben takes what he describes as a more subtle approach. He says, "So what I try to do is remind her, not every day (I don't badger her). I pick my times and I remind her subtly of things. I'll say, 'Hey, what time you getting home?'" With this kind of remark, Ben means to pointedly admonish Caroline to not treat their home like her office. He elaborates, "She's already home, but it's a subtle hint, like 'join the family.' Other times I'll just say, 'Hey, I really think you got a lot on your plate. You ought to think if all these meetings are necessary.' Not stopping her from going, but I just put the thought in her head. We don't argue about it. Because if I did, I'd feel like I was telling her not to be who she is."

Ben understands that Caroline's career is important to her, But he continues to worry that Caroline's focus on job searching may be detrimental to her time with her family. When he gets frustrated and feels as though he is not getting through to Caroline with subtle hints, Ben sometimes takes a blunter approach, telling Caroline, "No one's got a gun to your head saying, 'Get a job.'"

Wives of unemployed men often function as supervisors who keep men on track with their job search. Ben frames himself in similar terms, but with the opposite goal of getting Caroline to cut back on the job search. He says, "Well, I do address [her fixation on her job search], but I don't do it like a supervisor. I don't want to seem like a supervisor, because I know she's very capable of handling all the situations." Both unemployed women and their husbands in this study understood behavior like Caroline's to be out of the ordinary. Instead of encouraging this laser focus on reemployment, husbands usually sought to soften it.

Ben explains to me that all of this is for Caroline's benefit. Thinking back to his own unemployment, Ben recalls the intense pressure he felt to find a good job, and soon. He worries that Caroline feels similarly pressured: "I don't want her to feel the pressure of getting a job just to get a job. . . . First thing I told my wife was, 'Do not feel the pressure to be looking for a job and apply to every job that you see. Don't feel that pressure. I'm working. Yes, we need your pay. We can get by without it. . . . but don't get into that frame of mind where you feel pressure and obligations to job-search for eight hours a day.'"

Caroline appreciates Ben's downplaying of the need for her to work, saying, "I thought you were going to ask if he's been pressuring me like, 'Oh, are you looking for a job?' He has not. . . . He's supportive in that he doesn't pressure me. He knows I'm looking." Ben understands that their lifestyle depends on both his and Caroline's income, saying, "We need [her to be employed] if we want to have a nice, comfortable living." Nevertheless, Ben actively discourages Caroline from spending too much time on her job search. He does not expect her to treat her job search like a full-time job. Nonetheless, Caroline has been conscientious about using her time wisely to find a job. She explains, "He sees me and he knows . . . I'm doing everything I can." Caroline's immersion in the ideal job-seeker norm suggests that if Ben did encourage her attempts to find a new job, Caroline would feel more supported in pursuing her own priorities of becoming reemployed as soon as possible. Instead, Ben's narrow conception of support—by which he encourages Caroline to focus on the domestic—undermines Caroline's preferences for speedy reemployment.

Redirecting Unemployed Women to Focus on the Home and Children

For Ben, the most irksome part of Caroline's focus on job searching is his perception that it detracts from her attention to their home, and especially their two sons. In Ben's view, this should be Caroline's focus. He draws on his own experience of unemployment to urge Caroline to redirect her focus to the home and their children: "I did bonding time with my children. And when I look back on it now it was a blessing in disguise. I loved bonding with my boys. It was the best time I had with them. . . . The two little knuckleheads and I'd have a lot of fun. She never got that opportunity. One of the first things I told her when she got laid off, I said, 'I don't know how long you're going to be laid off, but you now have an opportunity to bond with your kids.'"

Ben thinks Caroline may later regret not spending this time with her children. With some irritation, he tells me about a recent incident when he thinks Caroline made poor choices with her time. "So last night was my son's birthday. I was away. . . . I knew when he got home from school nobody would be there. My wife was going to be out all day with her mother." Caroline was taking her elderly mother to a few routine doctor's appointments. As discussed earlier, unemployed women frequently spend more time on carework, often for their elderly parents. We saw that Gina Forrester, a Black woman, was unapologetic about using her unemployment as a time to focus on her mother. Gina's husband did not raise an eyebrow at this. For Ben, a White man from the professional middle-class, however, it is self-evident that their children should take priority over their kin, including parents. Many of the unemployed women I spoke with mentioned their gratitude for the ability to spend time at home, for the respite from long work commutes, and from the frenzy of managing chores and paid work. Caroline, though, did not. She sought opportunities to be out of the home, usually for reasons related to job searching, and although she continued to do the bulk of the housework, she did not frame it as a respite or gratifying; she continued to see housework as necessary drudgery.

Fuming, Ben continued his anecdote, "So when my son got home from school, on his birthday, he came home to an empty house." Shaking his head, he says "And I feared that would happen. So I left him a note, big note: 'Happy fifteenth birthday, buddy. See you for dinner.' And it said, 'Love, Dad.' I knew as soon as he walked in, I could put a smile on his face. I feared that she wouldn't be there. She wouldn't think to be there." Ben finds what he sees as Caroline's oblivion to household chores and care-work galling. Professional middle-class families such as the Anderson's tend to engage in intensive parenting where they curate each aspect of their children's lives from education to extracurricular to social development.[11] Most of this work is actually, however, done by mothers. By the standards of intensive parenting, and especially of intensive motherhood, Caroline's casual treatment of her son's birthday is odd. Ben is reacting angrily to Caroline's departure from the (gendered) norms of their social class. He sees her behavior as emanating from Caroline's focus on her job search. He continues, "But I had to go get a cake. On my way home. I had to get a cake and a card for my son. I didn't get into it with her, but I tried to allude to her: 'I thought you would have taken care of this. I'm working. You're not working.'"

Ben, according to both Caroline and himself, is an involved father. Commending Ben, Caroline says, "My husband's always been the one to do homework and help them memorize things. I've never been good at that. So that is a little disappointing to me, because I probably should when they get home [from school]. As Caroline explains, though, echoing how unemployed men job search, her time is spent in networking and focusing intently on finding new jobs to apply to, "but I'm usually involved in something. Or yesterday I got home after they got home, because I was out meeting this person and having lunch and running errands and stuff like that."

But Ben's job requires him to travel; he is away Monday through Wednesday of each week, spending Thursday through Sunday at home. During this time, Caroline is the sole parent at home. When traveling for work, Ben calls his younger son to wake him up for school each day. Of course, the Andersons could have focused on teaching their younger son who will soon be a teenager, to get up and ready for school by himself. As the accounts of many parents in this study, and as research on intensive parenting suggests, Ben's understanding that one of the parents (and ideally Caroline) should monitor their younger child in the early morning is very much a part of intensive parenting, endemic to this social class. Ben also describes calling both his sons after school to make sure he remains involved in their lives. "Every day after school, the first thing I ask my kids, what do you have for homework? Well, 'Hello, how you doing, how was school, love you. What do you have for homework? Do you have any tests coming up? Do you have any projects coming up?' I have a system for them. And I told her, 'I'm going to be away, you need to make sure you follow up where I was. You need to be that person.' She doesn't follow through on it."

Caroline disagrees with Ben's description of her involvement with her sons. In her own, separate interview, she emphasizes that despite her focus on job searching she is involved in her sons' morning routines: "These days I wake up at quarter to six to wake my son up to get to high school. I make his lunch. Sometimes I make him something for breakfast or he'll just have cereal. So I make sure he gets up on time." An hour later, Caroline says, she wakes up her other son, gets him breakfast, makes his lunch, and gets him off to school. Ben, likely because he's traveling for work most of the week, may be unaware of how much Caroline does for their sons even as she job searches. Or it may be that he simply expects Caroline to focus entirely on the home now. A desperate tone creaks into Ben's voice as he tells me how he is trying to make Caroline understand some simple things: "Get involved in your life. Enjoy your life. Enjoy the people that are in your family. That's my goal." Ben is piqued by what he considers Caroline's neglect of their sons because of her focus on her job search. He says, "But when it affects my kids and they're not getting out to school on time or she's not taking time to think about a nice, nutritious dinner for them or hey, get involved in their homework. We go see a teacher and the teacher's telling us, 'Oh, he missed all these things.'" Sighing, his voice trails off, and he lowers his gaze to his hands, tapping his fingers against the bar table in a gesture of annoyance.

Caroline is aware of Ben's expectations. She says, "I think most parents would say the number one priority in their life should be their kids." Looking at me earnestly, she says, "and I try to do that." Biting her lower lip, she continues: "I think there are times when I get, maybe, not distracted, but I get engrossed in something and I might say, 'Oh, well, maybe the kids will just make themselves a hotdog for dinner because I'm not home yet.' Or I have to leave early and I didn't have time to make a good dinner for them." Caroline's more laissez-faire parenting style is not the norm in contemporary, American middle-class families like theirs. For Ben and Caroline, meals, in particular, have become a sore point. She says, "My husband gets upset when I don't cook. He said now that I'm not working, we're eating less home cooked meals than when I was." Home-cooked meals are an important, feminized way of showing love and care across social class and race, especially in the context of family life. But the effort, skill, and time needed for this work often pulls women into subordinate and oppressive positions within the home.[12]

Caroline recognizes the symbolic and nutritional importance of home-cooked meals but explains that getting dinner on the table every night does not jive with the reality of searching for a job, which requires flexibility. She says, somewhat apologetically, "Every day is different. Since I don't have as much structure, I think it's very easy for me to get engrossed in something." She provides a concrete example: "Like Monday, I was on the phone and doing all this kind of stuff. When you're working, you know you will get home by a certain time. Or you know this night you have to do it early." Caroline references a particular form of employment—standard and stable—increasingly available only to professional workers like her and others in this sample (and declining for them too). In this kind of employment, workers know their schedules and know in advance when they may have to work late.[13] As she describes, searching for a job, however, throws that certainty out of the window, since job-seekers are more reliant on others—for example, in networking.

Ben has explicitly urged her to cook more now that she's not working. Caroline explains: "I agree with him [that I should cook more], but I don't like agreeing with him. It's not my focus. He feels that part of us as parents should be home-cooked meals, and I guess I get so enthralled in other things that I don't make spending an hour on dinner a priority and I should. I really should do that more often, because then they might eat a little better." Caroline, adhering to the ideal job-seeker norm, feels guilty about not taking the time to cook as well as about not meeting Ben's gendered expectations that she should be responsible for preparing meals.

Ironically, she feels an acute sense of work-family conflict, even when she is unemployed.

Caroline's approach to job searching is similar to how unemployed men job search. But while wives of unemployed men encourage this focus on reemployment, both Caroline and Ben frame this same behavior in an unemployed woman as deeply anomalous; zooming in on Caroline's cooking (or what both perceive to be the lack of her cooking). Caroline continues to defy gendered expectations by privileging the prospect of paid work, and Ben continues to wish she would turn her attention to the home more than she does.

"IT MAKES ME WONDER WHO I MARRIED"

Rebecca, a thirty-five-year-old unemployed White woman who is currently looking for a job routinely dresses in black calf-length yoga pants and a loose T-shirt. Her T-shirts have logos of beer companies whose product she likes, or perhaps a funny slogan. These T-shirts match her gregarious personality. Her wavy brown hair is usually pulled up into a messy ponytail, and she keeps her hair off of her forehead by wearing an eighties-style elastic headband. Five years ago, she married Chuck, who is a tall and lanky thirty-six-year-old with a shaved head and glasses that tend to slide down his nose. The Masons' home is filled with food (mostly cooked by Chuck), drinks, their two friendly terriers, and—most of all—laughter.[14] Their attention and mirth center on their one-year-old, daughter, Ellie. Ellie is inordinately fond of their vacuum cleaner, which is usually kept propped up against the banister leading downstairs to their basement. Whenever Ellie, who is not entirely steady on her feet yet, stumbles past the vacuum, she pauses to hug it. Every time, Rebecca and Chuck guffaw.

Ellie is also why Rebecca finds it difficult to focus on her search for a job. The pervasive lack of access to affordable childcare in the United States means that unless the Masons decide to spend a considerable part of Chuck's paycheck on outsourcing childcare for Ellie, Rebecca's time is spent looking after her. Chuck is one of the more unusual husbands in my sample, in that he is deeply disappointed in Rebecca's fragmented job search. A close examination of the Masons illuminates contradictions and complications often intrinsic to gendered beliefs versus behaviors. While Chuck profoundly wants a dual–income family, his everyday behavior belies this feeling and does *not* shape how he interacts with Rebecca. Despite sharing a loving and affectionate relationship with Chuck, Rebecca is not fully aware of Chuck's earnest desire to see her fully employed again. Chuck and Rebecca talk and interact in a manner that often, unintentionally, glosses over Chuck's feelings about this situation.

"It's All Gravy, as They Say."

Rebecca has a bachelor's degree, and Chuck finished an MBA while working full-time several years ago. Rebecca's employment history has always been choppier than Chuck's.[15] In the best of times, she brought in about a third of Chuck's total income. Rebecca viewed her money as extra for the family, saying, "It's all 'gravy,' as they say." She elaborates on this, "Chuck took care of the bills, and I had the fun money. And it worked out great. If we wanted to eat out three times a week, 'Yeah, let's do that.' If we wanted to go overnight somewhere for a weekend, we could." But Chuck is aware that Rebecca's irregular income history is a drawback for their financial trajectory, telling me, "There's no long-term wealth-building or anything for the future going on. It's all day-to-day." With great emphasis, he continues, "And it's *extremely* frustrating for me to take on that burden." For the moment, Rebecca says that she is focusing on searching for a "quote-unquote 'real' job, you know: the benefits, the time off, the whole thing. Because right now, we pay for benefits out of pocket. Chuck's job only covers him, not family."

Rebecca, who has a deep sense of fairness, is unhappy with what she sees as her lack of economic contribution to their family. She wishes to contribute economically, seeing her own employment situation as a burden to Chuck, "It's not fair to Chuck. He has everything on his shoulders, you know, work, bills. To take some of the stress off of him, I would love to get some kind of income." Chuck acknowledges Rebecca's feelings, saying, "She has a hole in her heart because she's not able to contribute the way that she thinks she should be able to contribute."

Nevertheless, Chuck is also keenly aware of the precariousness of their financial situation and believes Rebecca is not. He says, "If I was to screw

up, we would be out of a house. We'd be living in a shelter somewhere."
Pausing to weigh his words, Chuck continues, "I feel like there's less of an
urgency and, and seriousness and ability to take direction from Rebecca."
But instead of telling Rebecca that he feels burdened, he says that he holds
it back. "Because I know that she's really sensitive. She sees me as in a
position of power, and I don't want to undermine her confidence, or make
her feel any worse than she actually feels already." Holding his hands up,
Chuck shakes his head and adds, "So she needs a third person to be able to
tell her those imperfections, you know? Otherwise she's going to react
defensively. And I understand that, so I'm kind of helpless." Unlike families of unemployed men, for instance the Radziks, Chuck does not overtly
push Rebecca to find paid work, for instance, by issuing an ultimatum that
she get a job, any job. He takes a far more subtle approach.

Rebecca tells me that any pressure she feels to contribute is coming
from herself, saying, "This is not coming from Chuck. It's all me. He does
not complain about it. You know, he's great. But I know it's hard." Rebecca
knows this through their interactions. Recently, Rebecca was feeling particularly despondent that her job applications were not getting any trac-
tion. She says that Chuck told her, "'You know we knew it was going to be
tight, and it's OK. We can still pay our bills. It's just hard.'" Chuckling,
Rebecca adds, "That's what he would say. Which, of course, didn't help at
all!" Instead, what would have helped her, Rebecca says, is if he had said,
"Oh, don't worry. Things are gonna be OK." With a hint of pride, she adds
that Chuck is too truthful to "coddle" her and that "he speaks the truth. He
doesn't always say what you need to hear, but he speaks the truth." Chuck
does not conceal the fact that he prefers that Rebecca would do paid work,
but neither does he push her into it. His feelings about how much he
would prefer her to be in paid work are far stronger than Rebecca has
gauged.

Rebecca is worried about what not working says about her. "I don't feel,
I guess 'complete' is the best word that I can think of. I feel like if I found
a job, then I'd have it all, you know: kid, job, family, dogs, whatever."
Sighing, Rebecca continues, "But, I just feel like the missing piece to my
life-puzzle right now is a job, and that, if I could just find that, then I'd be,
like, picture perfect." It's important to Rebecca to model the life of a working mother for Ellie: "I always knew that I wanted to be a working mom."

She adds, "When Ellie's, like, five, six, seven, eight, I would like her to be able to say, 'Yeah, my mom and dad work.'" Chuck sees Rebecca's not working as a comment on himself and perceives Rebecca as someone who is lost when it comes to the professional realm. This is very troubling for him. He says, "It makes me question whether I'm making too much of a sacrifice in having someone who's my partner who's not willing to put out the same sort of professional motivation." But Chuck jumps to add that Rebecca's qualities outside of her professional endeavors make her an excellent partner. "She's so wonderful and forgiving, and understanding enough towards me. And knows me well enough that we're able to have such a wonderful relationship together." To put his disappointment with Rebecca's professional trajectory in perspective, he says "So, there's a period at the end of a sentence. There's a whole sentence to go through. What punctuation is on the end doesn't matter—as long as the understanding is there."

Even though Chuck does not particularly push Rebecca toward job searching, the two of them have an understanding that Rebecca's paid work matters. Despite Rebecca's desire to be employed, the default responsibilities of her daily life, including caring for an infant, mean that her job search is fragmented. Chuck, for his part, does not fully recognize how much Rebecca's domestic responsibilities limit her ability to concentrate on finding a job. Inadvertently, Chuck is helping to produce the situation that leads to Rebecca's fragmented job search.

How Child Care Contributes to Unemployed Women's Fragmented Job Searching

Rebecca's days are ruled not by her job search but by Ellie. One afternoon, I arrived at the Masons' home a little after three in the afternoon. Rebecca was doing laundry, and Ellie was sleeping in her room upstairs. We went down to the basement while she sorted the laundry into different piles: whites, Chuck's work clothes, and Chuck's non-work clothes. Rebecca put some sheets from their spare room and some blankets in the washer. When the dryer finished its cycle, she pulled out Chuck's clothes, folding his pants and shirts. This went on for about an hour. Rebecca intermittently checked the baby monitor she kept close to her, watching for Ellie to wake up. When Ellie still hadn't woken up a half hour later, Rebecca picked up her guitar. When Ellie finally woke up after about another half hour, the two of us went upstairs to Ellie's bedroom. After an initial period of crankiness and shyness, Ellie soon started smiling. The next few hours were for Ellie and Rebecca to play.

Rebecca points to exactly this type of routine as the reason her time at home is not really conducive to looking for paid work.

> But you have to [job search] while she's sleeping. . . . Sometimes they can take a while, online applications. So I would start it, and then if she woke up, if I wasn't done, get her, do whatever, nap again. Go back to it. So it was very segmented. . . . When she was younger and not as mobile, I'd be able to lay her down and maybe take ten minutes to do something quick. But mainly while she was napping, because that's when my brain can fully focus. If I was doing stuff while she was up, it'd be like: do stuff, look over, is she OK? It's not really full attention to the application or the search. It's split time.

Rebecca paints a picture in which her search for a job constantly serves as background for other tasks in the foreground. For unemployed women, job searching is fragmented as other life concerns take the focus.

Chuck is envious of the time that Rebecca gets with Ellie. He says, "So that's been the hardest part for me—carrying the resentment that Rebecca gets to stay at home and enjoy Ellie while I don't." But taking care of Ellie is not necessarily relaxing for Rebecca. Spending time with children, especially young ones, can be both valuable *and* tiring, since young children often require extensive physical and emotional labor.[16] Chuck underestimates the toll of maintaining constant vigilance over a young child day in and day out. This same afternoon, Rebecca played with Ellie nonstop for several hours after she woke up around four-thirty p.m. All three of us then moved to the stoop outside. We went back inside at six in the evening and Ellie, still very energetic, ran straight to the stairs and started trying to climb them. Rebecca, who was checking that the front door was locked, moaned and said, "No! Not up the stairs! I'm so tired." She bent down, letting her head and arms fall down beside her, fatigued. She looked over at me, shook her head, widened her eyes and repeated with a self-knowing, mock-whining sigh, "I'm so tired!" Then she slowly walked over to Ellie to pull her back from climbing farther up the stairs. Constantly keeping an eye on Ellie, fitting chores in between, and thinking about her job applications had tired Rebecca out by the end of the day.

The Logistical Difficulties of Networking

White-collar job-seekers believe securing a job depends on networking. Networking is more than simply handing out business cards at industry-specific events. Instead, as social scientists have shown, networking requires tremendous amounts of emotional labor.[17] Because networking is an activity based on human interaction, race and gender shape how people network and how networking impacts individuals' careers. Whites in America are far more likely to get hired through informal networking, while Blacks are more likely to be hired through formal applications. Women in particular use networking to build tight circles of women colleagues who can eventually advance their careers.[18]

The activities associated with networking are time consuming, and they usually cost money. Networking is not equally available to all job-seekers. It also requires mobility: you have to be able to go for coffee or lunch in the middle of the day, or dinner in the evening. Networking events typically take place at a location more convenient to the person you are trying to network with. The sort of workshops where job-seekers can learn ancillary job searching skills, such as using LinkedIn effectively, interviewing well, or creating an attractive résumé, also require mobility. Women's household responsibilities can constrain their mobility; this is certainly the case for Rebecca.

Chuck sounds exasperated as he explains to me how Rebecca doesn't seem to grasp what job searching in the contemporary labor market entails. "I mean, applying for jobs online is like throwing shit against the wall and seeing what sticks, you know? There's a point where you need to network face-to-face, rather than blindly send your résumé out there." Laughing, Chuck adds, "You need to go to Cheers, where everybody knows your name, you know? And that's how you get jobs. That's how it's done."

Chuck recognizes that Rebecca is taking care of their daughter, and that these caretaking responsibilities limit her ability to network. "As a tangential point, it kind of goes along with raising Ellie." But nevertheless, he is annoyed by what he sees as Rebecca's lackadaisical approach to finding work, saying, "So, I've encouraged, encouraged, *encouraged* Rebecca to go out, meet people, go to these things, you know, go to whatever. When I'm home, I'm home. And Rebecca can go out and be social, you know? Because she's at home with Ellie all day, and that's not professionally developing, you know? It doesn't build any skill set."

Chuck's advice asserts that networking needs to be active, dogged even. But Chuck has not experienced unemployment, and he does not quite take into account how networking events occur at times and locations that are not as easily accessible to Rebecca as he imagines. Rebecca does not see her job search as lackadaisical or unfocused. Instead, in her conversations with me, she highlights how the default role of caretaker for her daughter limits her ability to conduct an effective job search:

> You know, going out, going to stuff, it's hard. So we have one car, and a lot of those things are not [nearby]. As far as I can go with [Ellie], is the easiest to get to. Because of Chuck's long commute, he's usually back by between six and six-thirty. I've googled stuff and everything that's come up has been, like out in the suburbs, or it's at four o'clock. And how do I get there without a car? Or you know, it's seven o'clock. But Chuck's not back 'til six-thirty and I wouldn't get there until whenever. And it's just hard timing.

Rebecca's mobility constraints thus limit her ability to network effectively. She doesn't have a car, and she needs to be able to take Ellie with her to any networking event—a difficult task that runs the risk of appearing unprofessional.

Chuck and Rebecca live in a bustling, walkable city. When something is too far to walk, they're surrounded by a well-connected system of public transportation within the city. And yet, most of the networking events relevant to Rebecca don't, according to her, take place in the city. They take place in the suburbs. Getting there would require Rebecca to transfer between multiple, and at times infrequent, modes of public transit. Rebecca thus says "So it's just not worth it, really." Unemployed women, like Rebecca, find it challenging to organize their days to look for work. The professional, middle-class version of the ideal job-seeker is a person who has copious amounts of time in which to network, a car that enables them to easily move around, and the resources to pay the fee for attending networking events.

Negotiating Whether to Invest Resources in Rebecca's
Professional Development

Rebecca's frustrations with unemployment run deep. Having not received any positive news from the job applications she has been submitting for months now, Rebecca is now considering whether to return to school for a new degree. She is unclear on what this degree would be, perhaps something in human services. During my visits to the Masons' home, I also noticed fliers and pamphlets from a renowned and nearby nursing school scattered on the computer desk in the basement.

Chuck is currently discouraging her from this option, because he does not see a human services degree as necessary for working with kids as Rebecca wants. Dismissively, he says, "You can work with kids and do event planning with children without a human services degree. I don't want to be responsible for $400 a month for the rest of my life." The "$400 a month" remark is a reference to student loans, but Chuck's comments also reveal his broader skepticism about Rebecca's follow-through. What if she starts this degree, and doesn't finish? Or what if they go deeply in debt to obtain it, and then she keeps working in the same sorts of jobs she had before?

While Chuck and Rebecca are affectionate and generally forthcoming with each other, they rarely discuss her job search. They do, however, discuss the question of whether Rebecca should go back to school. Chuck has vetoed Rebecca's human services degree idea, but nursing school is very much still on the table. One evening, after Ellie had been tucked into bed, they settle onto the living room couch, very dry vodka martinis in hand. Turning toward Chuck, Rebecca says, "Oh I got my transcript today!" Chuck responds, "Oh yeah, because you have that meeting with the nursing school person? When is that, the eleventh?" Rebecca gets up and walks over to their dining room table, picking up an open envelope with a university logo stamped on it, her folded college transcript inside. Shaking her head, she says, "Nah, the tenth. It's on Friday." Chuck is looking expectantly at her. Instead of reading the transcript, she says, "This cost eight bucks!" She finally walks back, sitting close to Chuck so that their knees touch. She waves the transcript at him, smiles, and proudly says, "I was your typical average mediocre student. I had like a 2.9 something GPA." Chuck takes the transcript from her and giggles, saying, "All my A's were in my electives! My major classes were all B's and C's!" He and Rebecca both laugh over this. Rebecca continues looking through the transcript to see which classes she had taken.

Later, Chuck tells me that Rebecca has jumped from job to job; an additional degree would be an expensive way to continue the pattern. He works out a hypothetical scenario for me: "You're not happy with your job and you're coming home crying and then you're gonna end up doing something else in three years anyway? So, I really discouraged her from doing it." Although Chuck has definite opinions on how Rebecca should approach her career, he does not always share them as bluntly with her. He is afraid of hurting her. Rebecca and Chuck are excellent at laughing together, often at themselves. Their interactions, however, do not focus on Rebecca's professional trajectory in the way that those in unemployed men's families do.

The families of unemployed men in this study were willing to invest time and money on extra certifications and professional credentials that they thought might improve the unemployed man's chance of finding a status-appropriate job. It was much harder for the unemployed women to access these resources. Both of the Masons say that they support Rebecca's reemployment, but they exhibit reluctance to direct the resources—such as time, money, and a second car—to fully support that. Given all this, it's perhaps unsurprising that, for Rebecca, looking for paid work comes second to the chores of daily life, most of which revolve around Ellie.

Over half a year later, in following up with the Masons, I ask Rebecca about her job searching; she explains that it's going slowly these days: "We're just trying to get my mother's birthday. Then we have two weddings actually this month. We have one this weekend. So, it's a wedding this weekend, her birthday the following weekend, and a wedding the following weekend, and then we're away the first two weekends of next month. So, once we get past this craziness, then maybe that [networking more] would be something to consider."

Rebecca's social life is rich, in part because she herself is warm and outgoing. Although Rebecca wants to find employment, she continues to find it difficult to make that happen because of housework and especially childcare, which falls to her, and which is often rendered invisible. Chuck is not fully aware of how Rebecca's time is actually occupied during the course of her day.

CONCLUSION

Job searching is not a gender-neutral activity. For the unemployed women in this sample, job searching is a fragmented experience squeezed in between domestic obligations. Unemployed men, in contrast, see themselves as encountering an imperative to demonstrate that they are morally unemployed, which is usually upheld by their wives. They must make a diligent show of searching for paid work, especially to their wives. Unemployed women encounter no such requirement. Instead, the race and class position of these White, professional middle-class, unemployed women allows them to emphasize their role as stay-at-home mothers and almost demands that they do so. Consequently, these unemployed women simply spend less time than unemployed men on job searching and related professional development activities, typically with the support—and sometimes encouragement—of their husbands.

I used the case of the Boyles as an example of the most common approach among this group of largely White, professional, married, and heterosexual unemployed women to job searching. Women's fragmented approach to job searching is not limited to those women who earn less than their husbands. This way of contending with unemployment emphasizes women's unpaid work, particularly caregiving, over their paid work. But this approach itself is possible because racial and class-based ideas about gender ideals loom large in the imaginaries of these couples. Even marriages that had not been traditional—for example, having female-breadwinner nonetheless evoke these ideals as instructive for how to organize their family life in this tumultuous time. Couples dig in their heels, drawing on nostalgia for a situation that no longer obtains for most and had never actually existed for them.

I found two main divergences from this experience of a fragmented job search experience. In the first variation, represented by the Andersons, we see an unemployed woman who *does* strive to be an ideal job-seeker, but is stymied by her husband. Caroline explicitly wishes to demonstrate to her husband, Ben, that she is morally unemployed—that she is striving hard to find paid work. But Ben is perplexed, annoyed, and even angry that Caroline chooses to focus on reemployment rather than their children and home. In my study of twenty-three families with unemployed women, I only saw four cases like the Andersons. For the most part, couples quickly reverted to an interactional script in which unemployed women focus on the home, and their husbands encourage this.

In a second variation, represented by the Masons, we see the opposite pattern. Here, we see a husband who is eager to see his wife back in the workplace and is disappointed by her fragmented job searching. Yet, there are also fissures between their stated beliefs and their behaviors. Chuck wants Rebecca to have a stronger, more defined career than she does. Rebecca, too, wishes that. The couple has not dedicated financial resources, like paying for childcare or a second car, that would allow Rebecca to conduct her search more effectively. Rebecca's time vaporizes in daily chores that often center around their daughter, Ellie.

Why some husbands wish for their wives to focus more on the home, like Ben Anderson, and others wish for their wives to focus more on job searching, like Chuck Mason, is shaped by a variety of factors. Important are men's conceptions of masculinity and their ideals of family life. Ben, for example, is more traditional in his ideals of family than Chuck. A young urban professional, Chuck, along with Rebecca aspires to a dual-earner family structure rather than a male-breadwinner/female-homemaker model, which he sees as untenable in contemporary times. Chuck and Rebecca also view this latter family form as unfair in terms of rendering one family member, Chuck in their case, responsible for the entirety of family finances. The male-breadwinner/female-homemaker form is not tenable for Ben and Caroline's family either. While Ben acknowledges this, his acknowledgment in itself does not quite decouple the material reality of their lives from his ideals. So, he is quicker to fault Caroline for her focus on complying with the ideal job-seeker norm, at the expense (from Ben's perspective) of their family.

Overall, how unemployed women search for paid work and how their husbands respond, react, and interact around their wives' job searching suggest that unemployment is a key location in which couples contest gender norms, often reproducing gendered norms around paid and unpaid work.

PART III   Gendered Time in Housework

5 Why Don't Unemployed Men Do More Housework?

I'm home to job search. I'm not home to do housework.

—Terry Clarke, unemployed engineer

But, you know, you do have to take care of your family duties.

—Marcus Neals, unemployed management consultant

The hours that men and women spend on paid and unpaid work combined have become approximately equal in recent years.[1] Within this number, women spend more time on unpaid work and men more on paid work. One explanation frequently offered for why women remain responsible for more housework than men is that, in the majority of heterosexual marriages, wives earn less than husbands. Those who favor this economic explanation suggest that husbands' earnings buy them out of housework, while wives' lesser earnings render housework their responsibility.[2] But this economic explanation falls apart fairly easily; research has repeatedly shown that wives do more childcare and housework—the bundle of tasks related to the upkeep of the house, such as cooking, cleaning, grocery shopping, laundry, maintenance of the house—than their husbands, even in cases where men earn substantially less than their wives, or when men are unemployed.[3]

What seems puzzling from an economic point of view makes sense viewed through a cultural and social lens. From the social interaction perspective on gender, chores are a locus through which men and women perform their gender identity, primarily in order to have this identity validated by others. Doing housework—or not doing it—becomes a way for individuals to broadcast their identity as men and women on a relatively rigid and binary scale of gender possibilities. This understanding of "gender display" and "doing gender" offers a compelling explanation for why men's, but not women's time is protected from housework during unemployment.[4] For it turns out that, while unemployed individuals generally increase the number of hours they contribute to household chores, unemployed men increase their contribution by only half as much as unemployed women.[5]

While prior studies have recognized this phenomenon, they have been unable to describe the micro-level interactions and understandings through which the unequal division of household labor continues to be upheld. In this chapter, I delve into couples' negotiations around housework during men's unemployment to illuminate how gendered interactions among spouses lead to unequal outcomes, even during a time when economic explanations might predict a different outcome. In interpreting what follows, it is important to acknowledge that gender displays themselves emerge from socially specific ideas about what constitutes appropriate performances of femininity and masculinity. These ideals are typically shaped by intersection of race, class, gender, and (as an emerging body of research is showing) sexuality. For participants in this study, their gender displays are informed by their position as being overwhelmingly White, affluent, and heterosexual.

I reintroduce the Janssons, whom we first met in chapter 3. The Janssons represent the pattern that holds for the majority of families in this sample, in which the division of housework shifts only somewhat with the husband's unemployment. Like most of the families in my study, the Janssons assume that Robert's unemployment is temporary and will end shortly. We then meet the Neals family, who dramatically reconfigure their division of household chores, although they too assume that Marcus Neals's unemployment is temporary. Individuals make different assumptions about their gendered obligations and responsibilities within the home, and this informs their negotiations around housework. These contrasting negotiations in these two families illuminate critically different assumptions about gender roles in the home.

"I'LL HELP YOU OUT"

It is eight o'clock on a fall evening, and the home of the Janssons, whom we met in chapter 3, has been a hive of activity since about five. That's when their full-time nanny leaves and Robert, who has been unemployed for about seven months, starts getting their dinner together. His wife, Laura, usually returns home from her job in the city around this same time. Weekday family dinners are usually frenzied affairs, with Robert and Laura trying to have a conversation (usually about Robert's job search, Laura's work, or the kids' schedules) while simultaneously corralling their two children.

Today is no different. As usual, Robert and Laura's conversation is punctuated with directions to their four-year-old daughter, Tessa, to eat the food on her plate. One parent or the other intermittently gets up to check that two-year-old Taylor is eating properly in his high chair. By eight, Laura has bathed the two kids and put Tessa to bed. She and I have come to the kitchen while Robert is still putting Taylor to bed. We hover near the microwave where Laura is boiling water in mugs for tea for us. She explains her daily routine to me, "Usually I cook on the weekends and that way we have two or three meals ready for the week. But this past weekend we had to go to three birthday parties." Widening her eyes and shaking her head, Laura looks to me for a reaction. I responded by raising my eyebrows to mirror her look of amazement, and Laura continues, "So, I hadn't been able to make anything. So this morning I got up, went for a run, and ran by the grocery store where I picked up the ingredients for tonight's enchiladas, made them using Robert's mom's recipe, and then left for work by eight." She again looked at me expectantly.

Laura's description of her day is astonishing: it illuminates how deeply housework remains gendered. Yet the Jannsons' experience is not anomalous. My interviews with unemployed men and their wives reveal that these White, affluent families do not usually make major changes to the division of housework during men's unemployment.[6] Instead, they typically continue in a business-as-usual way. The ideal of the male-breadwinner and female-homemaker family is a powerful and influential image for this demographic regardless of the dual-earner structure. In these families, this ideal manifests as an emphasis on men's paid work and thus release from housework. Yet the absence of paid work does not seem to change this equation.

As I show, the vast majority of the employed wives in this study continued doing the chores they had done before their husbands lost their jobs. Unemployed husbands, too, continue with the chores they had done while employed. While unemployed men do contribute to household chores somewhat more than when they are employed, their increased participation comes with a couple of caveats. First, men usually accompany their contribution to household chores with an explicit statement that housework is not their priority or their obligation. Men make it clear to their wives that they are only "helping out." Wives in this study usually do not insist on realigning chores, although they do often find the situation unfair. Second, when men do add chores, they spend more time on "masculine-typed" chores that they have always done, including household maintenance such as overseeing the remodeling of a basement, working on the family's outdoor deck, or fixing bathroom leaks, rather than taking on "feminine-typed" work like laundry or cleaning.

Men's Unemployment as a Temporary State

Laura Jansson had scheduled their two-year-old son Taylor's haircut for the upcoming Thursday. When she was bathing Taylor and Tessa the evening before, Robert came up the staircase, having filled Taylor's sippy cup with water and placed it in his room. Laura told Robert, "So Taylor has his haircut tomorrow. Either you or [the nanny] can take him." Robert, who was standing in the bathroom doorway holding Taylor's sippy cup asked, "What time is his haircut?" Laura responded "one-thirty." As she continued bathing the kids, she added "I scheduled it then so that [the nanny] could pick up Tessa from the school and take Taylor to the haircut place straight from there." Robert nodded and then asked, "So you don't really need me to go there?" Laura, who was kneeling beside the bathtub to bathe the kids, twisted her neck to look back at Robert and replied "Well, no. But he doesn't like haircuts so it might be good for you to go." Robert nodded again, saying "I'll be there. I'll go straight to the haircut place so that [the nanny] doesn't have to swing by the house. And I can meet them there and be there for the haircut." Laura nodded, "Yeah."

Laura remains responsible for scheduling and organizing the kids' activities. She instructs Robert on where he needs to be and when. Many of the husbands in my study, like Robert, explain that they often rely on directions from their wives as to how specifically they should help out. The phrase *helping out* means that both husbands and wives expect wives to hold primary responsibility for household chores—unemployed men are merely short-term executors of these chores. These couples understand men's unemployment as a temporary phase, no matter how long it has endured. As we saw in chapter 3, both husbands and wives assume that husbands will find a new job sooner or later. In this context, realigning housework responsibilities would not make much sense.

Robert is immensely grateful for the time he has been able to spend with both his children. He attributes his closeness to Taylor to his presence at home while unemployed, telling me, "You can see it even now today, like my daughter is much closer to my wife and my son is much closer to me. It all has to do with how much time we spent around those two kids." Robert is also amenable, and wants to be helpful to Laura as best he can. Yet this does not translate into retaining responsibility for Taylor's day-to-day schedule. It is Laura who has scheduled Taylor's haircut appointment and coordinated it with the nanny. Robert follows her instructions. This arrangement can, at times, be frustrating for wives. Wives often would like for husbands to be more involved with housework—including taking responsibility for chores. The mental planning behind allocating chores is tiring, and often irritating, for wives.[7]

Men's Incompetence with Housework

Husbands' need for instructions on when and how to carry out specific chores can be attributed to the stickiness of the prevailing division of housework, particularly given that doing—or in the case of men, not doing—housework is often a way of performing gender identity. Laura Jansson is aware of this discrepancy between her ownership of chores and Robert's execution of them. She frames this in terms of needing to learn to better vocalize her expectations in terms of housework while Robert was unemployed: "I think I was expecting him to just kind of figure it out, which doesn't happen. Because nobody's a mind reader. I think saying 'I need help with the laundry,' or 'I need help with the dishes,' . . . I feel great about our balance most of the time." Somewhat to my surprise, Laura expresses satisfaction with this situation. She also frames their household chores as her responsibility, which Robert can help out with: "I think most of the time I just need to ask and he's more than happy to help out. . . . I don't know if this is a male thing, but he's not automatically going to take the laundry down when the hamper is full. . . . But I know that I can ask, 'Can you throw a load of laundry in?' And he's happy to do it. He's happy to get dinner started. . . . He will do his best to make it happen and I appreciate that."

Robert has a slightly different take on their negotiations over household chores. While Laura frames these as discussions, Robert senses a hint of exasperation in Laura, perceiving her as admonishing him to do more around the house, since he is unemployed. He too talks specifically about the laundry: "She gets a little frustrated with the laundry. Like, 'Really? You couldn't throw in a load of laundry while you're sitting?'" Chuckling, he explains: "Because the laundry is like twenty feet from where my office is. . . . So I think that comes up: 'You couldn't throw in a load of laundry while you're working downstairs?' . . . Like she's frustrated today because the laundry had built up to a certain point. So I think I probably should do more and she gets a little more frustrated if I'm not doing more on those fronts." Robert's obliviousness to laundry can be understood as a general performance of masculinity, displayed here by not doing select housework.

I observed the Jansson family another evening as they went about bathing their two kids. Robert had put the toilet seat cover down and was sitting on it as he gave Taylor, the two-year-old, one last quick pat-down with the towel. Robert then got up, holding Taylor in his arms. He took Taylor to his room to put on his diaper and got the child dressed for bed. When Robert stood up, Taylor's towel fell down; Robert did not notice. The wet towel lay on the bathroom floor. Robert and Taylor were in Taylor's room when, a half-minute or so later, Laura emerged from their bedroom and went to the bathroom. She paused at the bathroom door, shaking her head. Heaving an audible sigh, she looked at the towel lying on the floor. She picked it up, rolling her eyes, clearly annoyed. She closed the door, so that she could hang the towel up on one of the hooks behind the door. These different responses may reflect gendered ideas about appropriate levels of cleanliness in the home, or they may reflect the couple's largely unspoken assumptions about who is responsible for cleaning up.[8] Either way, small moments like this illuminate how spouses assert their ownership over certain spaces, whether they intend to our not.

The Janssons had relatively minor disagreements over housework, and in this aspect they were like most of the families of unemployed men in this study. Housework is typically one of the major sources of friction for couples overall, however, so in some ways, their lack of conflict over this issue is surprising. Significant arguments over housework during men's unemployment only occurred in four out of twenty-five families in this sample. The families that experienced more tension around housework tended to be those in which men had been the primary earners. The wives in these families felt as though their husbands had broken their marital bargain by failing to provide for them, saddling wives with the responsibility of earning *and* housework. Wives in these couples were less convinced than other wives that being an ideal job-seeker should be so time consuming.

In chapter 1, we saw how men are considered trespassers in their own homes. In contrast, wives of unemployed men as well as unemployed women often claim the space of the home as their own. A similar process often occurs with housework, in which wives of unemployed men often retain control over key household chores. In the Jansson family, this occurs in the kitchen, particularly with cooking. Unsatisfied with Robert's grocery shopping technique, Laura elected to keep that to herself. Robert says, "Grocery shopping, I enjoy it more, so I like doing it. But she doesn't like the way I grocery shop, so she doesn't want me to grocery shop. So even though I would do that, she doesn't want me to. So she's like—because I buy junk that she wouldn't, where she buys more healthy stuff." In middle- and upper-middle-class families, mothers are more likely than fathers to insist on healthy eating habits. Children look to fathers when they want to eat a treat such as a bag of potato chips or a cookie.[9] Robert's greater leniency with the grocery items he selects means that Laura is less willing to redistribute this chore. Robert explains, "So she tends to want to hold on to that one and not give that one up. Even though that is something that I could do easily. And I do frequently, I go to the grocery store almost daily anyway. Like I'll drop her off at the train and then stop by the store on the way, because it's across the street. So, I'll like get bananas or milk or whatever, you know, for the kids. Because the kids eat a lot of milk and bananas."

Robert and Laura's interactions around kitchen work show similar tensions. While Robert has taken on more of the dinner preparations, Laura often supervises him there. One evening, I watched while Robert prepared dinner for the family. He had the water on to boil for pasta on the stove. He had chopped up some broccoli, which he planned to steam. But the garlic bread tripped him up. The loaf, a large baguette, was wrapped in aluminum. He held the loaf with one hand and dipped his head underneath it to check for instructions. Not finding any, he put the loaf down on the table, stuck out his lower lip, shrugged his shoulders, and said to himself, "I guess it'll go in like this." ("This" meant wrapped in the foil). He put it in the oven. At this point, Laura came into the kitchen to check on things. She opened the oven door, furrowed her brow, and, exclaimed, "You put the loaf in with the wrapping?" Robert took a slight step back, bewildered. Regaining composure in less than a second, he defensively said, "Yeah, that's how it's supposed to go in." Laura straightened up and raised her eyebrows skeptically, saying "OK."

As this incident from the Janssons illuminates, wives of unemployed men display ambivalence when it comes to domestic labor. On the one hand, they express a desire for husbands to take ownership of chores; on the other, they want husbands to perform the chores in certain ways. Wives implicitly claim the domestic sphere as their own, presenting their way of doing specific chores as superior, thus discouraging husbands from them. Couples are up against decades, indeed entire lives, of gendered socialization. Shifting practices around paid and unpaid work, even at this moment when it should seem achievable, is challenging precisely because of how deeply ingrained notions of gender interact with paid and unpaid work.

Doing Home Projects

Although unemployed men do not take ownership of household chores, many see their unemployment as an appropriate time to accomplish more masculine-typed chores. These tend to be projects relying on skills like carpentry or home maintenance. Overwhelmingly, when men told me that they spent more time on household chores, this meant that they spent more time on home projects. In this sample, the normative division of labor around gender might be described as, in the words of one unemployed man, "I do the outside and she does the inside." Indeed, this has long been the case among married, heterosexual American couples.[10]

Robert explains that, while he hasn't taken on a major home project during his current period of unemployment, he did the last time he was unemployed: "During my last one we actually redid the basement. And I had the ability to kind of project manage that job because I was unemployed. Had I been employed, it would have been much harder to remodel the basement, because there were so many decisions every single day with different people that had to come through, contractors, inspectors, whatever. It takes a lot of effort." Men in this study typically do not focus their time and effort on a new set of chores; instead, they devote more time to masculine-typed chores that they have always considered their responsibility. By focusing on larger home projects, these unemployed men are not breaking any gender norms—they are clearly fulfilling them. While men have taken on more housework, they are not "undoing" gender in any meaningful or enduring way.[11]

The experience of the Janssons, which is representative of the majority of the families in this study, illuminates the lack of a shift around housework during men's unemployment. Of the twenty-five families of unemployed men in my study, all but six of them displayed this dynamic. These families have prioritized men's job searching, as we saw in chapter 3. Because men's time is protected for job searching, it is not available for housework. Men do increase their contribution to housework, but both spouses continue to see household chores as the wife's responsibility. Husbands turn to their wives to know what tasks to execute and when.

A MODERN MASCULINITY

Marcus and Sylvia Neals, a Black couple in their forties, met as undergraduate students. They stayed in touch beyond college as both started careers and jobs. Their friendship, lasting for more than a decade before their marriage, has been a defining feature of their relationship. Sylvia says, "I think the biggest thing for us is the fact that we were friends for years. I mean, really good friends probably, well from like the late '80s up until like 2004. We were like really good friends." More than a decade after they graduated from college, they finally started dating and married two years later.

Both Marcus and Sylvia grew up in families with lots of siblings. Marcus comes from a working-class family, with a father who was in the US Army. When his father left the Army, he worked in security; meanwhile, Marcus's mother was a cleaner. Sylvia grew up in a more middle-class family, with a father who worked in the US government and a mother who stayed at home after marriage. Sylvia gave birth to their first daughter, Larissa, in her late thirties, followed by a second daughter, Toni, a couple of years later. Larissa is now eight; Toni, six.

The Nealses live an upper-middle-class life. When employed, they both earn a comparable six-figure income, depositing it in a shared bank account. They own a home in an upscale suburban neighborhood and have taken several European vacations as a family. Sylvia is especially particular about the girls' education and is currently in the throes of finding the perfect tutors for their older daughter, who has been diagnosed with a mild learning disability.

Both Sylvia and Marcus have MBA degrees, with Marcus earning his from a top-twenty business school. Both have had professional careers with recognized companies. Sylvia's working life has been somewhat unusual, in that she has only worked for one large telecommunications company in the course of her career. Marcus's career trajectory in management consulting has not been quite as linear—he has worked for name-brand organizations, but typically only for a couple of years at each, and often by being "contracted out" to the company.[12] Describing yet another employment transition in his career trajectory, Marcus, a portly man who dresses in slacks and Oxfords and wears wire-rimmed glasses, sums up his career history, "There was uncertainty, so I kind of jumped a sinking ship and linked up with someone." Reflecting on this career history of stops and gaps that he has just described to me, he sardonically adds, "This sounds like a broken record."

The Backdrop to the Nealses' Egalitarian Division of Housework

The Nealses, unusually for the families in my sample, strive for and largely enact an egalitarian division of household labor. This has been the case throughout their marriage, but it has taken on particular importance during the period of Marcus's unemployment. Three contextual factors combine to shape how the Nealses divide their housework. First is the sense of shame and stigma that Marcus feels at his unemployment, especially in terms of his role in the family. Second, Marcus and Sylvia share deep concerns about their future financial well-being. Finally, the Nealses' division of labor reflects ideologies and influences about gender shaped by race, class, and personal experience.

Marcus's last job, from which he was downsized just about a year ago, was a contract position as a project manager. He explains, "They were running into some type of money problems, and they forced all their contractors to go on vacation, because when you're contracted you don't get paid when you're on vacation. Two weeks I had to take off, and I came back on my second week. That's when my boss pulled me into the conference room and said, 'We have to let you go at the end of the month.' So that was the end of August last year, so now here it is the middle of August a year later, and I'm still out of work."

When I met Sylvia for our interview, she started off by saying, "Well, you know this isn't the first time he's been unemployed." She explains that, given the several employment transitions Marcus has experienced, this one did not particularly rattle her, "So, you know, when he told me that, he said, 'Today was my last day at work.' It didn't even faze me because it was like, been down that road before, you know? So I didn't get upset or anything because I knew it was like, OK, here we go again."

But this bout of unemployment, as Sylvia soon came to notice, would be different from prior ones. For one thing, it has lasted significantly longer than any previous period of unemployment that Marcus experienced. Marcus has taken this to heart. He says, "Oh, I mean it's extremely frustrating. You know, I doubt myself a lot of times because I'm like wondering, you know, I don't have a criminal record; I never got fired from a job for bad performance. I've been downsized, so it wasn't anything of my doing."

Marcus was the only participant in my sample to bring up the issue of criminality as a reason men do or don't find paid work. His comments likely reflect his experience as a Black man operating in a social context in which Black men are especially criminalized. But aside from this comment, Marcus never explicitly brought up the issue of race and discrimination in hiring.[13] We know, of course, that racial discrimination in hiring is rampant in the United States. An important body of research has used experimental methods to parse out mechanisms of racial discrimination. These studies have shown that Black men without a criminal record are less likely to be called back for a job interview than White men with a criminal record and that comparable Black candidates from elite universities receive the same number of callbacks for jobs as White candidates from less selective universities.[14] Unsurprisingly, the unemployment rate for Blacks in the United States typically averages twice that of Whites.

Marcus has an MBA from a prestigious program, but he wonders: Does it matter? He is worried about his career, "So I'm wondering, am I a middle-aged guy that no one wants anymore?" Marcus is full of unanswerable questions along these lines, "Is this basically the end of my career? After having what seemed to be a promising career, worked for some big named companies, working with high-level executives. And now it seems I've been relegated to getting onto a career of just contracting for short periods of time and then just being let go and spending another year or more looking for another contract." This has taken an emotional toll on Marcus. He tells me, "So I feel pretty depressed at times." He reiterates, "It's pretty depressing, to be honest." He ends with a deep sigh and a quiet "Yeah."[15]

Sylvia has noticed the emotional toll Marcus's unemployment is taking. Although Marcus neither saw a therapist nor went on medication for depression during this time, Sylvia worriedly says, "I really believe that he went into a depression and it was for a while." She explains, "I think he's been more distant because I think he's embarrassed. He's ashamed. He's depressed. If you knew him when he was working, his personality, versus now: night and *day*. Night and day!" Struggling to find the words to describe the change that has come into Marcus's personality, she says, "It's not—it's almost like—how can I put it?" She continues, "It's almost like he's just there, like matter taking up space, you know?" Trying to put her finger on how Marcus has become different, she explains,

> If we're downstairs watching TV, he'll go upstairs. Or if we're in the kitchen and I'm fixing them food, he'll take his plate and go in the dining room. Stuff like that would go on. I would come home from work, and I would start talking, he's like, "Oh, I'm going to take the dog out." I go, "OK, can I have a conversation?" Not often, but it would happen where I would have to bring it to his attention, "You know what, you got to communicate!" I think that all had to do with how he felt about himself.

Sylvia thought that Marcus was avoiding interacting with his family, and was isolating himself because of a deep sense of shame. Shaking her head, she says, "The personality is different." The Nealses' interactions about housework have to be understood in a context in which Marcus feels tremendous embarrassment about what he sees as his inability to contribute to his family.

Sylvia is saddened by Marcus's unhappiness, but she is also distraught that Marcus's unemployment may be putting their shared plans for the future into jeopardy. She says,

> I don't need you being depressed. I don't need you getting down. I need you to fight, OK? Because if it was me, and I think maybe because mothers are different, for me, I would look at it, oh my god, I've got to fight for my kids, and, you know, if I'm mopping the floors at midnight someplace to bring in some money, then I'd do it, you know, because my kids have got to eat is— that's kind of how I view it. You know, I don't view anything beneath me if it comes to survival. But if it meant me swallowing my pride, busing tables and not, and not being homeless, then so be it.

This type of emotional policing is a way for Sylvia to motivate Marcus to comply with the ideal job-seeker norm, where job-seekers are expected to be hopeful and optimistic in their search, regardless of whether those jobs materialize.[16] Sylvia invokes dramatic imagery of hunger and homelessness, even though the Nealses' financial situation is nowhere close to desperation. Sylvia recognizes that she is catastrophizing; she matter-of-factly adds, "And, truth be told, I make a decent salary. I do. But it's still a strain because even with the great salary for me, it's for four people, you know. And then, on top of that the thing that worries me more than anything is retirement. I think about that constantly."

Marcus is well aware of Sylvia's concerns. As we saw in chapter 1, affluent families in my sample typically treat men's income as indispensable, even if the wife has historically produced a higher income. Sylvia's worries are so acute that she suggested to Marcus that she may try looking for an additional part-time job, despite her heavy workload at her existing position. Marcus was especially hurt to hear this, responding that if anyone got a part-time job, whether at McDonald's or elsewhere, it would be him.

Sylvia's fears center on wealth building for themselves and providing for their kids' future. She says, "I want to work another fifteen years. I mean, we had our children late in life. I was in my late thirties when I had them. So even with college, like I know now I can't afford to pay for them to go to college. I mean, I do have some money saved, but it's not going to be enough. So hopefully they'll get scholarships or whatever." But she is also worried that Marcus's series of employment transitions, during which the Nealses contributed less to their retirement fund, is taking a toll on their future wealth because they are in what should be their prime wealth-building years. She says, "I took a hit those two years [when Marcus experienced unemployment earlier]. I mean, I literally dropped from the max contribution [for retirement] down to six percent, which is what my company matches. So that was a hit. A big hit. In those years, my money wasn't gaining because I wasn't contributing a whole lot, so I didn't gain a lot."

Marcus, who is also concerned about wealth, is more focused on the long term—specifically his career potential and his future income. He says, "I've become a contract worker who's bouncing around and don't really have a sense of career direction. I think that was probably my first reaction. Money, even though it was a concern—I mean, I was more concerned about the long-term direction of my career."

A final financial concern for Sylvia relates to her ability to care for her elderly parents. Marcus's parents are deceased, but Sylvia's are alive, and she is especially keen to help out with her mother's considerable health care expenses. Her mother has limited mobility. Sylvia explains, "I'll give you an example. The stairs in my parents' house, you go up three steps and then it curves, and you go up three more steps. Well, she's now totally disabled. To get a stair-lift for this is ten thousand dollars. So, I can't afford to help with that, you know. My father, he can't afford it. He's on a fixed income and he's supporting all of my siblings." Her eyes staring off into the distance, Sylvia continues, "Like, ultimately, like if I really had money, I would love to give them a little rancher, you know. So there are no stairs. I wish that I could buy them a little rancher." Monetary exchanges are common between parents and adult children, but the direction of the exchange varies by race. In Black families, adult children often provide help for their parents, while in White families, particularly affluent ones, adult children typically receive help from elderly parents. Wealth in the United States is racialized, with Black families possessing a dime for every dollar held by White families. These patterns in exchange of resources held true for the families in my study, with the White families often receiving support from their elderly parents. Black families, like the Forresters and the Nealses, in contrast, continued to find ways to support their extended families. It is in this context of qualitatively different meanings and experiences of care-work and kinwork that Black families such as the Nealses worry about their future wealth.[17]

In a family with high dual incomes, the loss of one income is a setback, but not necessarily disastrous. In the case of the Nealses, though, it is clear that unemployment has left Marcus feeling empty, as if he has nothing to contribute to his family. Through the course of their relationship, the Nealses have been a dual-earner couple, where both Marcus and Sylvia have contributed about equally. Their experience fits within larger data that have repeatedly found that women in middle- and upper-middle-class families, like the Nealses, are especially likely to have continuous work histories, with Black women in this social class being the most likely of all racial groups to have consistent work histories.[18] Yet, the practical setup of the Nealses' family life bucks the more traditional understandings of gender within their relationship. Even though Marcus has never been the primary earner in his family, the idea of providing for his family looms large in his mind, especially now that he is unemployed.

Acknowledging that his views may be old-fashioned, Marcus softly says, "Things have changed. I mean, more women, are working now and not just staying at home and taking care of the kids anymore, so it's a shared responsibility." That Marcus singles out the trend of women's labor force participation is noteworthy for several reasons. He himself grew up in a dual-earner household. In the United States, Black women have always been a part of the labor force, although they have often been in occupations that are devalued.[19] Sylvia's mother, who stayed home with the kids, was an exception.

Although Marcus understands both paid and unpaid work as some-thing shared by spouses, he still feels beholden to the provider role, explaining, "A lot of times I feel like I'm not owning up to my responsibili-ties by not having a job in a sense. So, I kind of feel that I'm kind of failing in my part to provide for my family, because we're just relying on my wife's salary and her providing health care and everything." Pausing, Marcus then adds, "And I'm not really providing anything financial for a while for the family." Marcus's comments are in keeping with Riché Barnes's finding that affluent, dual-earner Black families like the Nealses may prioritize a family structure with a male-breadwinner and female caregiver in keeping with a politics of Black respectability, where women's opting out of paid work may be understood as a radical choice.[20] Adhering to this family form becomes a way for privileged Black families to posit themselves as role models of stable marriage and family within the Black community. While not the most dominant family formation among the American Black middle-class, this norm appears to instruct Marcus's notions of masculinity. In this way, Marcus displays the same gender assumptions as most of the unemployed White men in my sample. None of their lives map on to the traditional male-breadwinner/female-homemaker pattern, but they nevertheless feel guilt and shame about their inability to perform masculinity by producing an income.

Sylvia is aware that Marcus holds himself to a more traditional standard—one that they have never really, in the course of their marriage, lived by. She says, "You know, he feels as a man he should be able to support his family." Sylvia understands that it grates on Marcus to feel that he needs to depend on his wife, "He doesn't want to be viewed as 'my wife is supporting me,' you know? 'Supporting the family; I'm not able to.'" Sylvia draws on her experience growing up, specifically her parents' gender ideologies, in explaining the pressure that Marcus feels as a man. She says, "My dad is old school. Because when he and my mother got married, soon as she got pregnant, he's like 'You're not working.' Like he's from the fifties generation, so the wife stays at home and takes care of the family, husband works and supports the family. So I think he kind of looks at Marcus like [raises eyebrows]. You know?" Sylvia references the idealized past of the 1950s—a past only rarely available to Black women—as the gold standard for traditional gender roles.[21]

Sylvia's vision of family roles has shaped her and Marcus's interactions while he is unemployed and looking for paid work. Marcus explains, "But she actually emailed me to tell me that we need to step it up and made the comment, 'Oh, my dad'—and I *hate* this—She's like, 'Oh, my dad worked two jobs to provide for our family.' Almost as to say that 'you need to go work at McDonald's or something just to have money coming in.'" Sylvia doesn't often bring up Marcus's obligation to be a provider, but when she does, it saddens Marcus. He is also conflicted by her support. "She mentioned that, 'Oh, maybe you should change careers if nothing's happening.' And she sent me a link to like an IT security certification. I mean, she was supportive, but she was also kind of getting on my case a little bit."[22] Marcus was also troubled that Sylvia delivered both of these messages by *email*, rather than just talking to him. He says, "I feel kind of bad that she had to go to an email to do this because she said that she felt that I get too defensive or I have this self-pity." Sighing, he adds that he was troubled by "the fact that she had to resort to the measure to communicate with me. That is, I don't want to say scary, but it's kind of a wakeup call to let me know that this whole thing is putting more of a burden on the family, you know? Both financially and in a dynamic of how we interact with each other."

In general, Black couples in the United States have a more egalitarian division of housework than do White couples. The Nealses' experience, in comparison to the White couples in this sample, is in keeping with that finding.[23] But within this sample, Marcus was not the only unemployed man to report feeling an obligation to contribute to housework. Just over a quarter of the unemployed men in this study (six of twenty-five) described feeling obligated to contribute toward housework, across the various racial categories in this sample.[24]

An Egalitarian Division of Housework and Childcare

Marcus's day now begins at five-thirty in the morning, when he takes the family dog out for a walk. The next few hours are for the kids. He explains, "I do the job search from home, but I spend a lot of time driving my kids around to their activities." Elaborating on what this means, he continues, "Like right now they're in summer camp, so I usually get them up, get them ready and then spend a good hour driving them because they go to two different camps. So I drive them to that. . . . After coming home I'll get breakfast and maybe get online again and start with the job hunt." Marcus has the morning and afternoon to work on his job search and do any household chores that may arise. But as evening closes in, around five o'clock, another kid-related rush starts, "And then I go pick them up, too. So that takes another hour out of my day doing that." If Sylvia is working from home that day, he explains, "She'll get their food together while I go pick them up." But if Sylvia is working from her office, then "I'll actually have to cook their dinner and all before I go pick them up." As with working parents who try to squeeze in hours of work in the late evening after children have gone to sleep, Marcus says, "I usually try to go back online in the evening after eight for a couple hours to see if there's any other [job] leads or anything."

To Marcus, it is obvious that these duties should be his, given that he is at home as he searches for a job. Besides, Sylvia is busy: "My wife, her job is pretty demanding. She's on conference calls all the time working, she has to [commute]." Marcus sees it as unremarkable that he should contribute more to housework and childcare during the period of his unemployment, "So I just take on that responsibility because I'm like, 'Oh, hell, I'm not providing any money to the household!' So the least I could do is do that." When I asked Marcus about what his unemployment meant for how he and Sylvia divided their housework, he explained that his approach differs from that of the other unemployed men he encountered. He told me, "There's another guy in our [job searching] group who has a young girl like me, and he was making a comment, 'Oh well, you know, even though you have family, but you can't just completely ignore your job search.' But, you know, you *do* have to take care of your family duties." Marcus's point here is that while his job search consumes a lot of his time, it does not absolve him from contributing to housework.

Indeed, Marcus feels a deep obligation to increase his proportion of housework. When I ask Sylvia about housework and how that may have shifted since Marcus's unemployment, she explains how the division was before, "Funny thing about that is I don't do any of that. He does it all. He likes to cook. I don't like to cook. So fine, that's your job. So, I mean, that was decided early on in the marriage. I don't clean. I mean, well, I'll sweep our bathroom here and there." Sylvia rattles off the list of all that Marcus does, "He does the laundry, cleans, cooks, picks the girls up. Now I have to do bedtime, of course, help Larissa with her schoolwork." Adding in matter-of-factly, "And, of course, I do their hair."[25] She explains their general division of work: "We kind of have role reversals, if you will.

Traditionally you would figure the female would cook and clean and the man would fix stuff. It's opposite for us. I'm the fixer, he cooks and cleans."

Both Sylvia and Marcus attribute their division of labor to Marcus's predilection toward cleanliness. Sylvia minces no words, saying, "He's a neat freak! I'm not." In a reference to the 1970s sitcom *The Odd Couple*, which chronicles the antics of the neurotic and neat Felix with his slovenly roommate, Oscar, Sylvia adds, "We're kind of like Oscar and Felix, you know?" Typically, the "neat freak" narrative is gendered feminine, so that couples explain women's involvement with housework and cleaning to their "naturally" higher levels of cleanliness.[26] Here though, the narrative is gender-reversed. Marcus uses the same phrase to describe himself even before his unemployment, "I was still doing most of the cleaning and stuff around the house. Maybe because I'm a neat freak, so I don't like the house getting in disarray." He adds, "That's another thing, a lot of time keeping the house in order because my kids are very sloppy," repeating as though it is an incorrigible trait, "And I'm a neat freak."

Most couples settle into a pattern of dividing chores early on in their marriages; while this pattern may of course shift over time, couples do establish relative, and often gendered, strengths in some areas. Marcus has long been responsible for maintaining the girls' schedules, a fact that the Nealses explain in terms of Marcus's capacity for organization. He explains: "Just making sure people get to the places they need to be on time, because if I leave it up to my wife, I think the kids would be late to school and functions. She's really busy with her job and getting on conference calls and all. So, the big thing I can bring is organizational strength to make sure that people get to places on time and making sure, you know, the calendar stays updated—we have a big calendar with when kids' activities are." Typically, this organizational work falls to women, but here it has fallen to Marcus.

Now that he's unemployed, Marcus simply does more of what he had already done before—especially childcare. Sylvia says, "Picking the girls up and dropping them off, that's shared, but he does it now, only because he's home. But when he's working, you know, whichever one of us is available would do it." Marcus concurs, saying, "It was more of a shared responsibility, but I was still, I think, doing the bulk of picking them up and everything, the dropping them off. Because my wife's job was really more hectic back

then." Research has suggested that mothers typically make more adjust-
ments to their paid work schedules than do men to tend to family responsibilities, but in the Nealses' marriage, Marcus was the one who would
sometimes leave work early to pick up the kids.[27] Now that he is unemployed, the Nealses have a strict policy that any pickups and drop-offs are
Marcus's responsibility, even on the days that Sylvia works from home.

There was, however, some negotiation around childcare when Marcus
lost his job. Once Marcus lost his job, Sylvia was adamant that they pull the
girls out of before- and after- school care: "Oh no. No, no, no, no, no! I
made that clear. Like that was one disagreement we had earlier in the year.
I told him, 'You need to pull them out of the before care and after care.'"
Marcus resisted this idea. The Nealses verbally tussled over how much
time Marcus needed to devote to his job search. Sylvia recalls that Marcus
protested, "He said, 'I need time. I need the extra time look up these jobs.'"
Sylvia was unconvinced that job searching needed to occupy the entirety of
Marcus's time. She says, "I said 'It's just two hours.' I said 'We're paying like
two hundred fifty dollars a month. Why would you want to have that extra
bill, you know?'" At the time, the girls had only two more months left in the
before-care and after-care program, so Marcus said, according to Sylvia,
"'Let me just finish the last two months.' I said, 'Whatever.'" When the two
months were up, and it was time to decide whether to reenroll Larissa and
Toni, Sylvia was firm. "When school started, I said to him 'They ain't going
back to the program. I'm sorry. They're not.' And he said 'I didn't plan on it.'
Because he knows, you know, paying an extra two hundred fifty dollars
when you don't have it. Are you kidding me?"

The ideal job-seeker norm looms in the background for the Nealses.
While Marcus is aware of it and trying to comply with it by actively spending at least a portion of each day looking for work, Sylvia expresses skepticism that the norm should take priority over Marcus's responsibilities at
home. A similar dynamic played out in two other cases in my study. Ten of
the twenty-five unemployed men had at least one child who was not yet in
kindergarten for at least part of their unemployment. Out of these ten
families, three families (including the Nealses) made extensive changes to
their childcare arrangements that directly involved the unemployed father
taking on more childcare responsibilities. In the remaining seven families,
the unemployed men typically became somewhat more involved—for

example, doing more pickups and drop-offs—but their employed wives retained primary responsibility for making sure children were where they had to be, when they had to be there. (Of course, these pickups and drop-offs reflect the extremely limited context of childcare policies in the United States.)

Although a significant portion of Marcus's day revolves around Larissa and Toni, he does not see this as "quality time," or something to be grateful for, as we saw with unemployed women in chapter 2. Instead, Marcus explains: "I don't think I'm spending as much time with them as I did before because I mean I feel like all I really do is I spend time shipping them off to their activities at school, picking them up, and then giving them their dinner, and then heading upstairs to the office to keep looking for work. And so, I don't think I spend any more quality time as a result of being out of work than you would expect." Marcus, in other words, does not find these additional child-centered chores especially meaningful or conducive to bonding with his daughters.

While Marcus shuttles the girls around and manages their schedules on weekdays, Sylvia takes over on weekends, leaving Marcus time to focus on job searching. He says: "On the weekends is mainly her dealing with activities with them. Occasionally, because she's busy with work or something, I'll do trips, we have a zoo membership and all. I'll take them to the zoo to get them away and to do things like that or to some amusement park. But typically, she spends more time with them on the weekends I'd say." Sylvia adds, "Larissa's birthday is Saturday and I'm throwing her a birthday party. Well, I should say *we're* throwing her a birthday [party] but he's not going to be around. He'll be there like maybe an hour after the party starts." While Marcus retains responsibility for the "organizational" aspects of pickups and drop-offs, as he terms it, the responsibility for big events for children—like birthday parties, or organizing childcare when neither she nor Marcus are available—ultimately falls on Sylvia.

Revisiting the Nealses: Shifting to a More Gendered Division of Housework

The case of the Nealses illuminates everyday processes of how couples discuss and negotiate housework when men are unemployed to instate a

more gender-egalitarian division. The Nealses already had a more egalitarian division of housework before Marcus lost his job, so after becoming
unemployed, he took on even more of these duties. In this study, six families of unemployed men were like the Nealses in terms of larger shifts in
housework responsibilities after men's unemployment. That being said,
these men typically saw their contribution to housework as temporary, as
a way to contribute to the household economy during the period that they
were not producing an income. Men in this study fully expected that
things would return to "normal" when they started paid work. The case of
the Nealses specifically—and these families broadly—thus raises the question of whether couples who turn to more gender-egalitarian divisions of
housework during unemployment continue to practice this over time.

I found that these changes were indeed often temporary. Revisiting the
Nealses shows how. I met Sylvia again about a year after the period
described above. Marcus had found a job—another contract position, but
a well-paying one—and things had shifted in their home. Both of them are
much happier now that Marcus is employed. For this follow-up interview,
I met Sylvia at a popular donut shop. She came without her two daughters, since she had just dropped them off at a nearby summer school.
Sylvia explains that instead of being distant and disengaged from Sylvia,
Larissa, and Toni, Marcus now, "tells me a lot of stuff about the job, his
coworkers." But Marcus's new job has presented challenges for managing
time. Their time together as a family is now so limited that Sylvia decided
to instate family dinners. "I said, 'We've got to eat together as a family.
Let's have Sunday dinners.' Traditionally in Black families it's always
Sunday dinners. 'I can't do Sunday.' He said, 'Sunday I'm getting ready for
work.' I get that, because Sunday is a hectic day, because you got to be
prepared for that whole week. He said, 'Let's do it on Saturday.' So Saturday
evenings we can eat together as family."

As we continued talking, I was shocked by how much Sylvia had on her
plate and that she had still made the time for the interview. Early on in the
interview, as she rummaged through her leather tote, she explained to me,
"I try to write down a to-do list." After pulling out a pack of gum, pens, and
a name-tag from a conference, she pulled out a crumpled piece of paper
with a list of to-do items. Waving the list, she continued, "These are just
simple things, like I have a clogged sink, and to pour Drain-O down the

sink. The bedroom is a mess. I'm moving pictures around. There was a leak in the roof, believe it or not, and I had that patched up a month ago, but I had to spray this stuff, because it went on the ceiling." She added, "I have to enter stuff on deductibles for our taxes, because we have to finish that. Just basic cleaning and things." Sylvia adds, "Now the burden has shifted."

The burden has shifted to Sylvia in some other key areas, too. She says, "Now I'm the one figuring out breakfast, lunch, and dinner. I'm not the cook. He's the cook, so it's kind of different." Previously, both Marcus and Sylvia had told me that Marcus was generally the cook, even when he was employed. Now, though, Sylvia has taken on the responsibility of managing the food, especially the girls' food, "So now I'm figuring out, OK—and they're picky eaters—what am I packing for lunch? What am I cooking for dinner? Even with trying to get them to eat more vegetables, I do this thing now where I'm steaming and puréeing vegetables. So buying all the vegetables. I did that yesterday. Now I got to cut them up when I get home and steam them and purée them and freeze them and label them."

Planning healthy meals takes time and organization; once Marcus got a new job, this chore shifted squarely to Sylvia. The girls often declare that they're hungry as soon as they get home from school, and this interferes with Sylvia's paid work, since Sylvia works from home about half the week. "It bothers me sometimes, too, because they get off the bus and they come home, but I'm still working, so now it's 'let me bother mom,' and technically I'm still on the clock for the next hour and a half, so that's been a transition for me to try and balance that." Marcus tended to the girls after school not only during the period of his unemployment, but also during his previous job, when his supervisor gave him flexibility. Marcus does not yet have the clout to ask for this at his new position, so Sylvia needs to take care of the kids.

Sylvia has additionally taken on the chore of searching for and organizing childcare, although they both agree that Marcus's organizational skills are better; and he had usually been responsible for managing the girls' busy calendar. Sylvia explains that the two of them are in the midst of "the dilemma of 'we have to hire a nanny.'" This is quite an undertaking, and Sylvia adds, "I am very particular with the kids. I don't just trust anybody with them. I'm not going to look on Craigslist or the internet for someone I don't know." Sylvia found a solution with a neighbor, "So I was fortunate enough that a former coworker of mine who lives maybe about fifteen minutes away, she retired over a year ago. And she said she would do it, so we pay her to come in once a week." This solution, Sylvia suspects, won't last long, "Problem with that now is she kind of just threw a monkey wrench into the plans because she told me just the other day that she has a job interview." The retired neighbor is itching to get back into the labor force. Sylvia is also preparing for a major disruption in the near future, when she expects some upcoming travel for her job. "I will not see them for a month. I got my sister-in-law; she said she can only do one week. She's retired and she doesn't want to be bothered, but she said she'll do one week. I have a girlfriend who'll keep them for a week." Sylvia approached this problem as solely her responsibility. But having only managed to cover two of the four weeks, she's now handed some of this over to Marcus. "I told him, 'You're going to have to talk to your boss. You're going to have to work from home those other two weeks.'"

Finally, Sylvia has also taken over primary responsibility for helping the girls with their homework. Earlier, they split this task, with each parent supervising one child, but Sylvia didn't care for Marcus's approach. Sylvia tells me that Marcus doesn't know how to speak to their daughters at a level appropriate for their age. She rolls her eyes as she says, "He doesn't know how to explain stuff. I'll give an example, like I think it was maybe like two years ago, Toni was learning time. He's like, 'What's quarter to two?' How do you expect her to know that when you're speaking in terms of fractions?" Sylvia was incredulous that Marcus thought such a young child could follow complex fractions like this.

Their elder daughter, Larissa, requires extra tutoring, which means that Sylvia has to discuss Larissa's progress with a counselor. Sylvia explains, "She has to exercise her working memory, her active working memory is not good and that's what's hindering her." When I ask how they manage the appointments and so on, Sylvia responds, "I handle mostly everything." She explains that she prefers it this way: "I want to control it. Because he doesn't know what questions to ask [the counselor]. I'm always googling stuff, reading articles, I purchased many books off of Amazon, reading stuff to figure out how to help her. Different things I look into. Number one, I don't think he has that amount of time—not that I do.

But I think it's different with mothers." In his own interview, Marcus told me that he thought the extra tutoring for Larissa was unnecessary. The responsibility for managing Larissa's learning challenges may fall on Sylvia simply because she is more concerned about it than Marcus.

In my earlier conversations with each of them, both Sylvia and Marcus reported a generally equal division of housework in their marriage, a balance that shifted toward Marcus doing more housework when unemployed. But now, as Marcus strives to settle into his contract position, he is less able or willing to ask for the kinds of workplace concessions that would enable him to take on more childcare responsibilities. Having been with the same company for decades, they both perceive Sylvia to be in a more secure position; she has more ability to negotiate working from home. Marcus, nervous about labor market precarity, is attempting to please his employers, shifting more of the housework to Sylvia. The Nealses are unusual though, and their case represents more egalitarian possibilities than most in this sample. The ideal job-seeker norm highlights that, generally speaking, gendered dynamics at home mean that only some workers (usually men) are supported by spouses to expend the time, emotion, and energy that it takes to please employers in this era of precarity.

CONCLUSION

The ideals that Americans hold about marriage, and the roles that they envision for husbands and wives, for mothers and fathers, are shaped by many factors. A hegemonic understanding of marriage, based primarily on the experiences of White, middle-class families, idealizes a family structure based on a male-breadwinner and female caregiver. In the United States, this particular family form has been a way to differentiate a family's privilege. White families broadcast their respectability by keeping women out of the labor force, and this is particularly evident in the most affluent families.[28] Families outside of this narrow demographic background—for example working-class and Black families—generally also have other ideals of family life that allow them to more easily rework these hegemonic expectations around housework.

For the majority of the couples in this study, as we saw with the Janssons, a man's unemployment did not create a major shift in the division of chores. Most of these families exhibited an uneven division of housework in which wives spent more time planning, delegating, and performing chores, and the presence of an unemployed man in the home did little to shift this dynamic. Couples, but especially unemployed men, perceive men's unemployment as temporary—even when it has endured for months, or even years. Men's unpaid housework continues to be framed primarily as "helping out" during unemployment rather than as a shared responsibility. Wives of unemployed men often appear to take ownership over some tasks and exhibit a reluctance to cede control—for instance, as illustrated through exacting expectations over chores like grocery shopping or helping children with homework.

Although there is less of a shift in the division of housework in families of unemployed men, in approximately a quarter of the families with unemployed men in my study, men increased the amount of time they spent on chores. We see this in the case of the Nealses. For the Nealses, it is important to reiterate that the couple was committed to an egalitarian understanding of marriage *before* Marcus lost his job. While Marcus desired to contribute to the household economy one way or another, Sylvia also made clear that she expected Marcus to do more around the house. Yet, even in this exceptional case, Marcus's reemployment catalyzed a more gender-traditional division of housework as Marcus and Sylvia both sought to ensure that Marcus did well at his new job. Spousal interactions and understandings during unemployment combine with individual motivations to encourage some men to take on more housework than before their job loss.

Unemployed men obtain some reprieve from housework, but the focus on their reemployment also means that men do not have much room to grieve for their job loss. Sylvia, for example, became annoyed when Marcus displayed any signs of depression or sadness, which she saw as weakness. Wives of unemployed men view men's despondency as detracting from their job search, given that the white-collar job search process requires explicit demonstrations of cheer and optimism. Thus, while masculinity may protect men from housework, it comes with the expectation that unemployed men will comply with the ideal job-seeker norm.

6 Why Do Unemployed Women Do Even More Housework?

In general, women do an additional six hours of housework per week after they lose their jobs, although they were already doing more housework than men while they were employed.[1] Families in the professional middle-class protect the time of unemployed men from housework on the theory that they need that time to look for paid work. Why doesn't that logic hold for unemployed women? What cultural understandings propel unemployed women to spend a significant amount of their time on housework?

In this chapter, I draw on three different case studies to show how husbands and wives think about who is responsible for housework when women are unemployed. The family ideal of a female-homemaker and a male-breadwinner looms large here. In these professional, middle-class families, the gendered allocation of housework is additionally exacerbated by high expectations for what constitutes good parenting. Contemporary middle-class parenting is time intensive, and much of it is performed by mothers.[2] These ideals about family life—intensive parenting in particular—are a persuasive counterpoint to the ideal job-seeker norm among these families.

I first present the Blums, whose experiences represent the dominant experience (fourteen out of twenty-three) of those families with unemployed women in my study. Unemployed women often take over the responsibility for the majority of housework, and their husbands encourage this. Unemployed women frame mundane chores as invaluable opportunities. Yet, as I show with the Blums, this does not mean that wives absolve their husbands of housework altogether—a situation that at times presents marital challenges. Unemployed women do more housework because it becomes a way for them to find meaning in their unemployment, because they expect it of themselves, and because others around them, especially their husbands, encourage it.

The remaining two cases diverge from the more dominant model. The experiences of the Levy's depart significantly from those of the other couples in this study because Monica experienced a brief period of unemployment followed by several years of underemployment, rather than a sustained period of being unemployed. Underemployment is an important part of the general trend toward precarity, with some occupations being particularly adversely impacted by it, including higher education—Monica's area. I include the Levy's case to address a scenario in which the spousal interactions most closely approximate that of unemployed men. In this case, the division of housework is shaped by an understanding that Monica's time needs to be protected.

Finally, I delve into the lives of the D'Angelos to show how mental health challenges can shape a spouse's ability to perform housework. Depression often inhibited the ability of the unemployed men in this study to adhere to the strict expectations of the ideal job-seeker norm (as with Jim Radzik in chapter 1). Christina D'Angelo is experiencing the same phenomenon, but her husband is not expecting her to comply with the strict demands of the ideal job-seeker norm. Christina rebukes herself, however, for not complying with the expectations of domesticity.

TURNING CHORES INTO A CALLING

Grace and Finn Blum, a White couple, both worked in government agencies. Grace is a petite woman who dresses casually in jeans and blouses with ballet flats, has shoulder-length chestnut-brown ringlets and hazel eyes. She exudes a calm confidence. Grace is an urban development specialist with a master's degree. Her husband, Finn, a runner, cuts a lean athletic figure, routinely wearing a suit for work. His conversation is infused with a muted sense of humor. Finn holds a JD. The Blums have two daughters, five-year-old Clare and eight-year-old Stacey.

Grace and Finn have been a dual-earner couple with continuous work histories, except for the few months that Grace took as maternity leave after the birth of each of her daughters. Until Grace lost her job a year ago after fourteen years at the same workplace, both Finn and Grace had been earning about $70,000 a year in their respective jobs, making for a combined household income of $140,000 a year. Finn describes their relationship as quiet and content, saying, "I love my wife very much. I think we're a great couple, great parents. I think we do well together." He adds that part of this stems from a shared understanding that "family's the most important thing."

Speaking about Grace's job search, Finn says, "I'm not gonna push Grace to do something that she doesn't want to do." Finn does not encourage Grace to take jobs about which she is decidedly lackluster; indeed, Finn has a hands-off approach to Grace's future employment. A key question for the Blums is what will happen to Grace's career and how Finn will react to her choices, particularly as Grace is trying to decide if she even wants to go back to full-time, paid work.

Grace's ambivalence toward jobs she comes across as she searches for employment stems from her experience in losing her job. As Grace describes it, the atmosphere in her long-term workplace turned unbearably toxic in the last few years, with bureaucratic hurdles making day-to-day work increasingly unpleasant. An atmosphere of camaraderie gave way to fear as, one after another, members of the team lost their jobs. Many other women in this study, more so than men, recounted exceptionally unpleasant workplace experiences where they had been passed over for promotions they felt they deserved, their expertise was routinely questioned, and they constantly worried whether they had adequately demonstrated their commitment to their employer.[3] Their experiences echo those of women in professional workplaces.

So, when Grace, too, was let go, it was not exactly shocking, but the negativity of those recent years had left a "bitter aftertaste." She was wary of getting embroiled in a similar toxic workplace. Finn says, "She had been

there forever. But she had been looking to move on for a while." Being let
go in these circumstances did not feel as debilitating as being laid off or
fired from a valued position. Finn says, "So I think initially it was kind of
a shock, but it maybe was not such a bad thing 'cause she was unhappy
where she was at." In the time since, Grace has been applying for jobs, but
she screens the positions she comes across for any evidence of toxic workplaces. Finn explains that while "her eyes are always open," she recently
"got a job offer and turned it down." Finn was fine with this decision,
because, he says, "She was miserable where she was at and this, I think,
was a very similar type of atmosphere." Finn reiterates, "I mean it's really
her decision; I wouldn't make her take a job that she would be miserable
in just to make a paycheck."

His hands-off approach means that Finn is not attempting to mold
Grace into an ideal job-seeker whose days are consumed by job searching
activities. Neither he nor Grace insist on her demonstrating that she is
morally unemployed, as we saw happen in the families of unemployed
men. Instead, as we will see shortly, their feeling rules around Grace's
unemployment focus on maximizing Grace's sense of personal fulfillment
and meeting the household's financial needs. While the Blums are concerned about money, they downplay the importance of Grace's income.
And because both Grace and Finn assume that she will one day rejoin the
labor force in one way or another, Grace feels particularly compelled to
use this time to perform the role of a deeply involved mother. These
aspects of how Grace and Finn understand her unemployment shape their
interactions around housework during this time.

(Almost) Getting By on One Income

Grace has been unemployed for a year when I first meet her. Her unemployment benefits—which had been extended in the years following the
Great Recession—are winding down. The Blums are starting to feel a bit
of the financial pinch now. But rather than focusing on finding a long-
term replacement for Grace's income, both Grace and Finn are more concerned with whether Grace can fill the shortfall between Finn's income
and their expenditures or, if not, how they might further tighten their
belts. Although prior to losing her job Grace's income constituted half of

the family income, neither Grace nor Finn seem particularly focused on Grace's financial contribution to the home. Grace says, "We live very modestly. . . . We always thought it important that we could keep our house on one income." Right now, that one income is Finn's.

The couple never quite met that goal: Both Grace and Finn explain that Finn's income does not fully cover their expenditures. They are currently focused on filling that gap. Grace says, "If I could make like $12,000 a year, honestly that would be enough to get us by." Finn concurs, saying in his own interview, "We need a little bit more money but not like a full-time income to make ends meet. . . . She does all the finances so she sees the budget and what our gap is with what I make and what we need to pay out every month. We didn't need a full salary, we just needed a little bit, so as long as she could make up that gap, then that's fine." Making up the gap, though, is Grace's responsibility.

For the first year, the Blums were able to ride Grace's unemployment out without making many changes to their lifestyle, in part because, as they both explain, they "were frugal."[4] They are keeping up with their mortgage payments. But they've instituted small cutbacks, like deferring their plans to finish their basement and upgrade the dishwasher. Finn says, "We haven't joined as many things. Like we used to be members of the zoo, the Nature Center." Both Grace and Finn try to do less expensive things with their daughters. Finn continues, "And just when you do things, we just think about the cost. We're not buying lunches out, we're packing lunches." That is, Grace makes the lunches. Finn adds, "We have a big group of friends in the neighborhood and the guys sometimes go out for beers or something like that. I might say 'no' more often than I used to." Grace concurs, saying, "Neither of us is spending money on clothes or anything like that." Echoing Finn, she says, "We're both pretty frugal to begin with." She tells me about the same home-packed lunches that Finn does, and she mentions that, instead of going out to movies, they do movie nights at home.

Yet, like most of the families I interviewed, it was also important for Grace and Finn to maintain some of the more expensive family rituals. For Grace, that is a family vacation to Maine that the Blums always take in the summer. She says, "We go to Maine and we rent the same house every year. This is our seventh year, and, you know, that was something I was not willing to budge on." The Blums view family time as precious and recognize that the girls' childhoods are of a finite duration. Grace explains, "I think both of us realize that it's, like, rejuvenating for all of us as a family." To save money, though, the Blums rented the house for a shorter time than usual. She tells me, "We actually wound up doing a week at the house that we rent every year, and we did another week of camping. So that's a pretty inexpensive way to vacation." Brows knitted, Grace adds, "We would have to be really in dire straits to drop that. I can't say we're there yet."

Longing for Life as a Stay-at-Home Mom

Although the Blums have been a dual-earner couple for the duration of their marriage, Grace's adverse experience at her work in the past few years has caused her to think more deeply about whether they will continue that way. Finn shares Grace's uncertainty, telling me that he does not think that a career is "an essential element of being a wife or a mother, really." Aside from Grace's serious reservations about the changing nature of her field, part of her uncertainty about her career trajectory stems from her conceptions of motherhood. She says, "I was always so jealous of those non-working moms, 'cause I wanted to be one! And now I am one." This is an envy vested in idealizations of being able to afford the luxury of staying at home, an ideal itself based in raced and classed approaches to gender and marriage.

While employed, Grace often felt as though she ought to be even more involved in the caregiving for her two daughters:

> It's just been, honestly, it's been freeing for me. It really has been. . . . When I was working, I felt like I tried to hold on to things that made me a mom. And felt frustration that there were just things I couldn't do, you know? Like I couldn't pick my kids up every day, or go on the field trip, or do this after-school activity, or this play date, or just be there at like three o'clock and we're hanging on the playground. . . . It really was liberating for me in that respect that I just thought this will probably not happen again, where I can just stay home and just do this one thing, you know? And take care of my household.

Being unemployed has provided Grace with what she considers an opportunity to practice a more involved approach to motherhood.

A few years before Grace lost her job, Finn had lost his. Recalling that time, he notes how Grace's experience has been far different from his, saying, "I didn't want to stay home with the kids. I hate saying that, but I don't know if I could deal with staying home with kids day-in, day-out, all summer. Grace loves it, and relishes it, and would be perfectly happy I think doing that forever, really." Pausing, he adds, "So I think my layoff was harder than hers."

The Blums' interactions around the division of housework while Grace is unemployed are shaped by how they understand Grace's unemployment. They both see her paid work as important to filling an income gap, but they both also see the period of her unemployment as an opportunity for her to practice an intensive motherhood. The Blums' feeling rules are vested in recognition of how Grace felt about both her job loss and her desire to be more intensively involved in her children's lives. These rules, which frame her job loss as a highly negative experience and emphasize her feelings of longing for the ideals of life as a stay-at-home mom, have been key to how the Blums have divided up chores during Grace's unemployment. Grace, in some ways, has turned mundane chores into a higher calling.

Chores as a Calling

Prior to her unemployment, the Blums practiced a gendered division of housework typical among White middle- and upper-middle-class families.[5] Even though Grace and Finn spent a similar number of hours in paid work for a similar income, Grace did the majority of the housework. The Blums, like most of the families of unemployed men and women in this study, followed a housework regime where Finn was responsible for the outside and Grace for the inside. Chuckling sheepishly, Finn says, "I do all the yard work, she does everything else." Recognizing the unevenness of this division of housework, he points to the small, square coffee table in between us at the Starbucks where we met for our interview and adds, "Our yard is about the size of this table."[6] Husbands often recognize that the division of "outside" chores for husbands and "inside" chores for wives is not equal, but the recognition does not necessarily mean a move to change this situation.

The unequal division of housework when they were both employed rankled Grace. Her brown eyes widening, Grace says, "The trash is once a week, and you mow the lawn every two weeks. Those are not the equivalent of dishes every day, bathing the kids, most of the time putting them to bed." Sighing in frustrating, she continues, "Like I *always* bathe the kids. I almost always did bedtime." Grace's comments here highlight the gendered discrepancy between what scholars call "core tasks," which need to be done frequently—for example, cooking, laundry, cleaning dishes, grocery shopping—and "peripheral tasks," for example, fixing a bathroom leak or mowing the lawn, which are typically less frequent and, on average, less time-consuming responsibilities.[7]

Since Grace's unemployment, though, things in the Blum household have shifted so that Grace has taken over almost all of the housework. In part, this reflects Grace's desire to take on more of the work associated with raising their daughters. To Grace, these tasks are tied up with being the kind of mom she felt her work prevented her from being. But it also reflects, at least in part, the implicit expectation that, because she is unemployed, unpaid work in the home is entirely Grace's responsibility.

When Grace talks about the current division of housework, she emphasizes that this period of her life represents an opportunity to spend more time with her daughters and on child-centered chores. She says, "This is kind of a special time for me." Grace particularly acknowledges the young age of her daughters as what makes this work especially meaningful, "You know, they're still young enough where they want to do things with me." Laughing, she continues, "We have fun and play and things." For Grace, mundane chores such as pickups and drops-offs constitute valuable time together, precisely because she sees her unemployment as temporary. Finn echoes Grace's perception that she lacked time with her daughters when she worked. He says, "Well, as Grace points out, aside from weekends, the two girls and her never had that much time." Now, especially during the summer, the girls have been excited to have time together in a way they never did before, "Grace did things with them like special trips, swimming, and stuff like that. I think they had a great time!" From Finn's perspective, this is because he sees the relationship between Grace and Clare and Stacey as being singular: "She's more the nurturer, and they definitely defer to their mother."

Grace and Finn do not see childcare chores as tedious, but rather as filled with meaning for Grace. The Blums have never outsourced chores such as cleaning, although many families in the upper-middle-class do. In this study, families with an unemployed woman who had outsourced chores—most commonly housecleaning and childcare—tended to cut back on outsourcing these types of chores when the woman became unemployed.

For many unemployed women like Grace, the expectation that their unemployment is temporary becomes a reason for cherishing childcare chores, turning them into a calling. Household work in general, and childcare specifically, becomes a way to embrace a certain type of domestic role—especially in terms of motherhood—that women in this study had felt accountable to but unable to perform when they were working. In families with an unemployed man, in contrast, the very temporariness of unemployment becomes a reason why men do not do more housework.

While Grace is unemployed, she contributes to her family by providing her time. Although unemployed men's time, as we saw in chapter 5, is fiercely protected, overall I found that unemployed women feel obligated —and are expected by their husbands—to provide their time as a resource for the family when they can't provide money. Grace explicitly explains how her time allows the Blums to spend less than they normally would. "The plus side of me being home," she says, "is that we don't have to pay for aftercare [for their two daughters], which is three hundred dollars per month." Because Grace has been unemployed for a year, including a summer, the Blums have saved on expensive summer activities.[8] She says, "And we didn't have to pay for [summer] camp. Which could be two thousand to five thousand dollars per kid, depending on where you go. And if you have to do camp aftercare, that's additional." The money that the Blums saved does not equal the loss of Grace's income, a fact that Grace quickly acknowledges. The Blums describe skipping summer camp as a way to save money while also encouraging mother-daughter time. This is in contrast to the families of unemployed men, where families viewed even the smallest cutback in expenses as a troubling indication of a loss of class status. Families of unemployed men clearly framed unemployed men's incomes as essential for maintaining status. Those of unemployed women, like the Blums, instead often downplayed the importance of women's income for their families, insisting that they could manage well enough without it.

The framing of Grace's time as her current contribution to her family means that Grace's days are busy. They seem to vanish quickly, even though she is unemployed:

> I needed to go food shopping or I had to do laundry or wash the dishes or, you know, household things. So, the days just went really quick. It was surprising how quickly they went. And then it's, you know, two-thirty and I gotta get back to pick my kids up. I never felt like there was just time to kill. It was always, "I only have a few hours, I gotta finish all this stuff." And it made me really think "How did I do all of this when I was working full-time?" Because I could barely do it with my free days. I felt like I was barely able to get the shopping done and the laundry. And people would ask me, "How is it being home?" And I said, "I'm a lot less efficient." Because I would go food shopping and I realized I forgot this or that and I'd have to run out to the market the next day.

Grace doesn't feel particularly regretful about her days disappearing, and she doesn't put pressure on herself to find a job, any job, as quickly as possible. Instead, she appears content, as she explains that even now, a year out of paid work, she continues to enjoy this involuntary time off.

She is alert to the reality, though, that given how much of the chores she has taken over, "there's gonna be a painful adjustment for everybody" at a later stage, "when I go back to work." Thinking through what this adjustment might entail, Grace suggests some possibilities, "Like, maybe we'll have to start ordering our groceries online because you know, you don't want to run out, like, Sunday to the market; everybody's at the market!" Because she is unemployed, Grace can shop during the middle of the week and save time that way. Shaking her head, she finishes with, "But, there are definitely some things that are gonna have to—the balance will have to shift a little at the point that I go back to work."

The chores themselves seem to have multiplied. Instead of simply shopping at a single store, Grace now comparison-shops, picking up one item at the supermarket and one at Trader Joe's. This was common across unemployed women in this study who embraced chores as a calling (fourteen out of twenty-three). Instead of buying new clothes for herself or the girls, Grace spends times at thrift stores. She explains:

Whereas before, when I was working, I didn't have the time to go you know, "let me check this thrift store, or that consignment shop," or whatever. I just knew that I'll go to Target if they need sneakers, or a winter coat. Now I have the time, I can run out to that store, this store, without spending as much. And they love it. Because they know when I come home with a bag they're getting new stuff. . . . My older daughter *loves* going to thrift stores because she can buy so much stuff for very little money and she's kind of a little fashionista, so she thinks it's great.

These savings are not extensive for families of this social class. Yet being unemployed means that women often expend time in devising ways to cut costs. Although the women in these studies are looking for jobs, their time does not end up being protected for job searching. In contrast, comparable unemployed men in my study rarely looked for opportunities to cut costs—if anything, they incurred additional expenses by setting up home offices and assuming that housework and childcare would not fall to them, since they should spend their time searching for paid work.

Meals, too, have become more elaborate. Finn, for example, explained how when both he and Grace worked, they ate quick and convenient meals, such as frozen dinners. But now that Grace is unemployed, mealtime is a completely different affair. Finn says, "Now we have these great dinners, which is fantastic." The Blums are members of an urban farm that delivers produce each week. Finn describes these deliveries as abundant, and sometimes mystifying: "I mean crazy kinds of greens, collard greens, kale, just stuff that I wouldn't know what to do with, but Grace spends the time looking up how to cook them." As Grace explores new menus and recipes for produce she is unfamiliar with, her time preparing meals has increased.

Cooking in the home and for one's family has long been a feminized activity through which women express love and affection, but it can also be a means of subordinating women.[9] Across my sample of unemployed women, I found that, along with time spent with and on children, unemployed women especially spent more time cooking elaborate meals for their families. Some of these women had long enjoyed cooking and baking as a hobby, but even those who didn't particularly enjoy it nonetheless spent more time on it as a way of expressing care for their families during their unemployment. Finn describes their meals now as "So well-balanced, always kind of like a good vegetable and usually a meat. But really good home-cooked meals like from beginning to end." And, of course, eating at home saves the Blums money, as well.

"You're Part of This Family, Too!"

Despite the joy and meaning that Grace claims to experience in chores, she is nonetheless troubled by her perception that their division of housework has become skewed. Shaking her head, she says, "There should be more of a split." Reflecting on how things used to be, Grace says, "Like whoever cooked, the other person would do the dishes. So, I always cooked, but now I always do the dishes too." As in many families, Grace finds that her husband is often oblivious to the chores that need to be done; if she wants him to do more housework, she has to tell him to do it. Grace tells me about how she has to prod Finn to do basic household tasks, saying, "'If you see a laundry basket that needs to go up the steps, like, take it up the steps!' So, I try to give subtle hints you know, 'Take this up the steps.'" My sample of unemployed women reported that this masculine oblivion to housework becomes more acute during women's unemployment than when they were employed, presumably because of the expectation that wives will take over most housework.

Grace explains that her exasperation about Finn's reluctance to do housework stems from her conception of family. To Grace, it seems obvious that everyone should pitch in: "For me, I'd say it's coming from the presumption that I will do everything because I'm home all day. And for me back to him it's like 'I am home all day, but you're also a member of this family.'" Thus, while she accepts Finn's expectation for her to take over the housework during her unemployment, and even enjoys some of the work, the imbalance nevertheless irks her.

Grace elaborates, "Because I'm home more, even though I'm home with the kids now, but I'm home, so, you know, I still am responsible for the majority of the household chores. And that can be frustrating." For Grace, the frustrating part is figuring out how to make time for herself in a context where others likely perceive that she has all the time in the world. Grace feels that her time is not her own anymore. She has to squeeze in leisurely activities surreptitiously, "So if the kids are engaged in an activity,

I will sit down and read my book and not feel guilty because I'm not doing something around the house that needs to be done." Comparing herself to Finn, Grace says, "And I understand it from his side, you know. He's out of the house the whole day, and then when he comes home, he wants to relax and not have to clean the bathroom or whatever."

Grace resists the expectation that because she is at home she *should* do all the chores. She says she wants to "not feel bad" about taking some time for herself, away her daughters. Those moments to herself, she tells me, "don't come very often, where I feel like I can sit and read my book for a little bit." Unless she specifically carves out time for herself, Grace's whole day easily dissipates in doing things for others, "Because otherwise I am not gonna get that downtime." Grace is not talking about an entire evening to herself or hours at a stretch—just a few minutes here and there to catch her breath from looking after the kids and their home.[10]

Grace wants Finn to "help" more, especially with their daughters. She explains: "But I'd say, probably chores surrounding the kids: get a bath ready, help one of my kids with the shower, or sort of chase after them to get ready for bed. You know: "Put on your pajamas! Get your teeth brushed!" That's something where I think we butt heads all the time because that's part of what happens during the time where he's home and, that's his, you know, downtime." Grace's comments imply that Finn's need for downtime is easier to recognize because he works for pay outside the home. While she is also performing work in the form of providing care for their daughters and their home, no money is being exchanged, and there are no clear boundaries for when her workday starts or finishes. Grace explains that she has to actively claim her time and ask for help from Finn. "So, I'd say probably one of our biggest issues is, like, 'You need to help me get these guys ready for bed, because I've been with them all day, too.'" Grace enjoys being with her daughters, but it is also tiring to provide the constant attention that small children typically require, and to do so without respite or downtime.[11] "I'm exhausted by then," she tells me. "I need help. I can't do it by myself."

Finn, too, feels he and Grace have fallen into a routine during her unemployment in which he is far more distanced from his children's lives than he would normally be. He attributes this change to the fact that he no longer handles drop-offs: "Like when I was dropping off every day I would stay and meet with the teacher, meet with parents and stuff, and I was a lot more engaged with the school." Shrugging, he adds, "Like we go to social things and I don't really know the parents." When I ask him whether he wants to reinstate his responsibility for the drop-offs, he laughs, and responds, "I should. I'm just too la—" Hesitating to admit indolence, he continues, "I mean we could both, I'd just sort of have to get up a little bit earlier." He draws a deep breath and tells me that dropping the kids off *now* would not necessarily make him more familiar with teachers and parents of other kids: "But it's different now; so that was in pre-K. Our oldest now is in second grade, so she walks. Like you walk her onto campus and she goes up to her room. You don't walk her up." He adds, "The little one is in kindergarten now, and I think you can still go in and kind of linger and spend ten minutes in the classroom." Although Finn is not especially keen to reinstate his responsibility for drop-offs, he does, nonetheless, regret that he is less aware of the details of his daughters' lives than he was earlier. He appears to share Grace's view that childcare chores are a way to participate in the family life.

Revisiting the Blums: Two Years after Grace Lost Her Job

A year after I first interviewed Grace and Finn, I talk with Grace again. It is the middle of her daughters' summer vacation, and it has now been two years since she lost her job. She remains unemployed. While earlier Grace told me she hoped to find a part-time job with a "mommy schedule," a 9:00–2:00 workday, she is now reassessing.[12] She says, "I'm open to the part-time still, but there are just not a lot of options. So, I am still also looking full-time." Grace reasonably wonders what her prospects are, given how long she has been unemployed, "Being two years out, that starts to weigh on me now." She adds, "So maybe that is, you know, something I need to consider more. Because I can imagine it doesn't look good when somebody's on the other side of the table looking at my credentials."

Grace has good reason to worry. Research shows that unemployment has a "scarring effect," such that potential employers often see active unemployment as a sign of a flawed worker. They view lapses in employment, whether involuntary or opting out to care for family members, unfavorably.[13] With a slight defensiveness, Grace invokes her long tenure at her previous workplace as a sign of her employability, "Even though my last place of employment, I was with them for, you know, almost fourteen years."

Although Grace is more concerned about finding a job now than she was a year ago, and despite her growing awareness that the clock is ticking, her time still goes primarily into housework and childcare. With the girls out of school for the summer, they require most of her time. She describes her mornings and afternoons to me: "So, we wake up, and now I take them to swim lessons first thing in the morning. And then we maybe run an errand or we come home, or, you know, doctor's appointment or whatever. Hang out at home for a little bit; usually eat lunch here; and then head out and do something in the afternoon hours. Go to a playground, go to a movie, go swimming again. They love to swim."

She estimates that she's only spending about a fifth as much time looking for paid work as she would during the girls' school year. The girls' summer vacation, in other words, has eaten into approximately 80 percent of the time for her job search. But for Grace and Finn, the calculus on how she should spend her time is clear: "Well, I think it seems a little crazy to ship them off [to summer camp], Grace says, if I'm home. And it costs a lot of money. So it doesn't really seem like a viable option for us. It's just extra money that we really don't need to spend if I'm home."

An important addition to their weekly schedule is spending time with Grace's father-in-law. "We are also two days a week going to my father-in-law's and providing, you know, some support for him." Grace explains what visiting her elderly father-in-law entails: "I straighten up, make sure his mail is in order, make sure there's food in the refrigerator. The kids just hang out, you know, watch TV or play with him. And then that's kind of it. Yeah, so we're there for maybe, like, two or three hours a day." Unlike the care that Grace provides for her and Finn's children, the carework that Grace provides for her father-in-law is remunerated, albeit indirectly. Finn's father now covers part of her daughters' tuition at their private school. Grace elaborates on what she does for her father-in-law: "I handle most of his bills, I handle *all* of his bills, and just kind of managing, like, his household things." Grace replaced a female home health worker who took sick leave. At that point, Grace says, "My husband and I discussed, since I'm home, I would be helping out instead. So I took on that role." She ends with, "And the arrangement we've made is, he's contributing to [my daughters'] tuition." In his earlier interview, Finn explained that, if their financial position got worse, he knew he could always get help from his father. At the time I first spoke with them, the Blums did not feel as though they needed that help. Now that another year has passed, they feel less secure financially, and so this arrangement is very welcome.

An additional year of unemployment does not seem to have significantly changed the Blums' feeling rules for understanding Grace's unemployment. Both Grace and Finn continue to understand Grace's paid work as a practical matter that involves bridging the gap between Finn's income and their expenditures. Given Grace's negative experiences at her previous workplace, both of them envision Grace finding a job, not a career—an agreement that justifies her focus on the children and their home rather than on reemployment. Their interactions around housework, specifically the shift in Grace taking on most of the housework, are shaped by these understandings. Yet there are some fractures in these feeling rules. While Grace wants to be an involved mother, she also wants Finn to remain involved as both a parent and a spouse by participating in housework. Through subtle hints, she urges Finn's participation, with limited success. Grace glorifies motherhood, but she does not relish sole proprietorship of parenting. Mothers, who already do more housework than fathers, end up doing even *more* while they are unemployed, and they do so at the expense of looking for paid work. The labor market is gendered—women's experiences range from receiving slights and subtle digs to outright sexual harassment and discrimination. The jobs that women can access are often less gratifying in terms of professional status than those available to men, and women also encounter more hurdles to increases in pay and promotions.[14] Women in professional occupations, like Grace, encounter higher wage gaps than in working-class occupations.[15] All of this may mean that when unemployed, the domestic realm offers many women both more social status and greater satisfaction, especially when it comes to practicing socially prized intensive mothering.

WORKING HARD AND EARNING LITTLE

Monica and Rayan Levy, both in their mid-thirties, met online about eleven years ago, right before they were both about to start their respective

PhD programs on different continents. Rayan, the son of Lebanese immigrants, was moving to Europe, while Monica, herself the child of one Moroccan and one American parent, was starting a doctoral program in the United States. Their early courtship was characterized by long phone calls and meeting each other as often as their budgets and schedules would allow. After several years of a primarily long-distance relationship, Rayan finished his PhD while Monica was still completing her studies. Luckily, he found a job in the United States not too far from her. In eight years of marriage, Monica and Rayan have had two children: a five-year-old daughter, Zahra, and a two-year-old son, Salman. While Rayan had a difficult ninety-minute commute for a few years, he eventually found a job at a university closer to Monica. He received early tenure a year ago, at the age of thirty-five.

Monica's academic journey was far more fraught. It took her close to a decade to obtain her PhD. She unexpectedly got pregnant with her second child while in the finishing stages of her dissertation. This timing was unfortunate, in that she had a painful final trimester that made it difficult to polish her dissertation to the extent that she had wished. She had also hoped to produce some more publications before she went on the academic job market.[16] Monica's heart was set on obtaining an academic job, and she was crestfallen in not reaching the final stages of any of the applications.

Since that time, Monica's experience in paid work has been one of underemployment. When I meet Monica for an interview in the summer, she is about to start a contract of a year-long visiting assistant professorship at the same university where Rayan is tenured. This is more secure than the work she had been cobbling together by teaching courses as an adjunct at four different universities for the past several years.

Underemployment, as distinct from unemployment, typically refers to working in a job below your skill level, working in a job below the average pay for your skill level, or working fewer hours than you would prefer. Underemployment is a different manifestation of precarity than unemployment, and some occupations and industries—including higher education—are increasingly likely to be subject to it. Monica, has been adjuncting for four different educational institutions, teaching about eight college-level courses each year for annual earnings between $15,000 and $20,000, with no benefits or job security. She and their children are on Rayan's health insurance plan, at significant cost.[17] As Monica succinctly describes her situation, "I am so underemployed and yet so overworked." Monica's work experience has been critical to how the Levys approach the division of housework—a division that, as we will see, is far more egalitarian than is typical among heterosexual, married American couples with children. The Levys' experience nonetheless sheds light on the marital dynamics of employment by providing a glimpse into how spouses feel about and experience various kinds of precarity.

The Emotional and Financial Impacts of Monica's Underemployment

Monica's enduring underemployment has taken a toll on her professional identity and self-esteem, as well as on how she thinks about her contributions to the household. Reflecting on her attempts to find a tenure-track academic job, Monica says, "I think the hardest part is the hit it took on my self-esteem probably. Just not feeling really successful." She adds, "I sometimes felt, like, really worthless." Rayan has been an important source of support, and she describes him as a source of unfailing optimism in her future career.[18] She explains, "He would just listen to me. He'd be like, 'I know, I hear you. It must be really hard. You're going to get something.' He'd be like, 'You're really talented or you can do this. You're really smart.'"

Beyond her persistent self-doubt, Monica is also worried about her family's financial situation. Rayan earns an annual income of $55,000, which he can top up by teaching more classes during the summer—which he has done on occasion. Monica adds another $15,000–$20,000 a year to this by adjuncting. But the Levys also have considerable expenses, including a $1,900 monthly mortgage payment and childcare for their two young children. The family invests in childcare, despite Monica's spotty job history, because it is obvious to them that Monica must remain connected to the academic world if she is to have any chance of landing a tenure-track position.

Monica explains, "We have to have childcare because I was trying to publish and trying to work and I was teaching in four different places at a time." Teaching at four different institutions means that Monica spends considerable time driving from one place to the next for classes. She also has different email addresses for each university, requiring her to check multiple accounts, and she has to fulfill different administrative requirements at each university—for example, taking multiple online training modules for dealing with sexual harassment. Now that she has a more stable position at one institution secured for the next academic year, she reflects back and says, "I felt really scattered and it was just very hard to focus and to be present and it was hard to publish during that time. It gets you further behind." Sighing deeply, Monica says, "We are so in debt right now because of those two years."

The Levys are considerably in debt, mostly to Rayan's parents. In addition to multiple $10,000 gifts, his parents loaned them $20,000. Rayan describes his parents as not being tremendously wealthy—the couple emigrated from Lebanon to Canada as teenagers and built up a portfolio of small businesses. His father finished high school, but his mother did not. They packed up their last corner store over a decade ago and have since been living as retirees in Canada. Rayan, an only child, explains the tremendous amount of material help his parents have given to Monica and him over the past several years as a cultural phenomenon: "For me, it's totally normal. Totally normal. For Monica, it isn't. That's a kind of cultural thing I think as well. For me, the household assets are the family's assets. Like, well, my parents have these homes, who's going to get that stuff? I'm not saying that because I'm a jerk. I'm saying that because that's how they thought. Things got passed down." Rayan is matter-of-fact in saying, "Basically, we sustained our life because of my parents."

Monica's parents, too, gave them a big gift in the form of purchasing the Levys' starter home in full, so that Rayan and Monica did not have to pay a mortgage. Rayan and Monica sold that house, buying a bigger house in an upper-middle-class neighborhood of their choice. Monica acknowledges that, as she puts it, "We're living out of our means. We definitely are living out of our means. We're doing it in anticipation." By this, Monica means that the Levys are building a middle-class lifestyle in anticipation of being a fully-employed, dual-earner family, looking forward to the time when Monica will finally be in a more secure and better-paying job. Their debts to Rayan's parents and their mortgage make sense to them in that they are both anticipating that her underemployment will end in the near future.

That they need these gifts and loans troubles Monica, who blames herself and her underemployment. "It feels embarrassing to me, because I know that I'm the reason. Rayan has a full-time job. He's been working for years doing this. I'm the one who is not bringing in money."[19] Furthermore, Monica, who identifies as a feminist, says that not being able to contribute to her family financially bothers her in terms of how she sees herself as a wife. "What frustrates me about it is we are in an equal partnership, but it's not really fair that one of us doesn't bring in the money and I'm not even taking care of the kids." Unlike the unemployed men in this study, who tended to think about their contribution to their families *only* in terms of money, Monica perceives multiple ways of contributing to her family; she feels dejected because she does not think she is contributing in *any* of these ways. She continues, "It feels like there's a ridiculous burden on Rayan."

Rayan, in contrast, is more troubled by how Monica's underemployment has corroded her sense of self. He frames the issue primarily in emotional terms. Shaking his head vigorously, he says, "I mean, her sense of professional self-worth was so low. So low! That was probably the number one thing that was difficult for me, is, like, here's this woman that I love and I admire and is so intelligent and so capable and such a good teacher and such a good researcher, like all the things that an academic should be she is. She's just treated like shit. Just treated like crap everywhere she goes."

Rayan is trying to do whatever he can to help Monica find a better position. This means facilitating time for her to focus on her research and getting out peer-reviewed publications while she is adjuncting. He describes how he approaches their division of housework: "A lot of it had to do with her emotional well-being and trying to balance supporting her both in terms of giving her time to write, to teach, and also to be present for her, to be a sounding board. To be around, to take care of the kids. That's a big one—because we have two children who are five and two." Their division of housework, as we will see, has been shaped by the couple's understanding that Monica's more insecure career trajectory means that she needs more time to focus on research so she can get a tenure-track position.

Housework Shaped by a Time Crunch

Time has been a scarce resource for the Levys, with both Rayan and Monica feeling pulled in different directions. They want and need to advance their careers, parent their children, spend quality time with each other, maintain independent social and athletic activities, and take care of their house. In much the same way that the families in this study protected the time of unemployed men, the Levys have attempted to give Monica space to position herself for a tenure-track academic job. Consequently, as Rayan says, "Our collective efforts have to be towards making her professional life easier and to helping her." Having multiple pulls on their time means that Rayan takes on more chores at home; they both worry about how Monica's professional life impacts her time with the children, and Rayan, in particular, has been worrying about their marriage.

In Monica's assessment, the couple divides housework fairly evenly. She explains:

> He does most of the cooking. He learned how to cook a few years ago and just loves it. I like cooking, but sometimes I feel overwhelmed by everything, so he'll do the cooking. Cleaning we sort of split; we clean different parts of the house. . . . He'll make the lunches for the kids. A lot of times he'll drop off, because he wants to get to work early. We have a schedule for drop off. . . . So we switch back and forth dropping off and picking up. I did a lot of pickups this past year, I would say, with the kids. He did more drop-offs. I do the kids' laundry. He does our laundry.

Rayan has a different take on their division of chores. He underscores how Monica's underemployment has been a central structuring factor in their home life, saying, "It's a division of labor in the home that emerged specifically out of her professional circumstances, specifically. A hundred percent." Rayan is deeply frustrated with what he perceives to be an unequal division of chores.

Many of the unemployed men in this study were often oblivious to chores piling up around them. Rayan evokes something similar when he talks about Monica's obliviousness to time. He says, "My personality type is that I know—I say this with all love and affection towards my wife—but I know that if I don't get up and get the lunches ready and the breakfast ready and the bags ready and all that stuff, the kids are not going to get to school on time." Shrugging his shoulders, he adds, "I just know it. She has a cavalier attitude towards time." Couples with unemployed men in this study were the ones most likely to evoke natural skills to explain the division of housework as Rayan does here. He explains that he is far more attuned than his wife to the realities of their kids' schedules.

Spending time with, and taking care of, their two children has been an emotionally fraught issue for both Monica and Rayan. Rayan explains that, in order to enable Monica to work on her research, he provides most of the childcare when their children are at home, especially on weekends. Rayan spends a lot of time with his kids, but he fears the very quantity of that time detracts from its quality. He says, "So it does two things: one is that it doesn't give me the space I personally need from my children to be the kind of father that I want to be all the time. Now I'm like, 'Just watch a video.'" The other issue is that Monica's schedule has made it challenging for her to spend the kind of quality time she would like to spend with her kids. Rayan reports a recent incident with his five-year-old daughter: "The other day Zahra was whimpering before bed. I said, 'What's wrong, sweetie?' She said, 'I miss Mommy. I love you Daddy, so much, but you drop me off and you pick me up and then you come home and you read with me, and I just want to spend some time with Mommy.'"

For Monica, the fact that her underemployment and her attempts to make herself marketable academically have pulled her away from her kids is heartbreaking. Softly, she tells me, "I feel almost ashamed. I mean, I really do feel ashamed," she continues, "for the fact that my kids—that often I was just on an electronic device trying to deal with whatever I had to deal with." Parents value spending time with their children, often seeing it as intrinsic to developing a strong bond and relationship.[20] While adjuncting, Monica was saddled with an unenviable teaching schedule, some classes scheduled even on the weekends. Monica was upset with both the situation and herself, feeling that even when she was home, she wasn't present.

The Levys' decision to prioritize Monica's academic work has had consequences for their intimacy. Monica says, "Sometimes I'll be working until one o'clock in the morning and he would be asleep at eleven p.m. or something, and he wanted me to go to bed with him, and he felt like I wasn't being intimate enough and stuff." For his part, Rayan felt that Monica "neglected" him and their relationship, saying, "That stings on a level that is really, really tough to kind of verbalize. We have a wonderful physical life, an amazing physical life. It's great. But there are times where, like, I need to be physically close to her as a way to be emotionally close, so I will start equating the two." Rayan elaborates on how sex and love became inextricably intertwined for him—an issue that became a problem, given that Monica was frequently still working when he went to bed. Rayan says, "There was a time in the summer where I was saying, like, 'I don't know if you love me anymore.' It actually got that deep for me. You're not being physical with me right now. And I would say things like, 'I can't even remember the last time we were physical. The last time we had sex.' And she's like, 'Monday.' And it was like Thursday, and I'm like, 'Oh, my god, she's right.' But it wasn't about that. I just feel so emotionally neglected that the way I want to compensate for it is physical."

Rayan explains that when he is feeling particularly petulant, or when he feels fed up with the chores, he'll often say something like, "'If your work is so important to you, why don't you skip dance class once or twice?'" Rayan, who enjoys playing hockey and is part of a hockey team, says, "I would give her examples of times that I skipped hockey not just for me but for her. Again, it's a personality thing, it's a style thing. It is so important for her to have that time." Rayan and Monica, in other words, have different understandings of how Monica should spend her time. While most of the time Rayan understands the constraints posed by Monica's underemployment, at times his understanding ruptures and resentment peeks out. There is a disjuncture between how he feels and how he thinks he ought to feel.

How Much Gratitude Is Enough?

Monica and Rayan perceive the tensions in their marriage differently. Monica recognizes the sacrifices that Rayan has made to support her professional goals, describing him as "so supportive." She recounts a recent incident in which Rayan started a summer fellowship in Europe later than he had originally planned so that their whole family could accompany Monica to a conference in California. Rayan needed to be there to look after their two kids, who also had to be near Monica, as she was still breastfeeding the younger one. She adds, "That was amazing." After Monica's conference the entire family went to Europe for Rayan's fellowship. She also explains that she thinks Rayan has been "pretty fair" when it comes to how they split up housework and childcare. She acknowledges, "He works full time, too, and he also has to publish." She adds, "I think I wish that we could have navigated it better together. I don't know if I'd put it on him that we didn't."

While Rayan recognizes that both of them are making sacrifices to achieve the kinds of careers and lives they want, he feels many sacrifices are thrust upon him. Specifically, Rayan expresses a sense of loneliness, emphasizing the fact that he often has to "go to bed alone." For Rayan, the conflict is an internal one—he wants to be a supportive partner, but the reality of that at times grates on him. He says, "I felt like I had to martyr myself in order to make her professional life tolerable for her. And to also not just make it tolerable, but to put her in a position to be in a place where she could be happy."

What troubles Rayan the most is what sociologist Arlie Hochschild has described as a "scarcity of gratitude." Hochschild describes the economy of gratitude as what husbands and wives perceive to be "gifts" that their spouse provides and what they see as obligations that the spouse must provide.[21] A scarcity of gratitude arises when there is a mismatch between what one spouse considers to be a gift and the other, the receiving spouse, considers to be an obligation. The receiving spouse may not express as much gratitude for an obligation as for a gift, leading to a "scarcity of gratitude." Rayan sees doing more housework as a gift, not an obligation, that temporarily enables Monica to focus on her career. He wants this gift to be recognized with appropriate gratitude from Monica. Instead, Rayan perceives that "she refuses for whatever reason to see that imbalance. . . . I think her feeling is like, 'Well, it's an ebb and a flow.' In my opinion, it doesn't even out at all." He explains how Monica's insistence that they are equal in dividing the chores sometimes fuels his resentment. He adds, "She always tries to equalize the stuff." He elaborates: "There is a quantitative difference in the work that we do. Like I do almost everything in the mornings. And I do all the cooking, I do all this stuff, so there is an actual difference and she disputes that to the death. I always have to back off whenever that comes up, because she just refuses to accept it." In Rayan's assessment, Monica does not want to acknowledge their uneven division of housework because she feels guilty. "I think it's because she feels guilty.

I think she also doesn't believe necessarily that there is inequality there." Shaking his head, Rayan adds, "And that breeds my resentment, especially over the last two years and she doesn't get that."

With some sheepishness, Rayan narrates a recent incident in which his irritation at Monica's supposed lack of gratitude manifested itself: "When we were doing kind of an inventory of all the stuff that she has in the pipeline like research, things that she's published, things that are going to be published in the last year, and I remember we were counting five things. For an academic that's unbelievable, in a year, for things to come out that much. I still kind of regret my response to her. My response to her was, 'Where's my thank you?'" Widening his eyes as though still amazed that he could have made such an insensitive comment to Monica at what was supposed to be a celebratory moment for her, Rayan adds, "Not congratulations." Deeply ashamed, he chalks it up to his internal ruptures—of trying to be supportive, but with an underlying thread of resentment.

And in fact, Rayan's resentment sometimes does break through the surface in intermittent incidents like this one. Rayan invoked the notion of "martyring" himself several times as we spoke, elaborating on what this means for him, "Like Wednesday, she said to me, 'Oh, picking the kids up, it just cuts the day in half.'" Monica was making general conversation and not, as Rayan himself explains, trying to "game him" so that he does more unpaid work. But to help Monica focus on her research, Rayan explains that whenever he can, he offers to help out with her share of the chores. So, this time, "I said, 'I'll do it.'" Reflexively, Rayan continues, "So that's how it comes out. She's not gaming me. She's just expressing like, 'Oh, this sucks, or whatever.'" In this instance, and often, Monica tries to dissuade him from taking over chores that they have both decided belong to her. "She's like, 'No, no, no, I have to do these things.' I'm like, 'No, no, no, no I will do it.'" Their negotiations are often vested in consideration of the other's needs, yet, at times, they explode.

Rayan and Monica have experienced high levels of tensions in their marriage. Monica says, "It's been a rough few years," especially with her and Rayan fighting: "Just really nasty fights around stuff. Fights around time. Fights around responsibilities. We'd be yelling at each other. There were times when we were like, 'We should get divorced.'" Rayan, too, acknowledges that they have discussed divorce and attended couples' counseling, but he is far more sanguine about the state of their relationship than he has been in the past few years, saying, "Monica might actually disagree with this, but I don't actually feel like our marriage was totally ever really threatened." Pausing, Rayan adds, "I'm almost certain that she would disagree with that for various reasons." He continues, "But I always felt like at the end we knew how to talk about this stuff and that was important."

Revisiting the Levys

When I meet Monica and Rayan, individually, over a year later, just at the start of the fall academic term, Monica has parlayed her visiting assistant professor position into a tenure-track assistant professor position. After several years of trying to obtain a tenure-track position, she is finally poised to start her first year on the tenure-track in a few weeks. She looks happy, although her eyes are lined with dark circles. She says, "I feel happier as a person for sure. I feel more valued. I have colleagues who I really like. I really, really like my colleagues. I'm doing meaningful work. I have students that I like. I come in every day, I have an office that I go to and I do stuff in my office. I have a professional community!"

While Monica's professional life is looking up, she is trying to be as productive as possible to make sure that she gets tenure. She worked full-speed-ahead over the summer, trying to make the most of her unstructured time. She says, "I would be working during the day and then I'd be working at night again. Every night was that way, so things were tough between Rayan and me." She adds, "We were just both really busy, and especially I was really busy, so that was hard." She elaborates, "I spent most of this year staying up till like two o'clock in the morning, getting four hours of sleep and then waking up the next day, four or five hours of sleep and then wake up the next day. Monica's time was spent on prepping new classes as well as drafting several articles with hopes of publishing them in peer-reviewed journals. Alongside, of course, managing the daily business of life and family.

Rayan, too, sees this summer as having been an exceptionally challenging time, including a six-week period where they fought daily over how to allocate their time and how to get some time together as a couple. Yet, he explains that he is ecstatic that Monica is finally starting the kind of career she has been striving for, "And now her sense of professional happiness— she's so much more validated. And seeing her happy is really important to me." Monica, Rayan explains, has a greater confidence than she did before receiving this position, "She interacts with me differently. She interacts with her peers differently. She is confident in a way that she hasn't been in the last couple of years. All sorts of uncertainty that she had about being an academic are kind of gone."

In their personal life, things have continued to be difficult for Rayan and Monica. Rayan's prediction that their division of housework would not change much if Monica landed a tenure-track job has borne out, as Monica feels pressure to speed up her research and publications, to attend and organize conferences, and to take on university and departmental service, all in a bid to receive tenure five or six years down the line. Rayan thinks Monica is overdoing it. He explains, "I mean she has five publications." Because the university where he and Monica work is neither research intensive nor prestigious, Rayan says, "That's one a year already." He confidently adds, "She will get tenure, she will get promoted." Shaking his head in disbelief, he says, "But that train didn't stop, and it accelerated." He frowns as he says quietly, "It made me so sad." Biting his lower lip, he continues, "I can't quite articulate it, but I felt lied to. I thought, 'For the last three years why have we been doing this?' You know, like, 'now you got this. Like, slow down.'"

The Levys are, consequently, still having many of the same struggles they had when Monica worked as an adjunct. Rayan tells me a story about coming home on the day he teaches late to find the kitchen in disarray: "All this stuff is still here. The butter's still out, the ketchup's still out. It's not just about my sense of cleanliness." For Rayan, Monica's habit of leaving things for him to tend to rattles him. He recounts a conversation in which he urged Monica to take on more of the morning chores. He says, "So I'm like, 'Can I get ten more minutes of sleep and can you come down and make the lunch [for the kids]?' Or make it the night before, I don't care. Because that's fifteen, twenty minutes of my time." Monica agreed, "'Yeah, that's fair.'" He continues, "Guess how many times she prepared lunch? Once. Once since that conversation. Because it's like, 'Oh, I'm tired. I slept late.'"

In her own interview, Monica, in contrast, emphasizes how much more she has been able to contribute to housework and childcare simply because of having a more manageable routine. She says, "My university is very family friendly, especially in my department. A lot of people have kids, everybody understands." She adds, "Like the whole first semester I made sure I came to work at least four days a week. This semester I realized like actually people do not give a shit, like they don't care if you're in or not as long as they see you sometimes." This realization helped her plan her days so that she could cook more frequently at home and pick up their kids as needed. She says, "So I would do my teaching, meetings, whatever, leave at two-thirty to pick up our daughter at her school, go back and pick up Salman at his daycare, and then come back." She adds, "And we just sort of take care of the kids together. Some nights he's not here, some nights I'm not here or whatever." The accounts that Monica and Rayan present during their separate follow-up interviews do not match—while Rayan continues to feel a scarcity of gratitude, Monica is convinced that the division of housework has now evened out between them.

Like many of the unemployed couples in this study—regardless of whether the husband or wife had been unemployed—the Levys have discovered that a lot of the tensions in their marriage that they attributed to Monica's underemployment in fact have deeper roots. Rayan says, "I thought that job security would be a magic wand and it would give us emotional certainty and stability. And I did not in any way anticipate how difficult it would be to have that job. We were attributing so many things to job insecurity when there were other things happening." Despite this, both feel that their marriage is on strong ground, and they are discussing having a third child. Rayan closes on a happy note, balancing the challenges of work and life, "We both are very grateful for each other. We both really love each other."

UNABLE, NOT UNWILLING

Christina D'Angelo is a full-figured White woman in her late thirties with shoulder-length, wavy, chestnut-brown hair and blue-gray eyes behind glasses. Christina, who has an MBA, has had a career in the food industry.

She describes herself as an avid "foodie." While she sees herself as belonging in the food industry, her career so far has been speckled with job losses, the most recent of which occurred two years ago. Christina's husband, Aaron, is a small-framed White man in his late forties with graying hair. Aaron has a college degree, and he too works in the food industry. He's a pastry chef who concocts confections like Peach Bellini and Margarita cupcakes, infused with a generous dose of peach schnapps and tequila, respectively. Christina laughs as she tells me that colleagues and friends always perk up when Aaron arrives because they're anticipating creative, boozy, baked treats.

The D'Angelos met fifteen years ago when they were both working in the same restaurant. They married a decade ago. Christina and Aaron are enjoying parenting their fourteen-month-old son, Noah, whom they adopted at birth after eight years of waiting. About a month before our conversation, Christina found a convenient part-time job on the management side of the food industry. The past few years have been difficult, particularly for Christina, who has been wrestling with physical and mental health issues. Before Noah came into their lives, she struggled with the idea that she and Aaron had not been "chosen" for parenthood, due first to infertility and then to the adoption process, at the same time that she was not being "chosen" for a job. The combination was devastating for her self-esteem. She says, "I felt that I was damaged goods. You know, you're not worth being scraped off somebody's shoe." She "felt like there was something wrong with me, like significantly wrong with me." While Christina could theoretically accept that she had no control over her fertility or the adoption process, her inability to land and keep a job felt like a different kind of failure. She says, "With the baby issue, there was nothing I could do to work harder to fix it," but with unemployment, she felt like "I should have been able to work harder to fix [it]."

Christina suffered from severe physical ailments as a teenager, which impacted her fertility. She has had several surgeries, including one that lasted seven hours. Aaron explains that Christina's "thyroid problem" also impacts her mental well-being, since it "affects your energy level, which affects your mood." Christina and Aaron perceive her physical and mental health as being caught up in a vicious cycle, exacerbated by the extreme uncertainty they have encountered both in the family and on the professional front. A few years ago, Christina was diagnosed with clinical depression and needed medication. While the high cost of seeing a psychiatrist in addition to the medication was initially a cause of concern, together she and Aaron ultimately decided that their health, in all its aspects, was something they wanted to take care of. They had family help for this, but even without it, Christina describes the costs of mental health treatment for either of them as essential: "The one expense that we would splurge on was to keep us healthy."

Unemployment has severely negative impacts on well-being.[22] For Christina, the decision to pay for mental health care, even during a period of unemployment, was an obvious choice. Without access to a psychiatrist or to antidepressants she might have felt even worse: "There are people that teeter on the edge—and I think there's a lot of them. Something like unemployment throws them into the abyss, and then they have no tools to get out. I've seen that happen with a lot of my friends, and I've experienced it myself." Christina speaks of her mental health issues as if they are in the past—after all, she now has the family she wanted and has started a new part-time job in the field that she loves. She remains cautious, though, and is still on antidepressants because "the unemployment and the baby issue probably brought to light things that I had been dealing with" for a while.

For the D'Angelos, as we will see, Christina's depression shaped how the couple interacted around housework during the period of her unemployment.

Health and Housework

Christina's intense emotions around her job loss made it difficult for her to both look for paid work and do household chores. The chores slipped by, and Christina says, "We just got mad that it never got done. My husband usually just gives up and he's like, 'God dammit! All right, I'll do the laundry.'" Aaron is understanding of the emotional toll that repeated job loss and unemployment has taken on Christina. Yet, the lack of any help around the house from Christina is difficult for Aaron. He says:

> I would come home and the place would be a mess. . . . It would be like a bomb went off. Maybe it should be cleaned a little bit. . . . But I would try to remember to say, "Look, it stresses me out to come home to a place that's

just a nightmare." I would, verbally, I would shut down, and I would just start cleaning. And it was probably pretty obvious that I was a little bit annoyed. And sometimes she would ask, sometimes she wouldn't. And if she asked, I would have the ability to say, "Look, I just—I can't! If I come home and it's like this, it stresses me out. I can't deal with it." And she would feel bad about it and she said, "I'm trying the best I can." So not much I can say about that. I mean, you say you're trying the best you can and I know she is.

Aaron and Christina's interactions around housework are shaped by empathy, frustration, and ultimately understanding and acceptance that housework is difficult for both of them—for Aaron because of time, and for Christina because of her health. Neither of them sees the home as Christina's purview; in that sense, the D'Angelos have more gender-neutral expectations for who is responsible for paid work and who is responsible for unpaid work than the other families in this study. Aaron understands and accepts that Christina's depression can be debilitating.

That Aaron would interact with kindness toward Christina, despite his frustration with the undone housework, makes sense given that the D'Angelos embrace gender equity in most aspects of their marriage. While Aaron is considerably older than Christina, both have viewed Christina as the breadwinner. At the point that they began the adoption process in earnest, they frequently discussed how they would share paid and unpaid work. They both agreed that Aaron would stay at home to take care of the baby in the initial months, while Christina would get a job. Aaron explains: "Well, we went back and forth, because originally I was going to stay home. Years back when we started this, we felt like her income potential was better, being on the business end of the food industry. The earning potential is definitely higher. So the whole idea was that I would end up staying home, maybe working part-time." Christina, too, mentions both Aaron's comfort with childcare—"he has childcare experience [because] he was the nanny for his niece and nephew who are now in college, and I don't"—as well as her higher income earning potential. In a reversal of traditional gender norms, they planned that Aaron would "make cakes on the side for extra income," while Christina "would bring home the majority of the paycheck every week and would provide health care for the family."

About 21 percent of American fathers choose to stay at home to fulfill caregiving responsibilities.[23] While gender roles have experienced some convergence in the United States, married men usually only fulfill the role of stay-at-home dads when pushed out of the workforce through factors beyond their control, such as unemployment or disability. The D'Angelos' decision to arrange their lives such that Aaron would be the primary caregiver represents a relatively rare decision.[24] As so often happens in life, though, their well-designed plans had to be tossed aside when reality intervened. "When we got the phone call, he was the one with the stable job. I was the one who was unemployed, so I stayed home with the baby." In theory, Christina was job searching while she stayed at home with the baby, but her efforts to find paid work dwindled considerably given the demands of caring for a newborn.

Until about a month ago, when Christina started working part-time, she has been the one at home with Noah. But being a stay-at-home mother has never appealed to Christina, and caring for a newborn did nothing to change her assessment of that. Christina humbly describes herself as a "competent mother," saying, "For me personally, I think I need to work. I think I am a much more balanced and whole person when I work. I need to have some sort of adult challenge." The ideals of intensive mothering hold little allure for Christina. Instead, she invokes ideals of "extensive motherhood," a term coined by sociologist Karen Christopher to capture the experiences of mothers who are in charge of managing their children's care, but tend to outsource the care of their children to paid caregivers, such as nannies.[25]

While Christina enjoyed spending time with Noah, she never got the hang of doing other kinds of housework. She elaborates on the challenges of doing chores that are not centered on Noah: "I think that my attitude when I was at home was there's always time to do it later, and it never got done." Christina focused on Noah, explaining that she would spend her time, "Giving him a bath or you know, just playing with him. He's really cute when he goes to sleep. He likes to play little games before he goes to bed." Other chores fell by the wayside, and Christina chuckles as she explains, "My husband didn't eat! Like I didn't really have dinner for him for months." As a new mom, Christina's focus was on making "sure that we had clean clothes and the baby was fed and that, you know, I got some sleep."

Christina dove back into active job search mode about four months ago, at the point that she realized, "I can't do this anymore. Like I wasn't cut out to be a stay-at-home mom." This meant giving up the façade that she would do non-childcare chores, such as cleaning and organizing the house, laundry, and light cooking for the family. Aaron's family pitched in financially so that the D'Angelos could hire a nanny whose duties include keeping their home organized by picking up stray items here and there.[26] Aaron says, "I would come home and [our nanny] would organize before she left." Ironically, knowing that the nanny would pick up after them meant that Aaron and Christina became tidier. Aaron says, "I got to the point where I didn't want to leave too much for her to pick up. So I would organize a little bit in the morning, and then she would finish it. I'd come home and the sink was empty and everything was wiped down. And it was just like, 'Oh, my god!' It took so much stress off of us."

Although they are both in the food industry, the D'Angelos do not cook much at home. Aaron laughs as he explains that they end up "scrounging around" and eating either frozen foods or leftovers. He says, "Christina's at a full-service restaurant, so she's able to eat, but she often doesn't eat until towards the end of her shift just because she's focused on working. So oftentimes she ends up bringing like half of her meal home."

The D'Angelos, a sort of maverick couple, have mostly decoupled gender norms from their expectations about chores. Their interactions around housework, although sometimes marked by Aaron's frustration about the level of mess, suggest that they have no set-in-stone expectations that the person who is present in the home should be doing housework. Their ideas about who should provide an income and who can provide care for their son are fluid and flexible, shaped more by circumstances than by an insistence on gender roles. In this sample, they were extremely unusual. Their experience suggests the possibility that even heterosexual couples who are privileged when it comes to aspects such as their educational status, race, and access to financial support from kin, can, in some cases, dismantle gender norms.

CONCLUSION

The families in this study are making decisions about how to allocate unemployed women's time in a context in which childcare is privatized.

Childcare is an expensive responsibility that families are expected to manage on their own. The majority of families in this study, all of whom had children, reallocated unemployed women's time to unpaid childcare. This choice "saves" families money that they would otherwise spend on summer camps, daycare, or aftercare. These savings, however, come at the cost of an unemployed woman's ability to look for paid work. Even so, couples that include an unemployed woman show a larger spectrum of responses than couples with an unemployed man, suggesting that women's social roles have expanded in ways that men's have not.

The example of the Blums illustrates how women's unemployment can catalyze a shift toward more gender-traditional ways of arranging family life, particularly in the division of paid and unpaid work. The Blums' division of housework was unequal even when Grace was employed; her unemployment has compounded this inequality. Grace embraces many aspects of this role; the home has, in some ways, become a sort of haven for her. Both Finn and Grace expect that Grace should bear the major responsibility for the domestic economy, and this assumption shapes their interactions and decisions around housework. In contrast to unemployed men, unemployed women's time—because of its anticipated temporariness—becomes the very reason why women should do a deep dive into housework. Grace's time spent on the domestic—for example taking care of her daughters and cooking—also becomes a resource for her family that enables the Blums to save some money on these expenses.

In the case of the Levys, we see a variation in which Rayan and Monica protect Monica's time for professional development. The Levys are an unusual couple in this study. Their household practices more closely resemble those of the couples with unemployed men in this study, with both husband and wife explaining the uneven division of housework as an arrangement that allows the unemployed person to focus on locating appropriate work. Yet because she is underemployed, rather than unemployed, Monica does not have the resource of time. Rayan could have guided her toward giving up the dream of a tenure-track position in favor of a job elsewhere, an outcome that presumably would have improved their financial situation and minimized their stress. That he did not do so and instead for years supported Monica's attempt to land a tenure-track position strongly suggests that their interactions are driven by a shared understanding of the importance of an academic career for her.

The Levys are on the younger side of this sample, but their relative youth does not explain Rayan's support for Monica's career. The other young couples in this study are less progressive in how they divide their labor, a pattern that is supported by additional research.[27] There is still tremendous evidence of gender inequality among millennials in long-term heterosexual relationships. At the same time, emerging research has found that younger couples are more likely to try to work toward equality at home, particularly in terms of the division of housework, even though that equality is often hard to achieve given institutional and cultural constraints. For example, one study found that many millennial men would prefer a relationship based on gender egalitarianism; if that was not possible, they would favor a neo-traditional relationship. Millennial women, too, prefer egalitarian relationships, but in its absence, they prefer being single.[28] Some demographers have suggested that this mismatch between men's and women's preferences may partially explain declining rates of marriage in the United States, especially among highly educated women who are likely to desire financial independence.[29]

The Levys' case also illustrates the tensions that so often accompany marital negotiations over housework. Gratitude, for example, is a big theme in how couples divide housework and, more to the point, whether they argue about it. Prior research has shown that couples do not necessarily need an equal division of housework to feel satisfied with their marriages. Rather, what is important is that each partner's perception of how the housework is divided corresponds with the ideal division of housework that each partner has in mind. Typically, women in heterosexual marriages are least satisfied on this metric.[30] The Levys flip that script, with Rayan wanting more acknowledgment from Monica for his contributions, which he perceives as being larger than Monica's. Monica, in contrast, interprets their division of labor as "fair," even while she appreciates that Rayan has made some key events, such as attending a work conference, possible for her. There is a clear disparity in what each thinks they owe the other, resulting in ongoing conflict that erupts from time to time.

In a final variation, we see how Aaron and Christina D'Angelo's understanding that Christina's mental well-being should come before household labor shapes their division of housework. While a few other women in my sample also described experiencing depression that was exacerbated by job loss, this did not usually translate into a lack of accountability for housework, as it did for Christina. The D'Angelos are anomalous in other ways, in that they had originally planned for Aaron to provide unpaid labor in the form of childcare and Christina to produce the bulk of their income. Even though they ended up in a more traditional arrangement, with Christina taking care of their newborn son, their expectations about household obligations are decoupled from gendered norms. This situation barely lasted a year, as Christina soon expressed a desire to return to the paid workforce, and the couple hired a nanny to make her job search possible.

The division of paid and unpaid work remains a touchstone for understanding gender inequality within heterosexual marriage. Housework remains bound up in gender norms, with gendered expectations reproduced through moments of shared meaning-making. At the same time, occasional departures from this norm also suggest the possibility that couples can dismantle gendered norms through an explicit commitment to fostering and valuing women's desire for careers and paid work.

Conclusion

UNEMPLOYMENT AND INEQUALITY
IN AN AGE OF UNCERTAINTY

FORKED PATHWAYS

For the professional middle-class, unemployment has become an expected feature of working life. Sociological research on unemployment continues to treat unemployment as an aberrant event that primarily impacts low-wage workers. Consequently, the unemployment experiences of the professional middle-class remain little understood. The people in this book, the Radziks, the Bachs, the Clarkes, the Blums, and all the others, are well suited to contend with unemployment: they are highly educated, in dual-earner households, and married. Sociologically, why do their unemployment experiences matter? This book has argued that their unemployment experiences offer insights into the decisions that privileged families make as they frame their understandings of unemployment and consequently pursue specific paths of action during this uncertain, anomic time. By tracing their lives in great detail and over the course of months and years, we see that at moments when these families encounter the uncertain and risky labor market, they tend to organize their lives in ways that reify traditional gender norms. The ideal job-seeker norm captures this gendered organization of family life that occurs as a response to the unpredictable labor market.

Over time, the people that I met got new jobs; lost other jobs; and experienced divorces, illnesses, and deaths of friends and parents. One died. Unemployment was often a pivotal point in their lives, but it was always overlaid with these other life concerns, too. When it came to finding new jobs, as table 4 shows, the experiences of participants in this study fell along one major fault line: men were typically either employed or still heavily focused on searching for paid work, while women showed more variety of experiences and outcomes when it came to employment.[1]

At the time that I concluded my study, none of the men in my sample were considering withdrawing from the labor market, for instance by staying at home full-time. I had observed the Smith family, where William (who typically earned about half of his wife Shannon's income) had been without a job for a year. I asked Shannon if she and William had discussed the idea of William staying at home. Shannon sighed, explaining that she would very much like to end the uncertainty of Will's unemployment by deciding that he would be a stay-at-home parent. Yet, this is not something she feels she can say to Will, since "being a man, he thinks he needs to work." She continues, "If he could work part-time and do something he likes doing part-time and still be home with Alex [their four-year-old son], that would be ideal for me." William, like all the men in this study, continued searching for the elusive full-time, standard job with benefits. In contrast, the unemployed women in this study frequently found solace—at least for a while—in the domestic, usually with encouragement from their husbands.

More men in my sample than women engaged in some form of paid employment by the time of their follow-up interviews. Frequently the work was temporary, such as working as a short-term consultant. This aligns with research findings that suggest that a significant number of those who consult only do so after losing a job.[2] The men in this study were more likely than women to move across state lines to accept short-term consulting positions (e.g., participants Pierre Miot and James Peterson as table 4 shows). The pressure for men to engage in paid employment, in positions similar to what they had before, meant that they frequently accepted positions that took them away from their families or otherwise disrupted their lives.

Women displayed more diversity in the paths they pursued. Some remained unemployed. Among this group, some, for example Grace Blum,

Table 4 Where Are They Now? Employment Status at First and Second Interview (only participants included in follow-up interviews)

| | Unemployed Men | | | Unemployed Women | |
Name	1st Interview	2nd Interview	Name	1st Interview	2nd Interview
James Peterson	Unemployed, 7 weeks	Consulting, out of state	Cheryl Stanley	Unemployed, 17 months	Employed, full-time
William Smith	Unemployed, 10 months	Working as a substitute teacher	Lisa Brozek	Unemployed, 5 months	Employed, full-time
John Huber	Unemployed, 5 months	Employed, full-time	Darlene Bach	Unemployed, 3 weeks	Unemployed
Pierre Miot	Unemployed, 5 weeks	Self-employed, start-up	Donna Mayr	Unemployed, 1 year	Employed, full-time
Scott Mandel	Unemployed, 6 months	Consulting, in state	Julia Crouch	Unemployed, 3 months	Unemployed (wants part-time)
Robert Jansson	Unemployed, 7 months	Employed, full-time	Kiara Eklund	Unemployed, 4 months	Employed, full-time
Terry Clarke	Unemployed, 5 months	Employed (hourly wage)	Rebecca Mason	Unemployed, 5 months	Unemployed
Doug Easton	Unemployed, 2 years	Unemployed	Monica Levy	Unemployed & under-employed, 2 years	Employed, full-time

Table 4 (continued)

Unemployed Men			Unemployed Women		
Name	1st Interview	2nd Interview	Name	1st Interview	2nd Interview
Jim Radzik	Unemployed 1 year	Self-employed (franchise)	Grace Blum	Unemployed 1 year	Unemployed
Frank Amara	Unemployed, 4 months	Employed, part-time	Padma Swaminathan	Unemployed, 19 month	Employed, full-time
Todd Baron	Unemployed, 5 months	Employed, part-time	Eileen Boyle	Unemployed, 3 months	Employed, full-time
			Caroline Anderson	Unemployed, 11 months	Unemployed
			Gina Forrester	Unemployed, 2 years	Unemployed

continued to feel relatively comfortable at home, while others, like Gina Forrester and Darlene Bach, were conspicuously antsy, the novelty of staying at home having worn off. These women would have much preferred to be employed. Others who had told me that they found tremendous meaning in the life of stay-at-home mothering had reentered full-time employment. Padma Swaminathan represents one such case. She explained her full-time employment to me by saying, "Well, it's a job that really allows me to be home and with the kids when I need to be." The decision to enter full-time employment makes sense, given that part-time employment recompenses poorly and often insufficiently to meet childcare costs, with most childcare services being privatized in the United States.[3] These unemployed women do not have the time, space, and money necessary for focusing on their job search.

GENDER AND THE IDEAL JOB-SEEKER IN AN AGE OF UNEMPLOYMENT

In this book, I have introduced and developed the concept of *the ideal job-seeker norm*. This norm emerges from the conditions of the contemporary labor market, characterized by rapid economic churning, occupational obsolescence, and the creation of new professions. For the people in this study, these conditions also mean income volatility—they plan their lives and their expenses in a context where they do not know how much income they will have in a given month. As a privileged group, they often have access to resources, such as savings and help from kin, that help them minimize the uncertainty of their income volatility. In complying with the ideal job-seeker norm, they expect to facilitate a successful career trajectory in the context of paid work during late capitalism. This norm requires that professionals—especially those who are unemployed—should dedicate their lives to finding work by networking extensively and updating their skills training, employing career coaches, and so on. But dedicating oneself to complying with the contemporary demands of job searching requires resources. Securing privileges at home that direct space, time, and money toward job seeking is an important aspect of this norm. This is usually accomplished by demonstrating, through marital interactions, that one is *morally unemployed.* In this book, I illuminate how marital dynamics reward and punish those who adhere to this norm and how this is based on gendered expectations. Specifically, I have argued that adhering to the norm takes on moral overtones for unemployed men. Unemployed men who fail to conform to the norm risk threats to their moral standing. Unemployed women, in contrast, must juggle the competing moral demands of job seeking versus motherhood. The *ideal job-seeker* norm provides scholars with a useful conceptual tool to consider how families respond to precarity in the context of a volatile labor market.

In the case of unemployed men, wives monitor their husbands' job searching activities, worried that others might perceive their husbands as lazy and unmotivated unless they unequivocally prove themselves otherwise. This sense of urgency, felt by men and most of their wives alike, is palpable over dinner tables and peppers daily conversations. At times, it can be suffocating for unemployed men. But this obsession with finding a job is not reducible to financial necessity; it is driven by a sense that enduring unemployment marks a departure from the expectations of White masculinity. For men under capitalism, employment is a marker of moral worth, and its absence denotes the lack of morality. While temporary unemployment is accepted as a fact of life in the new economy, enduring unemployment is not.

Unemployed women, in contrast, face less pressure to quickly find a job. In the context of their families, reemployment is not a marker of women's morality. Instead, the mostly White, affluent families in this study often respond as though a long-standing wrong—that women combined paid work with motherhood—has been righted when a woman loses her job. The prism of the ideal job-seeker norm, allows us to see how couples' dynamics vigorously encourage men, but not women, toward reemployment.

That there is an ideal job-seeker norm and that it is gendered matters because it shows us that gendered beliefs and behaviors are often not directly tied to immediate economic circumstances. Conventional economic thought would suggest that if women are primary earners, then their reemployment should be urgent. Similarly, if men have a lower earning capacity than their wives, then their reemployment ought to be less urgent. An economic perspective would also suggest that the division of housework should be closely intertwined with earning capacity. Yet, the ideal job-seeker norm shows that couples remain hemmed in by outdated gender norms that bear little resemblance to contemporary economic realities.

The ideal job-seeker norm has emerged in the context of acute employment uncertainty. The erstwhile employee-employer contract has been irrevocably broken. The new economic and employment landscape is fragmented, tumultuous, and changing swiftly. We see this in the rise of contract work, temporary work, and gig work; increased mobility across national boundaries for paid work; and technological change in the workplace, including the arrival of artificial intelligence. These changes require that scholars rethink their understandings of the expectations and assumptions demanded of workers. If ideal workers are no longer defined through their loyalty to a company, then we need to ask what the new expectations are, and what they mean for curbing or perpetuating inequalities, at home, in paid work, and in the rest of the world. By offering the concept of the ideal job-seeker in this book, I hope to start a conversation on how inequalities of all stripes unfold in changing employment landscapes.

The ideal job-seeker norm has implications beyond marriage and family. In many countries, including the United States, individuals must comply with requirements that prioritize their search for paid work above other considerations, including the quality and suitability of potential jobs, to be eligible for unemployment benefits. In many US states, recipients of unemployment benefits must demonstrate that they are actively seeking paid work by keeping records of all the jobs applied to, attending reemployment classes if required, and meeting various weekly eligibility requirements. In Sweden and the United Kingdom, eligibility for unemployment benefits requires that individuals demonstrate an intensely active job search plan, which may include applying for jobs for which they are not qualified and may not have a reasonable chance of getting.[4] These and similar schemes incorporate assumptions that are similar to the ideal job-seeker norm in terms of what it takes to demonstrate one's moral worth during unemployment. In cases where job-seekers may have spouses and families, eligibility requirements for unemployment benefits operate on the assumption that job-seekers can easily negotiate schedules, location, and type of paid work with their families. Yet, as we have seen in this book, families do not perceive all workers and all jobs as equally important.

GENDER INEQUALITIES DURING UNCERTAIN TIMES

Feminist scholars have long conceptualized marriage as an institution that overtly and covertly subordinates women. In comparison to cohabiting or never-married mothers, married mothers do more childcare, more housework, and have less leisure time. Husbands could lessen the load of unpaid work that married mothers do—but they do not.[5] Married mothers are beholden to impossible ideals of being continuously nurturing to husbands and children, often at the expense to their own well-being.[6] They are tasked with producing family experiences and memories that capture some nostalgic, idealized essence of family life. Family members often expect that mothers will do this through both intensive material and emotional labor: for example, remembering alimentary preferences of each family member and then producing an elaborate meal that incorporates these. Married mothers are expected to remember minute organizational details specific to each family member—a specific tie for a husband's meeting in the morning, a different pickup time for a child whose track meet has been canceled. Generally, mothers are expected to be the linchpin of the family.

The American frontier writer Willa Cather noted this phenomenon nearly a century ago in her 1923 novel, *A Lost Lady*. Niel Herbert, the young narrator of the novel, thinks about the effort that Marian Forrester, the titular character, puts into appearing lighthearted even as (he suspects) her husband's recent loss of wealth causes Mrs. Forrester great anxiety. Cather writes, describing Niel, "He had the feeling, which he never used to have, that her lightness cost her something." As an emotional cornerstone for her home, cultivating a congenial atmosphere in her parlor and at a cost to herself, Mrs. Forrester is only doing what generations of women before and after her have done for their husbands and families. In the early twenty-first century, we still see women carrying a tremendous emotional load as they strive to serve as the bedrock for the families, even as the world around them changes.

But as the institution of marriage in the United States has evolved to recognize a larger variety of legal and spiritual unions, might it also evolve beyond such constrained expectations and ideals for heteronormative unions?[7] With the industrial foundations that shaped these ideals disappearing, might inherently inegalitarian gender ideals also vanish? For the families in this study, this book finds a decisive answer: No. Despite a new economic landscape, the gender dynamics among couples in this study were transformed rather than reformed. They take on new forms, but maintain the spirit of inequality.

A continuing thread of this study is that the material resources that allow men, but not women, to adhere to the ideal job-seeker norm are related to childcare. Material resources within these professional middle-class, mostly White households flow in such a way that men are absolved of childcare responsibilities while women shoulder its responsibility. Some scholars have produced more optimistic research on gender dynamics that suggests that younger men and women in the United States may prefer gender-egalitarian family structures in which men and women are equally responsible for paid and unpaid work. But in the absence of institutional support—for example, federally subsidized quality childcare programs, parental-leave policies, and access to flexible working arrangements—couples often fall back on less preferred but feasible, and deeply inegalitarian, practices.[8]

This book has focused on the interactional dynamics that produce and sustain gender inequalities in marriages and in the context of a new economy characterized by precarity for all. Institutional support, such as quality childcare policies and a humane organization of work, can foster more egalitarian practices in the home. As most research indicates, more gender-progressive values and beliefs are stymied in the United States by a policy landscape and organization of paid work that does not support these. Models of paid work and family roles need to be revised. In the United States, cultures of work, including for professional occupations, continue to emphasize a primacy of work, such as working excessively long hours, including to the detriment of one's physical health.[9] Such models of paid work overlook other dimensions of individuals' and families' lives, including caregiving responsibilities. Broadly, these models of work have negative impacts for both men and women workers—for example in terms of mental well-being. Of course, the specifics vary in terms of how dimensions of contemporary cultures and organizations of paid and unpaid work impact men and women.

Models of the family are undergoing a change, discernible, for example, in men's greater participation in unpaid work in the home, especially in childcare, when compared to prior decades. However, the home remains largely a feminized space, with women retaining the primary responsibilities. There are manifold reasons for this; cultural convention is one, but there is also the reality that, generally, men earn more than their wives in dual-earner families. Retaining men's jobs in this context of economic precarity may be seen by individuals and families as important. However, retaining women's jobs can also be seen as essential to ward off uncertainty due to income volatility. The point here is that neither cultural norms nor structural facts need to be treated as deterministic in pinning women to unpaid work and men to paid work. Rather, enlarging the possibilities for men and women to participate as fully as they can in paid and unpaid work should be the goal.

This goal can best be achieved through institutional and policy support. In particular, the institution of marriage can be reinvigorated with policy shifts that will alleviate the burden of caregiving that overwhelmingly remains women's responsibility. To name only a few of these policies, equitable marriages require access to high-quality, affordable childcare; parental leave; and flexible working arrangements. As this study shows, ideals of intensive motherhood, combined with a lack of support for childcare, mean that families downplayed the importance of women's employment and emphasized their responsibilities in child-rearing. These families experiencing unemployment prioritized a highly gendered division of paid and unpaid work.

LOOKING AHEAD

Family and marriage are deeply intertwined with the material conditions of life in a given historical context. The institution of marriage is a crucial element in propping up the dominant economic organizations of the day—that is, in the United States, capitalism. While the social institutions of marriage and family are impacted by capitalism, they also are building blocks of capitalism. The idealized middle-class, White nuclear family has been critical to cultural imaginaries of the proper division between pro-ductive and reproductive labor (itself a division that is a by-product of industrial developments) and how these relate to familial roles and authority. These ideals impact consumption and class status and ulti-mately social assessments of the morality of the family and the individuals therein.

Many of the conditions on which this idealized family was founded have been steadily eroding. Scholars of work and labor attribute the shift-ing organization of work to neoliberal capitalism, which has spurred pro-found economic, cultural, and technological shifts in American society. To fully understand either the world of paid work or the institutions of family and marriage, we need to examine how they intersect with each other. The couples in this study are, after all, responding to the demands of contem-porary manifestations of paid work through their behaviors at home. To examine either the organization of paid work or the institution of the fam-ily in isolation provides only a partial picture, since the two are deeply linked and bolster each other.

The responses of the families in this study reinforce, rather than ques-tion, the logic of capitalism. They emphasize the role of individual behav-ior—for example, in their approach to job searching or childcare—rather than systemic solutions to the widespread problem of insecure work and the privatization of childcare. Through their responses, the relatively affluent, mostly White families in this study affirm the types of gender inequalities that are specific to late capitalism, which are, in turn, based on gendered valuations of paid and unpaid work. This is not unexpected. As an affluent group of families, they have, on the whole, benefitted from capitalism.

This study presents a rather bleak picture of how forms of gender ine-quality proliferate in a novel context. Despite these findings, however, it is also true that shifts and fissures bring with them opportunities and glimpses of more emancipating possibilities: when the home and paid work can be equally accessible to men and women, in ways where the satisfaction found in paid work does not corrode the joys that unpaid work—taking care of loved ones by cooking a cherished family recipe or spending time with children—may bring.

Whether these possibilities will be marshaled to alleviate social inequalities remains an open question.

APPENDIX A Methodology

I read Katherine Newman's *Falling from Grace* in my first year as a graduate student. I was struck by her heart-wrenching findings, especially how she sympathetically detailed the painful experiences of unemployed executives in New York City. Newman chronicled the shame and stigma experienced by unemployed executives. She wrote about how downward mobility, resulting from unemployment, tore marriages and families apart. Her poignant portrait of unemployment and downward mobility remained etched in my mind as I continued with my graduate study. My interests around gender, already prominent after a master's degree at the Gender Institute at the London School of Economics, crystallized further as I continued reading, through coursework and independently, about gender in different realms: work, family, religion. My interest in the world of work, especially uncertain work, too, had been bolstered by my own recent experiences as a young professional at the United Nations (UN) in Geneva, Switzerland.

I completed my master's degree in September 2008, just a couple of weeks before the Lehman Brothers collapse. At this point, I was starting my first full-time, paid role, in the UN alongside hundreds of other young professionals from the world over. I was at the International Labor Organization (ILO) headquarters, in a unit focused on health and employment. My colleagues and I joked that although "decent work for all" underpinned the philosophy driving the ILO's mission, it was elusive in reality at the UN. Most of us jumped from one short-term contract—ranging from a few weeks to six months—to another.[1] This seemed to get worse as funding for projects that paid for the UN's operations in field offices and its headquarters dried up, with country after country seeming to get ready to freeze their contributions. I came to graduate school with this brief, but indelible, experience of employment, accrued at a point that has turned out to be pivotal in recent economic history.

In graduate school, I read about how the employment landscape has become more insecure in the last three decades, with words such as *downsizing* and *rightsizing* pervading conversations about work. I read about how those with college degrees who had previously been protected from the tumults of labor markets were much less so now. I also read about changing gender norms in marriages and family structure, for example the increase in breadwinning mothers and a convergence in time spent on paid and unpaid work for heterosexual spouses. The more I read, the more surprised I was by the dearth of recent studies on the white-collar experience of unemployment that paid attention to men *and* women's gendered experiences of unemployment. Studies still mostly focused on how men's unemployment mattered for their families. But if women are employed, care about their careers, and contribute substantially to the household income, at the same time that gender norms around paid and unpaid work are shifting, surely this should require a sociological examination? Keeping these gaps in mind, this study emerged as a way to sociologically inform our understandings of contemporary experiences of unemployment.

Given my own personal and professional background—growing up, studying, and working between Asia and Europe—binding the empirical focus to the United States was not an easy decision for me. I had moved to the United States as an adult and only for graduate school. I had always assumed that my research would be empirically relevant to places where I had spent the majority of my life thus far. Into the early stages of data collection, my research design included a comparison in India. Delving into data collection highlighted the sheer time required to collect the kind of deep data I wanted. Doing so across multiple country contexts was unfeasible. I revised my research design to focus on the United States. Empirically this was more viable, and it was also theoretically justified. The United States is a particularly acute example of labor market precarity combined with a "risk shift" that requires individuals and families to cope with this on their own.[2]

SAMPLE CRITERIA AND ITS RATIONALE

My inclusion criteria required the unemployed individual to be currently unemployed or to have been unemployed until at most three months prior to the original interview, be a heterosexual American citizen, have at least a bachelor-level degree, be married to a spouse who works at least twenty hours a week, and have children aged twenty-two or younger.[3] I designed these criteria to capture experiences of unemployment in the professional middle-class and in heterosexual dual-earner families with dependent children. In some ways, this is a limited sample—it does not include gender-nonconforming families (such as gay, lesbian, or queer families), nor households outside of the dual-earner married couple model. These are areas that future research should focus on.

For capturing unemployment, I used a definition congruent with those used by national and international bodies like the US Bureau of Labor, the Organization for Economic Co-operation and Development, and the International Labor Organization. Key elements of unemployment across these organizations are the following: does not have a job, actively looking for a job, available to work. I included one more criteria, not found in these organizations, which was important for this study: that participants should have *lost* their jobs (rather than, for example, quitting). This was important to capture the element of involuntary unemployment, a growing and understudied feature of economic precarity. This definition of employment assumes that there has been an unwelcome (from the worker's perspective) dissolution in an otherwise relatively standard employer-employee relationship. Such a definition of unemployment overlooks other broad transformations in the world of work that also result in uncertainty—for example work in the platform economies, contract work, underemployment, unemployment because self-owned companies have collapsed and so on. Others have written excellent books on many of these issues; however, this book focuses on unemployment due to this erosion of the erstwhile standard and relatively stable employment relationships that had characterized white-collar work for at least several decades.[4] This definition of unemployment also excludes discouraged workers— those who would prefer to work but have given up actively searching for work, usually due to long-term unemployment. By definition, discouraged workers would not be participating in venues such as job search clubs and working with career coaches. Another key issue is underemployment, where individuals either work for far less time (and money) than they would prefer or are over-credentialed for the work they do. I did not focus on recruiting the underemployed, but over the course of unemployment I found that some of my participants did fall into this category. Although this book does not focus on this category of work, one example of underemployment is represented in the case of the Levys.

Sociologists disagree on how to measure class, but most agree that some combination of education, occupation, and income (all of which are tightly correlated) capture the material and nonmaterial dimensions of social class. In the case of this sample, their high education levels, their occupational backgrounds (lawyers, academics, financial analysts, and program managers, for example), combined with household incomes of three to four times the US national median place them squarely in the professional middle-class.

I focused on this social class for several reasons. First, although there are ample studies of how unemployment is experienced by working class and poor families, our in-depth portraits of professional unemployment are dated. Katherine Newman's study, published in the 1980s, still remains the most detailed telling of the experiences of unemployment for otherwise affluent families. Yet trends in the economy have changed such that college-educated professionals, who used to be far more protected from the tumults of the economy, no longer are. This is due to a variety of factors, including the shift from fat to lean companies and a shift in the employer-employee relationship, including an erosion of the employer's obligation to the employee.[5] The Great Recession of 2007–2009 made this point starkly clear. There is an empirical need to examine this social class's experiences through a sociological lens. Conceptually, too, this social class is interesting because women from this social class are highly educated and have scaled the highest professional echelons. They have well-paid careers and expect to work continuously over the course of their career. Paradoxically, they are nonetheless also likely to be in neotraditional marriages.[6] Lastly, women here are the "cultural arbiters" who shape hegemonic gender norms around paid and unpaid work through their own beliefs and behaviors.[7] These factors combined make this social class particularly salient for examining the gendered experiences of unemployment in marriage.

I focused on the dual-earner family structure because I wanted to ensure that I was capturing the experiences of comparable families with unemployed women or unemployed men. Although including a wider array of family structures, such as male-breadwinner or single mother households, might have added nuance to my arguments, they would also have precluded my ability to make tenable claims about how the experience of unemployment is gendered and what that illuminates about gender inequality in heterosexual marriages. The study design, consequently, retained a focus on dual-earner families.

Since gendered divisions toward paid and unpaid work become particularly salient after the birth of a child, I included the criteria for parenthood.[8] Additionally, research of emerging adulthood suggests that in the professional middle-class, children are dependent on their parents until, and even beyond, college education—hence my definition of "children" as young people up to age twenty-two.[9]

I did not focus on a specific type of job loss—for example being downsized or being fired. The differences have legal implications, including access to government unemployment benefits. Instead, the unemployed individuals in this study had lost these jobs through a variety of means. In earlier decades, the *reason* for losing a job was paramount; Katherine Newman recounts how the stigma of being fired versus being let go shaped families' reactions to unemployment in the 1980s. But the contemporary moment is rife with job losses, with downsizing built into organizational logics. Professionals expect to encounter job loss. As scholars such as Sharone (2013) have explained, the stigma that used to be centered on the very fact of losing a job is now centered on how long you remain unemployed. The post-Great Recession landscape that has highlighted these structural shifts may dilute the stigma such that the unemployed now place greater blame on the economic system than on themselves.[10] The method of losing a job was thus not a factor I prioritized when recruiting this sample. In my analysis too, it did not emerge as critical in shaping families' responses. In this way, my study aligns with Sharone's (2013) assertion about the importance of job searching as an organizing principle for individuals, and as I argue, families.

RECRUITMENT METHODS

Table 5 describes the fifteen sites through which I ultimately obtained my forty-eight unemployed men and women. I started the recruitment for this project by searching online for job search clubs and reached out to one of the largest groups, Pursuing Your Career Passions (all names of organizations and people are pseudonyms), operating in the metropolitan area where I was conducting research. After an administrator responded the next week via email, we scheduled a brief phone conversation so I could tell her more about the research. She invited me to attend their next monthly meeting group. Over the next year, I attended about four meetings in person at this group. Meetings usually featured a speaker who would give a lecture on a job searching-related topic, such as "Crafting Your Best CV" or "Acing the Job Interview." On the first Saturday morning that I attended, there were about one hundred attendees present. After introducing me as a PhD student at the University of Pennsylvania who wanted to learn more about unemployment, the administrator allowed me to make a two-minute pitch about my research. I then hung around the front of the room during the break and at the end of the two-hour-long workshop so that people could approach me. I always carried my business cards with me, as well as a one-page description of the study and the sample criteria. When potential subjects showed interest in participating, I would take their contact details (phone and email), usually in the form of their business card. I made sure to follow up the day after with an email requesting an interview. Every two or three months, I also asked the administrator to send out my "call for participants" to their list-server, which she did. Additionally, I created a LinkedIn profile, with my accurate information and credentials, and joined the group's LinkedIn page. I would post my call for participants almost monthly at this page. The fifteen participants I recruited at this site came from a combination of responding to my verbal pitch at a PYCP meeting, a PYCP listserve email, or a PYCP LinkedIn post.

Job search clubs aim to provide information on how employed and unemployed professionals should strategize to find new jobs. They have been criticized

Table 5 Sample Recruitment Sites

Recruitment Site* (n = 15)	Participants Recruited (n = 48)
Pursue Your Career Passion (PYCP)	15
Tyler Kerswell, career coach	8
Associations of professionals (n = 2)	5
Parent list-servers (n = 3)	5
Christian job search club	3
Referrals from study participants	3
Neighborhood peer-led career groups linked to PYCP	2
Stacie Shedd, career coach	2
Pastor in an upper-middle-class neighborhood	2
Help-Each-Other career groups	1
Jewish Community Career Services	1
Craigslist	1

*Names of sites and people here are pseudonyms, except for "Craigslist."

in their role for uncritically purveying neoliberal ideologies (for example, see Sharone 2013), with some critics arguing that they are a key element of an unconscionably profitable industry that capitalizes on the desperation of the unemployed (see Ehrenreich 2005). Recruiting heavily from job search clubs has several implications for the findings in this study, which I note below.

The recruitment process was similar for recruiting through associations of professionals, neighborhood peer-led groups, and through executive career coach, Tyler Kerswell. I reached out to Tyler at the recommendation of a PYCP administrator. Tyler welcomed me to the small weekly workshops he ran as well as to larger monthly workshops he held at a nearby private college. These workshops typically had eight to ten participants, charged $25—$30 per person for the two-and-a-half-hour-long session, and were focused around one aspect of the job search, for example, "Job Searching in the Right Places." The larger workshops typically had around forty participants and cost about $20 for the same amount of time. I paid these costs each time I attended. Because I had first explained my research to him, Tyler, too, endorsed me to his workshop participants and gave me the opportunity to make a two-minute pitch to see if anyone was interested in participating. Prior to attending any neighborhood peer-led group or association of professionals meeting (information for both were visible through different online platforms), I would email the organizer providing my institutional affiliation and a succinct description of my study, along with a request to attend a meeting. Mostly, I was welcomed because, as organizers told me, they considered the study important.

For several other recruitment sites, I initiated the recruitment process online. This held for two parent list-servers as well as for the Help-Each-Other and the Christian job search group. For the former, I first connected with the main organizer. Help-Each-Other had been started by an unemployed professional once he lost his job, and he had been featured in an article in the *New York Times*. He agreed to talk with me over Skype; we conducted an interview. While his interview did not make it into the final sample, as he did not fit the sample criteria, he did send out my call for participants on Help-Each-Other's extensive list-serve, through which I was able to schedule and conduct one interview. For the Christian job search group, I met over lunch with the organizer. Presumably assured of my credibility, she too sporadically sent out my call for participants to her list-server exceeding one thousand members, at my request. Not being a parent, I was not a member of any parent list-servers, but colleagues and friends who were parents posted my call for participants on three different such list-servers to which they belonged.

The remaining three recruitment sites were via Stacie Shedd, a career coach; a pastor; and a Jewish Community Career Services (JCCS). In each case, I was referred to these sites by members of the existing networks. At the JCCS, administrators invited me to a one-day career workshop they were hosting for white-collar professionals. I stood at the registration desk and explained my study to the participants as they registered for the workshop.

RECRUITING SPOUSES

As sociologist Jessie Bernard (1972) noted, there are "his" and "hers" marriages, in that each spouse in a marriage may have wildly disparate interpretations of even the same events. As such, when conducting in-depth interviews with spouses, these interviews must be conducted separately if researchers are to gain insight into marital dynamics. In qualitative studies of family life and marriages, couple-level interviews tend to be rare. This is because spousal interviews are generally difficult to obtain. Because many studies of marriages draw on information collected from one spouse, having reports from both spouses in this study provides valuable insights. Whenever possible, I sought to complete interviews with both unemployed individuals and their spouses. I ultimately completed interviews with thirteen wives and eleven husbands.

I compared the narratives of the unemployed participants whose spouses participated in the study with those whose did not participate in the study. Wives of unemployed men who participated did not seem to be systematically different from wives who did not. It appears that spouses who chose not to participate did so for reasons unrelated to unemployment. I requested that participants set aside two hours for the interview, which may have seemed like an overwhelming time commitment for some.

Interviewing husbands of unemployed women was more difficult. I reached out to spouses after interviewing the unemployed individual; unemployed women seemed to be wary of placing any burden on their husbands, particularly while they were unemployed. Frequently, I had to email and phone several times, sometimes over a period of months, before I was able to conduct the interview with the husband. It is a distinct possibility that the husbands I eventually interviewed were in more gender-egalitarian marriages, where wives felt comfortable asking their husbands to participate in a study, and where husbands were willing to do so. My findings, stark as they are, may thus underestimate the depth of gender inequality in the cases of unemployed women in particular. Alternatively, some of these husbands may have agreed to participate because they were deeply impacted by their wives' unemployment; for example, Ben Anderson was extremely frustrated with Caroline's focus on job searching. These husbands may have wanted to vocalize their experiences.

FOLLOW-UP INTERVIEWS

I also conducted follow-up interviews with about half the participants approximately six months after the first interview. I focused on conducting follow-up interviews with participants who fell into three broad groups: those who had appeared to be having a relatively easy unemployment experience; those who had seemed to be having a relatively challenging unemployment experience; and those who had seemed to be having a neutral experience. I would review their interview transcript from the earlier interview and my notes and tailor the interview protocol for each participant. Broadly, in the follow-up interviews I investigated how the experience of unemployment evolved over time for the unemployed individual and their families. Follow-up interviews averaged an hour, with approximately two-thirds being conducted in person, with the rest over phone or Skype. I conducted these interviews between 2014 and 2015.

RECRUITING FAMILIES FOR OBSERVATIONS

I was worried about how to recruit families for observations—I feared seeming callous or intrusive. But I was also certain that observations would add immeasurably to my understanding of how unemployment shaped the rhythm of daily life and would particularly illuminate spousal interactions. It was important for me to capture this. The first family I asked about observations was the Smith family. I had interviewed both Shannon and William by this time. In my interviews with each, I had explained that the broader study also involved observations as a means of warming them up to this idea later. I stayed in touch with William for the next month, particularly as I ran into him at PYCP meetings, which I continued attending and where I had first recruited him for an interview.

On one such meeting, when he casually inquired how my interviews were proceeding, I broached the topic of observations. He nodded, as though wrapping his head around it, and then said he would think about it and talk it over with Shannon. For the next several months I would follow up every three or four weeks to see if he and Shannon had had an opportunity to discuss it. Finally, William said he and Shannon had agreed that they would like to participate in the study and invited me to start observations in February 2014. I would later learn that Shannon had been quite reluctant to participate but eventually was worn down by William. Recruiting the first family for observations was key, since William and Shannon both indicated that they would be happy to serve as references in case anyone wanted to ask what their experience of having me "hang around" had been like. Although I never divulged their names, I did tell all the subsequent families that I requested to observe that they could talk to another family I had observed if they had any reservations. No one asked to talk—either they declined outright or they were willing to participate in observations without talking to the Smiths.

I ultimately recruited four families. I had asked ten families in which I had interviewed both the husband and wife to participate in the observation component of the study. Five declined, one could not participate because the wife had gotten a job, and four agreed to participate. I consider this a very reasonable rate for such an intrusive request.

I believe that families chose to participate because they considered their unemployment experience to be important and wished to help others like them by sharing their experiences. Since most of the spouses in these families had graduate-level degrees, they also mentioned that they found it worthwhile to help me pursue higher education. I offered a $250 honorarium for families to participate. For three of the families, the money did not seem to make a difference. Two families agreed to participate in the study before I had even offered any honorarium. The unemployed families who received the honorarium accepted it with a casual "Oh thanks!" with William Smith adding, "You know this wasn't necessary, right? We would have participated anyway." Despite experiencing unemployment, the families here—all dual-earner families in the professional middle-class where only one member was unemployed—continued to have comfortable incomes. The $250 honorarium did not seem to be a significant amount for them. I can't tell if it was a decisive factor, but the Masons did laughingly say that it was nice to get the $250. The honorarium may have mattered more for them.

THE RATIONALE FOR USING INTERVIEWS, FOLLOW-UP INTERVIEWS, AND HOME OBSERVATIONS

I draw on three types of data: in-depth interviews with unemployed men, unemployed women, and their spouses; follow-up interviews with participants; and family observations. I designed the study to privilege theoretical saturation and the collection of qualitatively rich data to understand interactions and processes.[11]

My approach to understanding the nuances of verbal and nonverbal interactions was based on observational and interview data. Direct observations allow the researcher to watch interactions unfold. Direct observations are particularly difficult when it comes to observing dynamics within families. Indeed, only a handful of studies of family life include observations.[12] These studies also usually have small sample sizes, with one of the most comprehensive studies drawing on family observations with twelve families across four cells.[13] These sample sizes of observations, complemented by a larger sample of in-depth interviews, have typically been considered appropriate for qualitative studies, since the aim is not to be representative but rather to illuminate, through a smaller number of cases, larger theoretical concerns. I locate this study as following in the footsteps of these prior studies of family life.

Direct observations, in themselves, are insufficient to illuminate interactions.[14] How participants in an interaction *interpret* what has happened is paramount. Here, interviews are invaluable. Through interviews, the researcher gains an understanding of how an individual in an interaction understood and made sense of it. Interviews are also useful for illuminating more intimate interactions that a researcher cannot access even with home observations. For example, in my interviews, participants talked about how unemployment shaped their sex lives and interactions around it.

I combine these methods to gain an understanding of how couples interact, and interpret their interactions, around issues of paid and unpaid work during unemployment.

SAMPLE LIMITATIONS

I tried to recruit additional participants via several other means, none of which ultimately yielded any participants. I had started off the study by first reaching out to 40+, the group based out of New York City where Katherine Newman had conducted her research on unemployed managers several decades ago. The group was still operational but met infrequently and appeared to be winding down. Although welcoming toward me (for example, they allowed me to attend a meeting in New York and after this to join and then post on their LinkedIn group), I ultimately did not recruit any participants through them.

At another point in the research process, I modified my recruitment strategy in an attempt to achieve a more racially diverse sample. Although I ideally wanted a mix of races, I decided that, given the demographic makeup of the metropolitan area where I was recruiting, focusing on recruiting more Black unemployed professionals would be the most efficient strategy to ensure that I would not end up with a solely White sample. I first approached a professional organization catering to black MBAs. I also wrote to pastors at several Black churches in middle- and upper-middle-class neighborhoods informing them about my study (under the assumption that places like churches often provide emotional and financial support in times of distress, like unemployment). I requested that they pass along my call for participants to those in their congregation they thought might fit the participation criteria. When neither approach yielded participants, I expanded my recruitment strategy by placing fliers in public spaces and by posting calls for interviews at more open sites, such as Craigslist (through which I obtained one participant, as noted in table 5). Last, I explained my desire to make sure all voices were represented in my study to my non-White participants in particular to see if they could put me in touch with colleagues and acquaintances who might fit my recruitment criteria. These methods were not particularly successful in yielding a more racially balanced sample. Although I focused on recruiting Black participants, I did not preclude other racial groups, and interviewed them as and when the opportunity arose.

I am not fully certain as to why these efforts did not yield a more robust racial comparison. This may be linked to my own racial and ethnic background (South Asian Indian), as men and women of Indian origin were explicitly interested in participating and helping me recruit participants because of the shared background. It may also have to do with the strict participation criteria I implemented that privileged a dual-earner family structure—a family form more common among some racial and ethnic groups than others. These criteria were necessary to make robust claims about gender in this study, but they limited my ability to capture how different types of families responded to unemployment. Since previous qualitative studies have not paid such comparative attention to gendered differences in unemployment experiences, this study, despite its limitations, nonetheless makes an important contribution to the sociological literature on work, gender, and family.

As I learned through the course of conducting my interviews, many participants were being encouraged by career coaches and job search clubs to "network" in order to expand their possibilities of learning about new jobs. Some participants explicitly stated that they saw their interview with me as a professional activity. Some explained that they saw me as opportunity to network—an assertion that surprised me, as I did not consider myself as having contacts that would be particularly useful for them. Treating their interview with me as a professional activity has implications for how these participants crafted their experience of unemployment that they chose to share with me. Specifically, these participants were likely often performing for me, for example as being morally unemployed, being an ideal job-seeker, or finding respite in the home. At times, the performative dimension of the interview was palpably evident to me, often around the narrative of job loss and job searching that participants and spouses crafted, throughout the interview.

Over the course of the interview, respondents sometimes changed the narrative about their job loss. Doug Easton, for example, started off by explaining that he had voluntarily taken early retirement. As the interview proceeded, Doug made clear statements indicating that his "retirement" was forced, and while he did not explicitly backtrack on his initial framing he made several statements that rendered this initial framing suspect to me, such that I noted in my memo on his interview "says early retirement—but does not sound like it? Probe in follow-up." I was cautious in how, and whether, I pushed back to ascertain details in cases where I suspected that participants may be modifying the truth. I worried that pushing back, with Doug for instance, could have meant threatening their identity as honorable people. I often relied on one of my other data collection methods—for example interviews with spouses, follow-up interviews, and observations—to piece together the job loss and its aftermath. Sociologist Marianne Cooper has described collecting interview and observational data as akin to detective work. She writes, "Being a qualitative researcher is, in many ways, like being a detective. Like a detective you arrive on the scene where something has happened. You interview witnesses, gather clues, and inspect the crime scene, studying events from one angle and then from another. After hours of fieldwork, you sit by yourself in a room and think. You feel lost—again and again. You follow up with key witnesses, hoping they will provide you with a big break. You look at all the evidence over and over."[15] This description captures my experiences with data collection for this study, given the triangulation I had in place. In Doug's case, his mode of job loss was clarified soon, when I conducted an interview with his wife, Alice. A few hours before our interview Alice emailed me saying that she had just learned that Doug had framed his job loss as a voluntary early retirement. She unequivocally explained that that is not what happened—that Doug had been asked to leave—and she wanted me to know this prior to our interview so that we were able to talk "honestly" (as she put it). Because my interviews delved into issues such as the division of housework, the issue of performativity became important here—for example how did each participant want to project their own and their spouse's gendered self? While the narrative around this was important in illuminating values and beliefs around gender, triangulating data (through observations and interviews with spouses, as well as asking specific questions around how participants divided housework) helped provide a baseline sense to me for the division of housework in each home.

To some extent, interviews are always performative, as people try to craft narratives about themselves. Interviews around a potentially spoiled and stigmatized identity, as in unemployment, are informative in their very performances in illuminating how individuals and couples seek to explain and "rectify" this spoiled identity. For men, as this study shows, this is through becoming ideal job-seekers—a performance that shapes interactions with spouses, acquaintances, and also with me as the researcher. This is far less the case for unemployed women.

On the one hand, an issue to consider is how this sample might be biased given that this study is about the stigmatized identity of unemployment. Perhaps those who participated saw themselves as having "normal" experiences that align with mainstream expectations around work and family. Those who strove to change gendered scripts in the home may have ended up getting divorced—meaning that their experiences would not be captured in a sample like this that focuses on married, heterosexual couples with children. The findings in this study, however, do line up with outcomes recorded in large-scale, quantitative data-sets, but they go beyond that. This qualitative data is well positioned to offer explanations for unanswered questions around, for example, why unemployed men do not do more housework and why unemployed women do even more.

On the other hand, interviewers also worry that the marginalized may be more willing to participate in studies, thus skewing the sample and impacting biases in it. As other scholars have noted, focusing on issues of generalizing to the population and so on are not the appropriate way to evaluate qualitative research.[16] Rather, for qualitative research a focus on the depth of explanations, and how deeply it captures mechanisms (of gender inequality in the case of this study) is more appropriate. Consequently, I decided to emphasize theoretical saturation.[17] Doing so meant actively recruiting to get not just "normative" perspectives, but including disconfirming evidence—for example, unemployed husbands who took over housework, or unemployed wives who did not. Focusing on this—an aspect that researchers can control—allowed me to see how the norm of the ideal job-seeker that was slowly revealing itself functioned and its various permutations as well. There is a healthy debate on whether interviews can reveal what people "do" or only what people "say."[18] My aim in using interviews—at multiple points and with multiple people in a family—and observations, was to get a sense of both what people say *and* do when it comes to unemployment. Conducting research on a sensitive topic such as unemployment, and asking people to share personal and private information means that researchers cannot control who ultimately will choose to participate. Out of those who do elect to participate, researchers can, however, be meticulous in data analysis to ensure that they have examined the broad topic and research question from multiple perspectives to enable them to sketch out plausible explanations, and alternative ones too.

Researchers have written about how doing qualitative research puts the researcher at the mercy of participants who may not show up, or may delay at the last moment, thus derailing your schedule.[19] But this was not my experience. My participants appeared to approach their meetings with me as a professional event. For example, although I always planned to reach the location at least fifteen minutes prior to the interview, I would often find them already there. This may have been because they had spare time due to being unemployed, but as I talked with them and learned about their professional lives it mostly struck me as a practice they had adopted vis-à-vis their work lives. If rescheduling an interview, participants did it well in advance and provided alternative dates and times. During my data collection period, I made it a point to prioritize interviews and observations above all else, and so I never "negotiated" an interview date or time that might have been more convenient to me. But other than this, my participants were unusually aware of respecting my time.

Some participants explained that they treated the interview with me much like they treated the neighborhood peer-led job search groups they attended: as a way to structure their day. Yet others explained that they considered unemployment to be an important and research-worthy topic and wanted to help others who may be going through it by sharing their stories. For many, talking about their unemployment was a way to get acknowledgment for going through a tremendously challenging experience—in these cases, I was often a "witness" to their struggles to accept that they had been asked to leave an employer and the pain that entailed.

LOGISTICS OF CONDUCTING INTERVIEWS
ON SENSITIVE TOPICS

After emailing or talking on the phone, I would schedule an interview with participants. I asked them where they would like to meet. Most suggested locations close to them, typically Starbucks, although some wanted to meet me on my university's campus. A very few asked me to come to their homes. I respected their wishes. I preferred conducting interviews in public places like coffee shops. I have been asked whether conducting interviews in public places on a fraught topic such as unemployment precluded me from digging deep and understanding the visceral experience of unemployment. I think, on the contrary, that such public places lend themselves to anonymity. Cafés often have intense, private conversations going on, and each table, despite its proximity to others, is like an island unto itself. Conducting interviews in cafés did not stop my participants from telling me deeply emotional and painful experiences about their unemployment or other relevant life experiences.

I also found these kinds of public spaces to be neutral spaces. The few times I conducted interviews at participants' homes, I found that the flow of the interview was frequently interrupted by phone calls on the landline, doorbells ringing, the arrival of a spouse, or a brief task when the participant may have, for example, had to run into the kitchen. Because the home interviews were in the participant's house, I also felt less comfortable asking more probing questions—for example about how unemployment had impacted participants' intimacy in marriages, especially when the flow of the interviews was already being interrupted. Cafés, as neutral and anonymous public spaces, offered better interview settings, from my perspective, for this study. Cafés did at times get loud—for example with the noise of a coffee machine, or the chatter of a large group. This noise at times impacted my ability to record the interview. But these occasions were rare.

I was conducting interviews several years after the Great Recession, but the national conversation at the time was still one of "recovery." Based on our conversations, the persons I spoke with did not seem to see themselves as particularly unique or flawed in experiencing unemployment.[20] Instead, they saw unemployment as part and parcel of the professional employment experience in contemporary times. Nonetheless, talking about their unemployment was often sad. The interviews were emotional. It was not unusual for participants to cry when describing their job loss, nor was it unusual for them to request a few minutes' break from the interview when we delved into marital dynamics. Although I told each participant that they could skip any question they didn't want to answer and that they could end the interview any time they chose, none ended the interview early and very few chose to skip questions. Interestingly, the questions they chose to skip or evade, if any, tended to be around money and the details of their finances in terms of savings, assets, expenditures, and salaries. To encourage them to provide some answers, I would say that they could just give a ballpark figure if they preferred, for example that they earned between $75,000 and $100,000. This was more amenable to most. In one couple, one spouse refused to answer the question about income, but the other answered it in their own interview. For the most part, participants in this study were forthcoming about their finances and wealth. Since I was "studying up," participants likely were not concerned that revealing their finances would threaten their class status in my eyes; even when unemployed, they were wealthier than I was as a graduate student.

As an interviewer, you can never be certain if you are getting the "whole story." I couldn't be sure if people were deciding not to share some aspects of their unemployment experience with me. Since people discussed suicide, depression and anxiety, emotional abuse in marriages, other extreme marital problems and alcoholism, among other topics, I am reasonably confident I obtained some degree of depth into their experiences. I wondered why individuals were so open about sharing some of their more difficult life experiences with me. My own speculation is that starting off the interview with an opportunity for participants to discuss their job loss before moving on to questions about family and marriage allowed them to open up. I think many of my participants had a "narrative" they were crafting—stories about their unemployment that they work on with career coaches and in networking groups about why they are out of work. Since the interview goes for a long time—longer than a professional networking interaction would typically last—even the ones who are trying to conceal their shame or embarrassment do end up eventually revealing less salubrious reasons for their job loss and their more naked feelings around it. I think of one participant, Nate Gura, who kept hedging about his job loss, citing "illness," until he eventually said it was alcoholism (which is an illness). Once he acknowledged that, he was pretty frank for the remaining part of the interview, revealing how his alcoholism messed up parts of his life. He would repeatedly say, "I won't get into that." But, without me prodding, he *would* get into "that." I think for him there was no other way to tell his story and share his experience without talking about alcoholism.

I also think it's easier to talk to a stranger about difficult things. Participants didn't have to worry about seeing me frequently or having me be involved in their lives. They could expose vulnerabilities without really being vulnerable. Unlike relationships at an ethnographic site, I did not have daily relationships that continued for years with most participants in this study. Their relationship to me in the interview would be very different from a relationship with friends and family, whose opinions and judgment regarding their unemployment they likely cared more about. In fact, with the families I observed, the longer our relationship, the more difficult it became to ask questions about finances or marital dynamics, particularly in the follow-up or exit interviews. Although I asked these questions, and participants usually answered them, I myself felt uncomfortable, as if I were being intrusive in a way I had not felt in prior interviews, even when I asked about what unemployment meant for their marital intimacy and sex life. My sense is that both parties—the family members and I—tried to get these parts done with quickly, so we could move on to other questions. Although intensive family observations offer many advantages, they do not immerse the researcher into the lives of the families such that the researcher becomes a part of the social world like classic ethnographic methods do. My familiarity with the families I observed, my rapport, was like that of an acquaintance. I was neither a stranger nor a close friend. I was, however, inquiring about some of the deepest aspects of their lives. It was disconcerting, for them, and for me.

Although I do think most people shared even very unpleasant aspects of their unemployment with me, I know some did not. Maeve Gura, whose husband talked about his alcoholism, never once said anything about it to me, never picked up on my probes for it. She was, in fact, misleading when I asked her whether her husband sought solace in drink, saying "no." Collecting data through multiple means meant that I was able to triangulate it. In the case of Maeve, for example, triangulating meant that I knew when some of her responses were not forthright, and were more about performing a specific kind of marriage and family life. Similarly, only one person (in the course of the larger study, who ultimately did not fit the sample parameters I determined) discussed infidelity. More members of my sample may have experienced infidelity, but that seemed to be the taboo in these interviews. Even with these hidden areas, I feel confident that my interviews provided me with a reasonable approximation of the challenges unemployment brings to marriages.

EMBODIMENT AND DATA COLLECTION

As a person of Indian heritage, I differed considerably from most of my respondents, the majority of whom were native-born and White. I found that in my interviews and my observations, my educational background was the main point of connection, which, to me, appeared to minimize the other significant differences between my participants and myself.

That my educational background should be at the forefront of our connection makes sense—I was, after all, recruiting participants for a study that formed the crux of my PhD requirements. My participants particularly emphasized my educational attainment. In our informal conversations, for example, participants often looked misty-eyed as they told me about their own graduate school experiences. Some described having toyed with the idea of a PhD, while a handful in this sample had completed one. Others said that they never thought about a PhD because it seemed like a huge time commitment, and perhaps not a financially sound decision. Being a PhD student at an Ivy League university, well-respected in the region, appeared to give me a status with this professional middle-class that my income as a graduate student certainly wouldn't have. They treated me as someone able to understand their aspirations and challenges. My respondents were not worried about destitution because of their unemployment, but they were worried about keeping up with their college savings' goals for their children, for the repercussions for a comfortable retirement, or how the lack of family vacations might impact marital quality and parent-child relationships. When they started listing these financial challenges—worries specific to the well-off—they appeared sheepish. I think they nonetheless provided details because I conveyed to them that these were legitimate concerns that I wanted to hear more about.

In key ways, I was studying "up." This was a group of professionals who, even when unemployed, had very comfortable lifestyles. Yet, it seemed to me that when I was conducting interviews or observations, my status was equalized because of my connection to a university these participants respected. Often, for example, the participants I interviewed or observed would chat with me about their concerns about college admissions for their children. I was, I think, seen as an expert who could provide some insight into this enduring question. For my part, I offered to talk with their children about college, or to show them around my university's campus, at a later date. In short, despite several key demographic differences between my participants and me, I think the similarity in our social class positions and their perception of me as a professional-in-the-making was important.

That said, two of my demographic characteristics departed in key ways from those of my participants, with important consequences for data collection. The first is my age. I started recruiting participants when I was in my late twenties, but I was often mistaken for being in my early twenties. Participants perceived me as naive, especially around issues of marriage. This proved to be helpful because my questions about details on housework and marital dynamics came across as the questions of someone without personal knowledge of these institutions. Since I was unmarried, this was true. For example, when I asked Claire Frankel about the division of housework in her home before and after unemployment, she chortled and responded with "You're not married are you?" I shook my head, "no," after which she detailed how the division of housework had unfolded between her and her husband during the course of their marriage and during her unemployment. My assumed lack of familiarity with marital dynamics and housework was helpful in enabling me to ask probing questions about these issues that might have seemed odd coming from someone older or married.

Being in the in-group or the out-group has advantages and disadvantages in terms of gathering data: in-group participation might preclude one from asking seemingly naive or probing questions; and being an out-group member might mean challenges to establishing rapport. For my purposes, I found that, insofar as my age and my marital status did not render me part of the in-group, they were helpful for my data collection.

Being Indian also mattered: it shaped the sample I gathered, and it made me very visible when I conducted family observations. My sample has just a few Indians, but in the places I sought to recruit participants, Indian-origin participants frequently approached me and either volunteered to participate or, if they did not fit my recruitment criteria, offered to put me in touch with friends, usually Indian. It also mattered in my interviews with Indian-origin participants in terms of their own assumptions of my knowledge about Indian "culture." In one interview, I was asking an Indian-origin participant about housework during his unemployment when he explained that his wife was reluctant to let him do more housework because, "you know, that's how it is in our culture." I did probe further to get specifics around housework and how he understood his own participation in housework, but he had clearly placed me in the in-group category and assumed that my own experience as an Indian would be similar to his.

My Indian-ness mattered with non-Indians too, in both the recruitment process as well as in the interviews. I often recruited participants from professional groups, as shown in table 5. Often the conversations turned to discussing how job-seekers could remain competitive in a global economy, with participants pointing to how American jobs were going to China or India. At one neighborhood, peer-led

APPENDIX A 237

job searching group, the host talked about losing jobs to outsourcing. He specified China. During the course of the group discussion, he asked me where I was from and, feeling awkward, I said India. I tried to hedge the answer, saying "Well I grew up all over . . ." before finally closing with saying, "I'm from India."

I had a similar experience when I met participant Terry Clarke for a follow-up interview outside of his workplace for lunch. Terry had taken a job in IT for a large telecommunications company, and he asked me what I knew about Indian engineers. He continued by saying that there were a lot of them in the building and that there seemed to be a lot in the engineering field in general. Terry was careful and polite, and he made sure not to say anything disparaging, but I did wonder what else he might have said if I had not been Indian.

My most explicit encounter in this regard was with a woman who expressed initial interest in participating in the study but never actually did. She wrote me a very emotional first email detailing the difficulty of finding jobs, and explicitly zoomed in on how jobs were being outsourced to India. Before I could reply to her email, she quickly followed it up with a second email, saying that she guessed I was Indian by my name. She expressly stated that she didn't have anything against people of any kind, but all the job advertisements she had seen were for outsourced jobs. She included a screen shot of recruiters, all of whom had Indian names. In the context of this research and the conversation around global outsourcing of jobs at all levels of skills and education, my being Indian certainly mattered in how individuals responded to me, and in how comfortable I felt in some settings.

Embodiment was extremely important in collecting my observational data. I have discussed the logistics and challenges to conducting family observations in detail elsewhere, but I want to make two points here about conducting observations in families with dependent children.[21] First, the presence of young children makes it difficult to blend into the background of the family. Second, small family sizes highlight the presence of researchers in the home.

The Smith home, for example, included Alex, the couple's four-year-old son. A high-spirited boy who loved dinosaurs, Alex would inevitably approach me with a book about dinosaurs and start stating facts he had gleaned from the book to me. Watching in amusement, his mother, Shannon, said, "He's showing off because you are here." Since I went every day, Alex did get somewhat used to me. While in the first few days he would keep circling me, by my fourth visit he would mostly stick to playing his own games, or doing an activity with his parents—my novelty had worn off. Yet there would still be moments, for example, when he wanted to show off a birthday card that he had received from his grandparents, that he paid attention to my presence in the home. Children of this age in particular amplify the visibility of the researcher.

The second note here is about the family sizes. Of the four families I observed, only one, the Janssons, had two children. These family units consisted of either three or four people. In this context, the presence of an extra person, me, stood out. With larger families, for example three or more children, or families where relatives and friends may drop by continuously (a situation unlikely to happen in native-born, professional middle-class American families), the researcher may better blend into the background. In smaller families though, it is harder to de-emphasize your presence.

Fieldworkers' embodied state (their age, race, gender), will, of course, impact the data they collect and the kind of access they have. While increased familiarity with the families I observed did not make me one of the "family," I think it did mean that family members slipped into their normal routines. After a few days, my presence was not the primary focus of our interactions. This likely allowed me to capture some semblance of their everyday routines, which I could also cross-check with the interview data that I continued collecting from the families. Despite some of the drawbacks of conducting family observations in their homes, these observations added a way to triangulate data.

My citizenship mattered in family observations. I observed the Jansson family, which consisted of Laura and Robert Jansson; their four-year-old daughter, Tessa; and their two-year-old son, Taylor. When I went over one evening, Tessa was very excited because she had just gone with her mother to cast a vote for local elections. As is the norm among professional middle-class parents, Laura had used this as an opportunity to start teaching Tessa about democracy and the importance of voting.[22] As we sat around the dinner table, Tessa asked me if I had voted. I said "no." With curiosity, she asked "why?" Before I could think of how to relate the concept of citizenship to a four-year-old, I found myself saying, "You can only vote if you are American. I'm Indian." Tessa looked puzzled, so I continued, as her parents watched, "India is far away, and it's my home, so I can vote there, but not here." Tessa didn't understand and asked, "So how far?" Given my limited interaction with children in my own life, I didn't know how to respond, so I stretched my left arm out and waved it to signal a far-away distance. At this point, Laura stepped into the conversation to explain the concept of countries to Tessa. This conversation lasted for about ten minutes in its entirety, about a third of the dinner time. The focus had clearly been on me, because of my status as a noncitizen.

OTHER FACTORS DURING DATA COLLECTION— FAMILY PETS AND DIETARY RESTRICTIONS

In many families, American or otherwise, it is common for either the family or a child to have pets. Often parents use pets as a way to teach children about responsibility. I, however, grew up in a decidedly pet-unfriendly family and have never owned a pet. I also have a slight, perhaps irrational, fear of many common animals, like dogs. This fear stems from some disastrous encounters with untrained dogs in my childhood in Delhi, India, but it has thankfully, diminished over time. In the families I observed, one family owned a Komodo lizard and two families had dogs. (These families also had other pets, like goldfish and hamsters, that did not bother me.)

The Smiths got a dog partway through my fieldwork, when it seemed like William Smith was close to getting a job he wanted. On one occasion, William asked that I join him at a neighborhood dog park. For many researchers, seeing dogs frolic might be a fun activity. But for me, while I had grown at least moderately comfortable with the Smiths' puppy, the idea of hanging around a park full of dogs was, frankly, frightening. I stood at the edge of the park, always close to the exit, unable to involve myself more fully with the games William and his son Alex were playing with their puppy and with other dogs. I stood apart, sensitive to when the dogs growled at each other or got rough, my discomfort visible in the slight grimace on my face and my tensed body language. At one point, William, looking over, smiled and waved me to come over. I looked to either side before I went and stood, perfectly still, unhappy to be surrounded by so many other dogs. I was glad when the hour was over.

Parker Bach, the teenage son of Darlene and Larry, owned a Komodo lizard called Sprinkles. I assume the giant lizard obtained his name in an ironic subversion of ideals of cuteness or delicacy. The family often let Sprinkles roam around the basement for its exercise. Since the bathroom I used was also in the basement, on those days I avoided using the bathroom. My discomfort around Sprinkles was particularly amusing to Parker, especially when I accompanied the family, and Sprinkles, on an eight-hour road trip. I was sitting in the front passenger seat, with Parker in the seat behind me, where he held Sprinkles in a soft towel. Darlene had told me that they normally let Sprinkles have free reign of the car, and this had worried me. Embarrassed about my discomfort, I whispered to Parker to "please keep Sprinkles well away from me" as his parents loaded the car. Parker smiled and then explained, "You know, Komodo lizards are a really common pet in American families. Little kids have them, so you don't have to be scared." I nodded, noting how he was positioning himself as an expert on American life, in contrast to me, whom he saw as unused to the norms of American life. I repeated pleadingly, "But please just keep him at the back?" Parker nodded reassuringly, and, to my great relief, Sprinkles did not venture to the front seat.

Lastly, elsewhere I have noted how researchers' own lifestyle preferences can be distracting in fieldwork.[23] This may particularly pertain to dietary restrictions, especially since fieldwork often involves participating in meals with families. At the time that I conducted my research I did not eat pork. Families often asked me about my diet, since I typically joined them for dinner, as that was frequently a time when the whole family would be together. I am sure my restriction factored into what they cooked, and consequently may have changed the family routine, but I cannot tell whether it also impacted *who* organized and did the cooking for the meal. In the Smiths' home, William Smith had been the cook before his unemployment and remained so while unemployed. One evening I saw that William was making spaghetti with pork meatballs, but he separately made stir-fried vegetables with noodles for me. My presence was thus visible through considerations of my dietary needs, and accommodating me may have added more work for different family members.

How we collect data and what data we collect are shaped by what we value theoretically. I value the power of ethnography in illuminating how minute interactions can have significant implications. My project was designed to understand the minutiae of unemployment at an economic and cultural moment when experiences of unemployment appear poised to become an enduring feature of the American economic landscape.

Interview Guide for
Unemployed Professionals
and Spouses

BACKGROUND

1. Can you tell me about yourself (education, occupation, age, family, ethnicity, religion growing up and now, siblings, where they are and what they do, previous marriages, names and ages of children, other members of the household). Can you briefly trace the trajectory for me of how you got from where you grew up to where you are now?

2. Tell me about who you live with at home:

   a. Details on spouse—job, education, length of marriage

WORK EXPERIENCE PRIOR TO JOB LOSS

3. Until your employment situation changed what were you doing? Tell me about the work.

   a. Work history—gaps, how you got jobs, earnings in last job, length of tenure at last job, future expected salary, hours

4. What did you like about the work?

5. What did you not like about the work?

6. What did being a [job title] mean to you? How do you think people saw you, your position and work? In terms of respect, status, income (wife, kids, others).

JOB LOSS

7. Tell me about the process of how your employment situation changed.

8. What did you do?

9. What were the first things you thought about when you found out you no longer had a job?

10. Have the feelings you had when you were told you no longer had a job changed now that some time has passed?

11. What did you tell your spouse? How did he or she react? The kids?

12. What did the change in your employment situation mean? Psychologically, emotionally, in terms of family.

    a. Perks/benefits from job, status, income, halt in career trajectory, etc.

    b. Household chores sheet

13. What is it like being in your current employment status? How do you spend your days?

14. Do you think that other people's opinions of you changed with your job loss? How?

    a. Do other people treat you as a [previous job title] or as someone who lost a job?

FAMILY FINANCES

15. Can you tell me how you and your spouse thought about and managed your finances from the start of your marriage?

    a. How did you decide how much to save?

    b. What were the goals you demarcated for yourselves (home, college for kids)? Did you always agree on these?

    c. What were the major credits or debits you started your working life with (help from family; inheritance; student loans)?

    d. Can you tell me about how you and your spouse divided contributions to the major purchases (houses, kids' education, savings)? Did you always agree on these or were there any arguments? Can you tell me about them?

    e. Who handles the money—bills, different accounts, etc., in your marriage?

16. How successful do you think you have been in meeting your financial goals?

17. Have conversation about finances changed in the past few months since unemployment? How? On what?

    a. Are there any major purchases you had been planning?

MENTAL AND EMOTIONAL HEALTH

18. Job loss can be really difficult, especially psychologically. I'd like to ask you about what it has been like for you in the past few months. Often people talk about feeling down, worried, or angry. What have your moods been like lately?

    a. Medication

19. Some people get depressed and it changes their behaviors—for instance, withdrawing, drinking more, maybe taking the anger out physically. Others don't. What has it been like for you?

20. How do you relieve any anxiety you experience? How have your spouse, friends, siblings, anyone else helped you in this time?

    a. If people are not understanding/helpful, what ways do you think they could be helpful? What could they do to relieve any pressure you are experiencing?

AT HOME

21. Now, I'd like to shift to asking more about your life at home. Different people think differently about what it means to be a man, husband, and father or a woman, wife, and mother. Can you tell me what you think about being a man/husband /father or woman/wife/mother?

    a. What are some of the characteristics?

    b. Does having a job matter? How and why?

    c. After losing your job do you think about these things differently?

22. Can you tell me about your relationship with your partner? How do you feel about your marriage? Can you describe it?

    a. Separation, divorce, counseling?

    b. Toughest problem? Where does unemployment rank?

23. How has your marriage evolved over time?

24. If I asked you to describe your life at home before your job loss and now, what would you say the major differences are?

    a. How do you spend time together?

    b. Probe for quietness in the house.

    c. Probe for change in topics of conversation.

    d. If there hasn't been a change, why do you think that is?

25. Do you think your relationship with your partner—the things you do together, things you talk about—has changed since your job loss? How?

26. What do you see as your main role in the relationship? What are the strengths you bring to the relationship?

27. What do you see as your spouse's strengths in the relationship?

28. Do you feel that your employment situation has changed your marriage, your contributions and your spouse's contributions? Can you tell me about them?

    a. Intimacy

    b. Fights—ask about last fight with spouse.

29. What is the toughest problem you and your spouse have faced? How did you handle it? How does this experience of job loss feature in there? Does it?

30. Can you tell me about your role as a father/mother? What do you like about it? What do you think you do well, what do you think you could do better?

31. Do you feel your role as a mother/father has changed (since your employment situation changed?)

ENDING

32. What is the hardest piece of this whole process of the change in your employment situation?

33. What are your hopes for the near- and long-term future?

    a. Have they changed from before your unemployment vis-à-vis children, career, spouse, etc.?

34. It there anything about this experience that we haven't talked about today?

Notes

1. See Cooper (2014).
2. For more on relative deprivation see Newman (1999).
3. See Bureau of Labor Statistics (2016).
4. See Bureau of Labor Statistics (2019a).
5. See Kalev (2014) for more. There is also more overt discrimination, for example firing women who are pregnant (this is an illegal practice, of course, but the formal reason offered by the employer is not about pregnancy. This can make it challenging for women to prove discrimination. See Byron and Roscigno (2014).
6. See Mandel (2018).
7. See Mong and Roscigno (2010) for more on discrimination experiences of Black men.
8. See Pager, Western, and Bonikowski (2009).
9. For more on the motherhood penalty and hiring discrimination see Correll, Benard, and Paik (2007). See Weisshaar (2018) for an audit study on which categories of non-work experience (parenthood, unemployment, or evidence of opting out for family responsibilities) are most likely to be discriminated against by employers at the hiring stage.
10. See Bureau of Labor Statistics (2019b).
11. See Bureau of Labor Statistics (2017).

12. See Board of the Governors of the Federal Reserve System (2019). Overall unemployment rates, of course, obscure the spread of unemployment, especially in terms of race and class. For example, for Blacks the unemployment rate is often double that of Whites. Hispanics often have unemployment rates that are lower than Blacks but higher than Whites. Generally speaking, the lower the average level of educational attainment, the higher the unemployment rate. For more on unemployment rates by demographic characteristics, see Bureau of Labor Statistics (2016).

13. See Folbre (2010), Thompson (2009). Note that although sectors in which women are more likely to be present were not as hard hit, recovery in female-dominated sectors was nonetheless slower. The recession can be seen as having had a longer-lasting impact on women workers. See Hartman, Fischer, and Logan (2012).

14. See Sharone (2013) and Newman (2008), both of whom cover in detail the implications for the health and finances of rising employment insecurity and unemployment among white-collar professionals.

15. See Sharone (2013) and Ilg (2010) for a definition of long-term unemployment.

16. See Newman (2008).

17. See Cha (2019).

18. See Kalleberg (2009) for a deeper look into how jobs have become polarized, such that jobs for lower-educated and workers tend to be extremely precarious and bereft of benefits; jobs for top earners increasingly come with ever-larger salary and benefit packages.

19. For more on how the growth of financialization led to sweeping changes in business priorities and practices (including in terms of labor market churning), see Carruthers and Kim (2011), Davis and Kim (2015), Krippner (2005) and van der Zwan (2014).

20. See Hacker (2006, ix).

21. See Cooper (2014) and Sharone (2013) for excellent backgrounds on how the global shifting economic landscape has shaped experiences of economic insecurity in general and unemployment in particular. Both authors also delve into the factors leading to more labor-market churning in contemporary times.

22. See Kanter (1993, 290).

23. See Pugh (2015a).

24. See Schor (1991), Jacobs and Gerson (2004).

25. See Rao and Neely (2019).

26. See Carruthers and Kim (2011).

27. See Newman (2019) for more on retirement and insecurity.

28. See Greenhouse (2009).

29. See Lopez and Phillips (2019).

30. This is particularly so when it comes to more privileged workers. For low-income workers, researchers are examining how changes in the organization of work—for example an aggressive move toward shift work spurred by automation—impacts their lives outside of work. For more, see Schneider and Harknett (2019).

31. See Villalobos (2014).

32. Pugh (2015a, 50).

33. See Lamont (2019), Cabanas and Ilouz (2019), Silva (2013), Rao and Neely (2019), Gershon (2017), Aitkin (2007), van der Zwan (2014) for how market forces, specifically of neoliberalism, shape and subjectivities.

34. See Komarovsky ([1940] 2004); Jahoda, Lazaersfeld, and Zeisel (1971); Newman (1999).

35. See Bianchi, Robinson, and Milke (2012).

36. Brines (1994)

37. See Gough and Killewald (2011) for more on housework during men's and women's unemployment.

38. For more on race and housework see Barnes (2016) and Sayer and Fine (2011).

39. See Livingstone (2014).

40. See Bureau of Labor Statistics (2018).

41. See Hays (1996) for "intensive motherhood." See Blair-Loy (2003) and Lareau (2011) for more on the concepts of "family devotion schema" and "concerted cultivation," respectively.

42. Dow (2019). Also see Glenn (2002), Barnes (2016).

43. See Cooper (2000).

44. Edin and Nelson (2013).

45. This line of analysis has benefitted from Viviana Zelizer's contention that all money is not equal. Her concept of "earmarking" is fruitful for understanding how we assign symbolic value and meanings to monies, such that even equal amounts may not be fungible. See Zelizer (2017).

46. See Sharone (2013) for job searching practices among white-collar workers. See also Max Weber on bureaucracy (Gerth and Mills 1946), specifically how bureaucracy serves capitalist interests. Under late capitalism, these interests include how markets permeate a wide range of social realms, including intimate life.

47. For more on sociological research on gender and interactions, see Ridegway (2011) for an overview of how identity categories, including gender, "frame" our interactions. Francine Deutsch (1999) explains how couples' interactions can be strategically molded toward gender equality by more equally shared parenting. Finally, scholars also argue that, just as interactions compel individuals to "do gender," interactions can also pave the way for "undoing gender" (Deutsch 2007) and limiting the power of gender.

48. See West and Zimmerman (1987).

49. This assertion stems from the Durkheimian view on *anomie*—a state of uncertainty where rules (in this case cultural scripts) are ill-defined. For more, see Durkheim (1984, Book III).

50. For more on the ideal worker norm see Acker (1990); Blair-Loy (2003) on "work devotion;" and Williams (1999).

51. Sociological research has focused on how mundane interactions accumulate over time to produce stratification and inequality. A particularly important part of this is how social class shapes interactional styles, leading to the accrual of advantage in educational institutions (Lareau 2011, Calarco 2018) and the workplace (Rivera 2012). When it comes to race, Anderson (1990) and Stuart (2016) provide context for understanding how strategies designed to ease one's life on the street, with the community, and in terms of interactions with police can have unintended consequences. The broad sociological literature on gender also has a rich history of deeply considering how interactions matter for gender inequalities (West and Zimmerman 1987, Ridgeway 2011, Deutsch 2007), especially in the workplace.

52. For further methodological details on research design and participant recruitment, please see the methodological appendix.

53. In her book on marriages, Jessie Bernard (1982) famously pointed out that each marriage is actually made up of a "his" and "hers" marriage. She points out that each spouse may have a very different understanding of their marriage. For this reason, it makes sense to conduct individual interviews with spouses to better understand both their perspectives.

54. For more on the methodology of "intensive family observations" see Lareau and Rao (2019) forthcoming.

CHAPTER 1. MEN AT HOME

1. See Rivera (2015), England (2010), Ridgeway (2011), Correll (2004) for more on occupational pathways, occupational segregation, and gendered discrimination that consolidate gendered economic inequalities.

2. See Bianchi, Robinson, and Milkie (2006) for more on decadal trends for parental time spent with children.

3. See Livingston (2014). In 1989 a substantial portion of stay-at-home fathers did so because they were ill or disabled. By 2012, staying at home for fathers was still driven by an inability to find work, but the *choice* to take care of their family also featured in the decision to stay at home.

4. See Pugh (2015b).

5. How much employment matters for social status is contextually contingent. It is possible to maintain social status without working, as among the incredibly wealthy (Veblen 1899). Some social groups may separate employment from ideas

of responsibility because of awareness of structural conditions such as race-, gender-, and sexuality-based hiring discrimination. For research on discrimination in the labor market, see: Pedulla (2018), Pager, (2003); Gaddis, (2015); Mize, (2016) for more.

6. For more on cultural scripts in times of uncertainty, see Swidler (1986). For more recent empirical examples of how people formulate (new) cultural scripts in uncertain interactions, see Bogle (2008) and Lamont (2014) for more research on hook-up culture. See Bearman's (2005) research on doormen in New York City. See Hochschild (2003) for more on the service work of flight attendants. See Pande (2014) for research on the labor of surrogacy in India. See Hoang (2015) and Rivers-Moore (2016) for more on global sex work.

7. See Mallett (2004) for a review of research on the home. As Mallett points out, the home from the mid-nineteenth century onward has been a space of authority for men, a haven from the travails of the world, but it has also often been the key site of subjugation for women and children. For Black women in America, the home can be particularly oppressive, but also at time serves as a space igniting political action, see Crenshaw (1989) for more on this. Finally, Stephanie Coontz (2016) evocatively describes how nostalgia shapes visions of home and family based on a specific, and peculiar, historical time period.

8. See Hochschild (1989), DeVault (1991), Gu (2017).

9. For more on domestic work, see Parreñas (2001), Ehrenreich and Hochschild (2003), Ray and Qayum (2009).

10. See Swidler (1986), Ridgeway (2011) for more on how times of uncertainty open up space for social change.

11. Networking is considered a key aspect of getting a new job for workers in professional settings. For more on the importance of networking, see Gershon (2017), Sharone (2013), Ehrenreich (2005).

12. For more on how the emphasis on networking encourages self-blame for enduring unemployment rather than a critical evaluation of structural factors that produce unemployment, see Sharone (2013) and Lopez and Phillips (2019). For an in-depth argument on how the job search industry targeting the white-collar unemployed is exploitative, see Ehrenreich (2005).

13. For more on age discrimination, see Roscigno et al. (2007). I was surprised to find that several participants in their early forties were extremely worried about age discrimination as well. Another dimension was that unemployed men, but not unemployed women, discussed how "old, white men" were the least likely to get hired. From their perspective, employer preferences for diversity meant that white men, older or not, were the least likely to get hired compared to white women or minorities, even in the same age bracket. This perspective—by which many participants were deeply convinced—is not fully supported by empirical evidence. For more on employer's hiring preferences when it comes to race, class, and gender, see: Gaddis (2015, 2017), Quadlin (2019), Rivera and Tilcsik (2016).

14. This ideal was deeply mediated by the particular historical context in which well-paying jobs were available to select, usually White, men. While this ideal discouraged middle-class White women from working, it bears noting that other women, for example Black women and immigrant women, have long been involved in the labor force, often as "the help" to enable White women to uphold the exacting demands of domesticity. See Glenn (2002) for more.

15. Friedan (1963)

16. See Putnam (2001).

17. See McPherson, Smith-Lovin and Brashears (2006) for more on how Americans' social networks changed from 1985 to 2004. The authors discuss how kin and non-kin networks have shrunk, with Americans generally having fewer people to talk to about things that are important to them. However, this has not been spread evenly: more highly educated people actually have larger networks. Women also continue to have somewhat larger networks than men.

18. See Wynn and Rao (2020) for more on the long hours that professional occupations demand.

19. Of course, unemployment occurs in the context of lives that have multiple threads. For Amelia, the difference in desire for intimacy is only partly related to Jim's unemployment. She explains that their sex life has diminished over the past several years for many reasons, including a surgical procedure she underwent a few years ago and Jim's medication for depression, both of which impact libido.

20. See Quadlin (2018).

21. See Cohen (2018).

22. See Guzman (2017) on the US Census.

23. See Cooper (2014) on how advantaged families often revert to a neo-traditional organization.

24. See Zelizer (2017, 18).

25. Brand (2015), Newman (1999). For the more privileged, the physical impacts of unemployment may be mediated by the mental well-being where their worse mental well-being leads to worse physiological health. For the disadvantaged, unemployment impacts physiological health more directly: via inability to access necessary medical attention and equipment, including medication.

26. See, for instance Zelizer (2015), Charles and James (2005).

27. Pepin (2019).

28. Thorne (2010).

29. For more on this, see Burgoyne et al. (2006, 2007).

30. For more on how market logics permeate into individual subjectivities, see Ailon (2019), Aitken (2007), Cabanas and Ilouz (2019), Lamont (2019).

31. See de Grazia and Furlough (1996) for more on how the male producer/ female consumer trope has persisted since the Victorian era, such that advertisements are largely targeted to women.

32. For more on race and the accumulation of wealth in the Unites States, see Benton and Keister (2017), Killewald and Bryan (2018).

33. Young (2012), Norris (2016), Thoits (1986).

34. Wendt and Shafer (2016).

35. Professionals, such as those in this sample, are typically conceptualized as having autonomy over such aspects of their work as scheduling and prioritizing, although within a hierarchical, bureaucratic system. They are also assumed to have more authority over their work, including over people they manage, than blue-collar workers. However, some scholars dispute this, arguing that "organizational control" is an important mechanism for maintaining a tight grip over professionals' authority. For more on the issue of authority at work, see Wynn and Rao (2020).

36. For more on how competence and expertise in professional workspaces is often adjudicated by factors such as race and gender, see Jackson and Wingfield (2013), Wynn and Correll (2017).

37. For more on this turn toward personal branding and companies of one, see Gershon (2017) and Lane (2011).

38. For more on the promises and realities of work on platform economies such as Uber, Airbnb, and so on, see Ravenelle (2019).

39. For more on how financial products and policies are racialized, see Seamster (2019), who discusses that the debt White individuals and families have can frequently be turned into an asset. The debt of Black individuals and families, in contrast, is far more of a hindrance for their wealth accumulation. Other issues, such as discrimination in the housing market, also mean that investments by Blacks show lower returns. See Besbris and Faber (2017).

40. For more on the trend of young adults living with their parents in order to save on money see Newman (2012).

41. For more on how unemployment has become an expected part of US professional life, see Lopez and Phillips (2019).

42. Visio is a Microsoft Office tool marketed to "simplify and communicate complex information using data-linked diagrams." The costs for the program vary depending on how many elements and advanced abilities it has. Visio Standard is in the realm of about $300.

43. For more on how wives emotionally support husband's during unemployment see Rao (2017a).

44. For a history of hegemonic masculinity as a concept, its empirical applications, and the debates surrounding the concept, see Connell and Messerschmidt (2005).

45. See Bureau of Labor Statistics (2016) for recent data on unemployment by racial or ethnic category.

CHAPTER 2. IDEALIZING THE HOME AND SPURNING THE WORKPLACE?

1. Rather than bolstering a privileged class position, staying at home for Black women may be rife with the "controlling image" of the Welfare Queen—imagined commonly as a Black woman with children from multiple fathers, who does not work and lives off of the state. For more on how employment is important to Black women as a way of attaining respectability, see Dow (2015).

2. See Norris (2016).

3. In her book on motherhood, *The Cultural Contradictions of Motherhood*, Sharon Hays (1996) describes intensive mothering as having three components: first, that mothers are primarily responsible for childcare; second, that proper childcare is child-centered, emotionally absorbing, and expert-oriented; third, that children, and consequently their care, should be seen as outside of market valuation because children are sacred.

4. See Jacobs and Gerson (2004), Blair-Loy (2003)

5. See Williams (1999).

6. See Damaske (2011)

7. Karen Christopher (2012) shows how even when working mothers resist the hegemonic ideal of intensive motherhood, they still feel accountable to it. That is, even if they think the expectations of intensive mothering are excessive and unnecessary in raising children, they do feel that they are judged, usually by others, in terms of whether they measure up to those ideals or not.

8. See Garey (2011).

9. As Dow (2015) details, rather than finding a sisterhood of stay-at-home mothers as Darlene does, the few Black unemployed women in Dow's study felt rebuffed by White women in public spaces such as parks and schools in their own middle-class neighborhoods. They felt unwelcome.

10. See chapter 5, "Club Member," in Susan Ostrander's *Women of the Upper Class* (1986) for more on the social role of exclusive clubs in the lives of affluent women.

11. See Legerski and Cornwall (2010), Bass (2015), Cohen (2016).

12. Arlie Russell Hochschild (1989, 5) discusses gender strategies in greater length in *The Second Shift*.

13. Compare this to how, in an anomic state, families of unemployed men treat unemployment as a grave problem. These framings inform the rules and cultural scripts families deploy.

14. While Darlene is comfortable wearing athleisure on a daily basis, unemployed Black women in Dow's (2015) study ensure that they are meticulously dressed anytime they leave their house. Anticipating that despite their class status they will not be seen as belonging in middle-class spaces, Black women take great care with their appearance and their interactions. They focus on conveying

their class status so that they are not viewed in terms of a negative controlling image. Black individuals and families save more than their White counterparts. They also spend less on everyday items such as food. On clothing, however, Black families spend more. Clothing—including investment in luxury items such as furs—is an important way through which Black individuals seek to be acknowledged as respectable and competent. They anticipate discrimination and view presenting a well-groomed self as a way to ward that off. See Bowen and Lago (1997) for more on the saving and spending trends by race. See Cottom (2013) and Sanders (2019) for more on the role of dressing well and racialized respectability.

15. For more on the world of white-collar networking, see Gershon, (2017), Ehrenreich, 2005; Sharone, 2013; Smith, 2001 for excellent descriptions and analysis.

16. Sociologist Youngjoo Cha (2010) finds that one important mechanism sustaining men's higher income is that men tend to more frequently be able to work overtime. Cha finds that men's overtime may be driving a "separate sphere's" ideology. Because of married men's overtime, their wives may have to curtail their own labor force participation in order to meet caregiving needs.

17. See the McKinsey & Company *Women in the Workplace* report (Krivkovich et al. 2018), which explains how being an "only"—where you may be the only person of your race and gender characteristics in a high-level position is an isolating experience.

18. Dawn Dow (2016) explains the concept of integrated motherhood.

19. See Barnes (2016)

20. For more on couples' patterns in terms of pooling financial resources see: Kenney (2006), Pepin (2019), and Treas (1993).

21. See Lunn and Kornrich (2018) for more on parents' education investment during economic downturns.

22. Carework is an expansive concept, and can cover work of looking after others for pay (for example, as home health aides, nurses), looking after others (family or neighbors) not for pay, and other volunteer work.

23. See Sarkisian and Gerstel (2004) and Fingerman et al. (2016).

24. See Rivera and Tilcsik (2016).

25. See Collins (2019).

26. See Weisshaar (2018) for an audit study of how different work interruptions are penalized differently by employers. See Ghayad (2013) and Gangl (2006) for the scarring effects of unemployment on reemployment.

27. See Whillans (2019).

28. See McKinsey's *Women in the Workplace* report (Krivkovich et al. 2018). For more on how workplace expectations, motherhood ideals, and lack of adequate childcare policies shape workplace experiences and decisions for highly educated mothers, see: Acker (1990), Blair-Loy (2003), Stone (2007).

CHAPTER 3. DINNER TABLE DIARIES

1. See Hochschild (2003, 56).

2. Men's occupational advantages mean that even in dual-earner families, men typically earn more than women. In a recent study, Jill Yavorsky and coauthors (2019) show that the discrepancy between men's incomes and women's is such that women's income is adequate for inclusion in the top 1 percent in only one out of twenty families.

3. In their book on fatherhood among poor and working-class fathers, Edin and Nelson (2013) show how these fathers rework fathering ideals to downplay the focus on breadwinning. Scholars such as Lane (2011) and Demantas and Myers (2015) suggest that masculinity is becoming increasingly decoupled from the ability to provide for one's family, given the changing landscape of employment and jobs.

4. Generally speaking, men's work spills over more into marital interactions than women's work. One study shows that men's workplace stress spills over into the home and impacts their wives' stress levels, but that this doesn't happen for women's workplace stress (see Levine, Bonner, and Klugman 2018). Focusing on the workplace challenges of a spouse who is in the process of losing a job is very understandable, but, as we will see in chapter 4, husbands' support for their wives' intensive focus on finding a job is not quite as forthcoming.

5. Sharone (2013).

6. For more on strategies that unemployed workers adopt to push their résumé to the top of the pile, see Gershon (2017).

7. In her study of contract professionals, Osnowitz (2010) finds that a large portion of her sample entered into contract work, such as consulting, only after losing their jobs.

8. I discuss how housework is negotiated for men in chapter 5 and for women in chapter 6.

9. See Hochschild (2003, 7).

10. Hochschild's concept of feeling rules encapsulates how our emotions are not just "natural," but rather governed by a set of social understandings that determine how, and when, we express our emotions. A general feeling rule, for example, is that one *should* feel sad when one loses a close friend unexpectedly. This is a feeling rule governing close friendships. Similarly, sets of relationships and contexts have feeling rules particular to them—for example, you do not cry in a professional space. Couples, too, have feeling rules.

11. Hochschild explains that "when couples struggle, it is seldom over who does what" (Hochschild with Machung 1989, 19). Rather, the contestation is over whether actions are interpreted as gifts by the spouse, and if they are, are they responded to accordingly. A traditional husband, for example, may see his wife's

cooking dinner as her obligation to him, while a more gender-egalitarian man may see the same act as her gift to him.

12. As Swidler (1986) explains, times of uncertainty mean a lack of clarity about expectations of culturally appropriate behavior. Typically, while people can resort to utilizing existing cultural scripts for behavior, they can also innovate on these scripts. One argument of this book is that cultural innovation that facilitates gender equality in marriages appears to be rare during men's and women's unemployment.

13. In their respective works, Pugh (2019) and Weinberger, Zavisca, and Silva (2017) note that omnivorous, "exotic" experiences, and especially travel around the world, are becoming a key facet of life among affluent Americans.

14. For more on how families in the professional middle-class seek to preserve their children's privilege in a context of economic uncertainty, see: Nelson (2010), Pugh (2019), Rao (2018, 2019b).

15. Black families in America are more likely than White families to exchange in-kind help—for example for childcare, housework, and transportation (Sarkisian and Gerstel 2004). This is in part because they are more likely to live closer to kin.

16. See Granato, Smith, and Selwyn (2015).

17. Many of my participants echoed the findings in other research on unemployed professionals that you should *always* be networking and job searching, if mildly, because you never know when unemployment may befall you.

18. Gershon (2017), Ehrenreich (2005), Smith (2001), Sharone (2013).

CHAPTER 4. CAN WOMEN BE IDEAL JOB-SEEKERS?

1. Newman (1999) found that men who lost their jobs for reasons that were seen as valid, even moral (for example, having participated in a union strike and consequently losing a job) versus having lost a managerial job because of a company's downsizing significantly shaped how families responded to the job loss. Recent research—for instance Sharone (2013) and Lopez and Phillips (2019)—suggests that the reason for job loss has become less important since workers, and their families, are aware that periodic layoffs and similar practices are organizational tactics aimed at profitability for organizations. Participants in this study had lost their jobs in many ways. Aligning with Sharone (2013), I found that these distinctions were ultimately less meaningful in shaping their family's responses than what workers did *after*.

2. For more on educational homogamy in relationships, including marriages, see Schwartz and Mare (2005).

3. For more on how social class shapes college pathways, including college completion, see: Goldrick-Rab (2006), Kornrich (2016), Silva and Snellman (2018).

4. For more on the racialization of wealth, see: Killewald and Bryan (2018), Benton and Keister (2017), Keister (2004).

5. Like the Boyles, several of my respondents had received or expected to receive inheritances. This is a particular feature of middle- and upper-middle-class American life. Immediate financial anxieties about paying for large bills and so on were often ameliorated by several factors, including the fact that the other spouse still worked; the couple's savings; and, finally, recourse to friends and family for stop-gap monetary measures. These avenues of recourse are often not available to poor or working-class families.

6. See chapters 5 and 6 for more on the division of household chores during unemployment.

7. For more on children's extracurricular activities and parenting in times of uncertainty, see Nelson (2010), Pugh (2019), Rao (2018, 2019b).

8. A menial job at a café may seem a peculiar choice for a sixteen-year-old from the middle-class. As the Boyle's example shows, however, they occupy a more ambiguous class position given Danny's educational and occupational status. This is further complicated by the wealth of his parents as well as Eileen's own educational and occupational status. Despite the ambiguity of their class status, though, research increasingly shows that "lifestyle" work in high-end cafés (like the kind Eileen's daughter worked in) and boutiques privileges young White, middle-class workers. Scholars often call this "aesthetic labor"—for more on this see Duffy (2017), Gatta (2014).

9. For more, see Rao (2019a).

10. Women typically earn less than husbands in dual-earner marriages. Recent data suggests that wives earn more than husbands in about a quarter of marriages. See Cohen (2018).

11. For more on intensive parenting, see Cooper (2014), Lareau, (2011), Nelson (2010). See Hays (1996) for intensive mothering.

12. See DeVault (1991) and, more recently, Bowen, Brenton and Elliott (2019) for more on how the idealized imagery of home-cooked meals exacerbates women's oppression and class-based inequalities.

13. For more on how schedule uncertainty at work has detrimental impacts on health and well-being, see Schneider and Harknett (2019).

14. A study using cross-national data shows that cooking is one of the few routine household tasks that men are spending more time on. However, this study indicates that data for the United States on this issue is tentative. See Sayer (2010).

15. Prior to having Ellie, Rebecca had been working casually, looking for freelance work in her area, and nannying as and when gigs came along. In this study, I did not encounter explicit instances of pregnancy-based discrimination resulting in being fired, probably because a significant portion of my participants already had their children as part of the "parenthood" criterion of this study. One

woman in the study was fired while she was pregnant with her second child. However, she attributed this more to a sexist boss who had fired a handful of senior women, rather than to her pregnancy. For more on pregnancy discrimination and job loss, see Byron and Roscigno (2014). For more on motherhood and discrimination in hiring, see Correll, Benard, and Paik (2007).

16. See Ruddick (1980) on the emotional labor of mothering.

17. See Gershon (2017), Sharone (2013) for research on networking. See Rao (2017a) for more on emotion work and emotional labor in families. See Hochschild (2003) for more detailed definitions of emotion work and emotional labor. Briefly, emotional labor is emotion work conducted for a wage and subject to an employers' control. Emotion work, in contrast, is not done for a wage, and occurs in the realm of private relationships, especially in sexual and romantic relationships.

18. See Yang, Chawla, and Uzzi (2019) on the importance of networks for women's placement. This study focused on the broad categories of "men" and "women" and does not offer an intersectional analysis (for example, variations, if any, within the broad category of women, on the basis of factors like race and ethnicity, and so on).

CHAPTER 5. WHY DON'T UNEMPLOYED MEN DO MORE HOUSEWORK?

1. See Bianchi et al. (2012) for more on housework trends over time.

2. Gary Becker's classic *Treatise on the Family* (1981) remains influential in advancing economic explanations for the gender division of labor.

3. See Bittman et al. (2003). The authors note that in the United States, the trend that men's housework declines the less they earn is driven by men whose earnings, relative to their wives, are the lowest.

4. For more on how interactions produce and affirm gender statuses, see West and Zimmerman (1987) and Ridgeway (2011). For more studies on gender displays and doing gender via housework, see Brines (1994), Bittman et al. (2003), Hook (2017), Schneider (2012).

5. See Gough and Killewald (2011).

6. This body of research has had mixed findings, with some studies showing that how much housework men do is closely related to how much income they or their wives provide. These scholars argue that ideas of gender display have been overemphasized. See, for example, Hook (2017).

7. For more on this kind of "invisible work" and "cognitive labor," see Daniels (1987) and Daminger (2019) respectively.

8. See Thébaud, Kornrich, and Ruppaner (2019) for an experimental study on how women and men are held to different standards of cleanliness and messiness.

9. See Fielding-Singh (2017b).

10. Starting from Hochschild's classic 1989 book *The Second Shift* and continuing into contemporary times. A recent study shows, though, that this inside-outside split is not very meaningful in urban areas, where outside work is limited. The authors find that the absence of an outside does not mean that men contribute more to housework. This study highlights the even worse implications for gender division of housework in urban areas. See Quadlin and Doan (2018).

11. The idea of "undoing" gender is a response to the concept of "doing gender" as fatalistic—where men and women are forever constrained by gendered imperatives. Both Deutsch (2007) and Risman (2009) push scholars to consider places where there might be scope to detach expectations of certain, specific behaviors, from gendered categories and to seriously consider that gender can be "undone."

12. As a contractor, Marcus is not a full-time employee. These kinds of positions are obtained through a high-level recruiter (or recruiting agency) as the key intermediary. While Marcus earns a high wage in such a position, these positions do not come with benefits like paid vacation or health care. In the Neals's case, Sylvia's job has typically provided the health care for the family.

13. I did not explicitly inquire about how Marcus thought race might impact hiring decisions. In my interviews, I consciously adopted an approach in which I did not ask leading questions. It is entirely possible that, had I been a Black interviewer, Marcus might have brought up race far more explicitly than he did in our interview. Because I was the only interviewer for the entire study, and I am neither White nor Black, it is difficult for me to detail how it impacted my findings. Individuals with the same ethnic origin as me—South Asian Indian—did explicitly discuss their conception of "Indian culture" and how they thought it shaped their experience by treating me as an insider who had the same experiences and could consequently understand and agree with their experiences. For research on racial discrimination and hiring, see Gaddis (2015), Pager (2003) Pedulla (2018).

14. See Gaddis (2015).

15. Jahoda (1982) offers an overarching theory of how unemployment impacts well-being and mental health beyond material deprivation. More recent studies on how unemployment adversely impacts mental health include Young (2012). Interestingly, Inanc (2018) finds that individual well-being in couples is most adversely impacted when men are unemployed and wives are stably employed. The author links this surprising finding to gender deviation from norms about the organization of paid and unpaid work.

16. See Sharone (2013) for an excellent analysis of the emotional labor of job searching. See also Rao (2017a).

17. Wealth in the United States is deeply racialized. For more on intergenerational transfers (which are important in wealth building) and wealth, see Cornwell and Cornwell (2008), Killewald and Bryan (2018), Oliver and Shapiro (2019),

Schafer and Vargas (2016). For more on the intergenerational exchanges around carework, especially the role of grandmothers, see Dow (2019).

18. See Damaske (2011), Landivar (2017).

19. For more on how gender and race combined to place Black women at the bottom of the occupational hierarchy, see Branch and Wooten (2012) and Wooten and Branch (2012). See also Glenn (2002) for a broad overview on race, class, gender, and employment.

20. See Barnes (2016) for more on affluent Black families who adhere to a more gender-traditional family form.

21. See Collins (1990), Dow (2016), Glenn (2002).

22. For more on the support that wives of unemployed men provide, see Rao (2017a).

23. See Orbuch and Eyster (1997). Note, however, that another study (Sayer and Fine 2011) does not find that married Black men do any more housework when compared with their white counterparts.

24. Other studies of unemployed men have found, in contrast, that unemployed men embrace a modern masculinity by emphasizing their caregiving, and spending time looking after children and doing housework. See Chesley (2011), Lane (2011).

25. See Thompson (2009).

26. See Pfeffer (2010) on how transmen take on the social and masculinized attributes of uncleanliness while in the process of transitioning for an excellent analysis of how clean/messy is more social than natural. See also Thébaud, Kornrich and Ruppanner (2019).

27. See Stone (2007).

28. For more on how women's absence from paid work became a marker of White, middle-class respectability in industrial United States, see Davies and Frink (2014), Branch and Wooten (2012), Wooten and Branch (2012).

CHAPTER 6. WHY DO UNEMPLOYED WOMEN DO EVEN MORE HOUSEWORK?

1. See Gough and Killewald (2011).

2. See Hays (1996) and Lareau (2011) for more on parenting.

3. This aligns with workplace research on gender that finds extensive evidence of discrimination against women in the workplace, including in hiring and performance evaluations, especially in elite and lucrative occupations. For more, see: Quadlin (2018), Rivera and Tilcsik (2016).

4. Families in this study often used the language of "frugality" to explain why unemployment did not yield a terrible financial blow. But this rhetoric obfuscates other available scaffolds, often including assistance from elderly parents.

5. Married women across social class and race continue to do more unpaid housework than their husbands. There are differences by racial categories; for example, studies have found that heterosexual Black couples have a more equal division of housework than White couples. Some studies, for example, Sayer and Fine (2011), dispute this.

6. In a recent study, Natasha Quadlin and Long Doan (2018) find that men in urban areas do not do male-typed chores, such as yardwork, simply because these chores are linked to suburban or rural life. However, urban men also do not increase their participation in female-typed chores such as cooking and cleaning.

7. Ridgeway (2011).

8. See Lareau (2011) and Levey Friedman (2013) for more on children's extra-curricular activities, including their costs.

9. See DeVault (1991) for more on cooking as a way to maintain women's subordinated status in the home. For recent research on gendered parenting related to cooking, see Bowen, Brenton and Elliott (2019), Fielding-Singh (2017a, 2017b).

10. This paucity of time is a feature of a context in which childcare is privatized—an expensive responsibility that families must manage themselves—rather than a public good, available to all parents. For more on how different, state-led provisions of childcare shape families' time and stresses, see Collins (2019).

11. See Ruddick (1980).

12. To integrate the privatized responsibility of childcare with paid work, US mothers often turn to part-time work. However, this work tends to be less well-paid and without benefits. Mothers in the United States encounter a fine calculus of whether participation in paid work outweighs the costs of childcare. For more, see Clawson and Gerstel (2014), Damaske (2011), Landivar (2017).

13. See Weisshaar (2018).

14. For more on sexual harassment, see McLaughlin, Uggen, and Blackstone (2017). For more on gender inequalities in promotion see Correll (2017).

15. See Blau and Kahn (2016).

16. The academic job market is peculiar in that job postings are typically concentrated in one season. In Monica's field, job openings are posted in September and October and interview invitations to candidates are issued in November or December. Interviews themselves typically occur from January onward, going into spring. This is the job market for tenure-track positions. Other positions, such as adjunct teaching, visiting, or postdoctoral fellowships may be sprinkled throughout the year. Monica's focus was on the fall market, as she hoped to receive a tenure-track position.

17. The plight of adjuncts—typically individuals with a PhD who are paid on a per-course basis—has been covered by mainstream as well as higher education publications. These publications have highlighted how adjuncts are paid a pitiful

amount, to the extent that some are homeless and others work for pay in other areas, for example, sex work. For more, see: Hall (2015), McKenna (2015), Chen (2016) Edmonds (2015), Harris (2019). As scholars have noted, universities have shifted to a contingent model for hiring faculty, with the number of tenure-track positions falling even as more students pursue doctoral studies. National figures show that more than half of faculty are now adjuncts in comparison to less than a third in 1975. For more, see Edmonds (2015).

18. Most research suggests that wives do far more to emotionally support their husbands than husbands do for wives. See Thomeer, Reczek, and Umberson (2015), Thomeer, Umberson, and Pudrovska (2013).

19. The intergenerational transmission of advantage is most concentrated among the affluent, and especially among White families. Children of middle- and upper-middle-class parents, such as Monica, often receive extensive help from their parents in the form of money and assets well into adulthood. Rayan's situation is somewhat anomalous for this study, as he grew up surrounded by financial insecurity (he recalls his parents receiving eviction notices both for their home and the property on which their business was located). Yet, over time, his parents amassed enough assets that they could retire and are able to (and desire to) support their son.

20. Research (e.g., Chesley 2011) on the convergence of time spent on housework by men and women has pointed out that couples view childcare differently from other chores, with both husbands and wives preferring child-centered chores, finding them more meaningful than other kinds of chores. The narrowing of the gender gap in housework is often due to chores centered on children.

21. Hochschild (1989, ch. 8).

22. Research findings on gender-specific outcomes related to well-being during unemployment continue to be mixed. For more on mental health, well-being, and marital relationships during unemployment, see Lane (2011), Norris (2016), Rao (2017a), Young (2012). In general, the stresses of financial instability and unemployment can lead to decreased marital quality, including domestic violence. For more on this, see Conger et al. (1990) and Schneider, Harknett, and McLanahan (2016). In my sample, no one reported these extreme outcomes as a result of a partner's unemployment, although I probed for them in my interviews.

23. This choice, described by Pew Research (Livingston 2014), is in contrast to being pushed into caregiving through job loss or some sort of health concern that may keep fathers either temporarily or for the longer term out of the labor force.

24. See Livingston (2014).

25. While the bulk of research on motherhood and on working mothers has focused on the sense of guilt that American mothers feel at not spending all their time with their children, some recent research has painted some alternative conceptions of motherhood. In developing the concept of "integrated motherhood"

Dawn Dow (2016) details how Black mothers see working as intrinsic to, rather than in contention with, motherhood. Karen Christopher's (2012) study on "extensive motherhood" explores how mothers see paid work as important to their sense of self.

26. See Bessen-Cassino (2018) for a broader a discussion of what a nanny's duties entail beyond care for children. These roles are shaped by the gender of the nanny.

27. Whether gender equality is progressing in a more or less linear way has a been a topic of robust debate among scholars. Scholars have pointed out that many trends toward gender equality, including the division of chores among couples and women's wages, have stalled or even reversed in the late twentieth century. When it comes to attitudes about gender, some researchers find that millennials (typically understood to be those born from 1981 until about 2000) hold gender-progressive views on all fronts (Risman, Sin, and Scarborough 2017), while others argue that, while millennials believe in gender equality at work, they do not believe in gender equality at home as strongly as older generations, especially baby boomers (Pepin and Cotter 2017). Marriage and parenthood in particular seem to present a challenge in terms of gender equality for millennials. One study finds that the male-breadwinner and female-homemaker model remains the most desired arrangement amongst millennials and those in Generation Z, (Dernberger and Pepin 2020). In her study of young men and women anticipating future parenthood, Brooke Conroy Bass (2015) finds that young women are likely to try to mold their careers in a way that is conducive to motherhood in the future. Young men do not do this.

28. See Gerson (2009)

29. See Cohen (2016).

30. See Cooke (2008), Pew Research Center (2015).

CONCLUSION

1. Other research also indicates such a plurality of outcomes, showing for instance that women take somewhat longer to find a job after unemployment. See Farber (2015).

2. See Osnowitz (2010).

3. See Landivar (2017) for more on part-time employment and pay. See O'Connor, Orloff, and Shaver (1999) and Collins (2019) for more on childcare policies.

4. The Swedish system was criticized by politician Bo Lundren (2006) for this reason.

5. See Pepin, Sayer, and Casper (2018).

6. See, for example, Ruppanner, Perales, and Baxter (2019).

7. See research by, among others, Ocobock (2013), Pfeffer (2016).

8. See Pedulla and Thébaud (2015).

9. See Wynn and Rao (2020), Michel (2012).

APPENDIX A. METHODOLOGY

1. For more on how young, international professionals contend with this pervasive practice of short-term contracts, see Rao (2017b).

2. See Hacker (2006).

3. Two male participants had only some college. Despite their educational attainment, their income and occupation when employed made them a part of the upper-level, white-collar work-force this study aimed to capture.

4. For example, see Ravenelle (2019), Rosenblatt (2019), Osnowitz (2010).

5. See Arthur and Rousseau (1996), Hacker (2006), Kalleberg (2009), Kanter (1993).

6. See Clawson and Gerstel (2014), Cooper (2014), Stone (2007).

7. See Stone (2007, 7).

8. See Walzer (1998).

9. See Arnett and Tanner (2005), Newman (2012).

10. See Lopez and Phillips (2019) for more on unemployment, job searching and self-blame.

11. See Roy et al. (2015), Weiss (1994).

12. See Cooper (2014), Lareau (2011), Ochs and Kremer-Sadlik (2013), Paik (2017), Reich (2005).

13. See Lareau (2011).

14. See Jerolmack and Khan (2014).

15. Cooper (2014, 63).

16. (Lareau and Rao 2016, Small 2009).

17. (Small 2009)

18. For more, see Jerolmack and Khan (2014) and responses to their article.

19. See Elliott, McKelvey, and Bowen (2017).

20. See Lopez and Phillips (2019), who explain that the post–Great Recession landscape is such that even the American focus in self-blame among the unemployed has been diluted by the undeniably visible structural shifts that have rendered unemployment so pervasive.

21. See Lareau and Rao (forthcoming).

22. See Lareau (2011).

23. See Lareau and Rao (forthcoming).

References

Acker, Joan. 1990. "Hierarchies, Jobs, Bodies: A Theory of Gendered Organizations." *Gender & Society* 4 (2): 139–58.

Ailon, Galit. 2019. "'Life Is about Risk Management': Lay Finance and the Generalization of Risk Thinking to Nonfinancial Domains." *Socio-Economic Review* (July 6) online. https://doi.org/10.1093/ser/mwz032.

Aitken, Rob. 2007. *Performing Capital: Toward a Cultural Economy of Popular and Global Finance.* New York: Palgrave Macmillan

Anderson, Eijah. 1990. *Streetwise: Race, Class, and Change in an Urban Community.* Chicago: University of Chicago Press.

Arnett, Jeffrey Jensen, and Jennifer Lynn Tanner, eds. 2005. *Emerging Adults in America: Coming of Age in the 21st Century.* Washington, DC: American Psychological Association.

Arthur, Michael B., and Denise M. Rousseau, eds. 1996. *The Boundaryless Career: A New Employment Principle for a New Organizational Era.* Oxford: Oxford University Press.

Barnes, Riché J. Daniel. 2016. *Raising the Race: Black Career Women Redefine Marriage, Motherhood, and Community.* New Brunswick, NJ: Rutgers University Press.

Bass, Brooke Conroy. 2015. "Preparing for Parenthood? Gender, Aspirations, and the Reproduction of Labor Market Inequality." *Gender & Society* 29 (3): 362–85.

Bearman, Peter. 2005. *Doormen.* Chicago: University of Chicago Press.

Becker, Gary S. 1981. *A Treatise on the Family*. Cambridge, MA: Harvard University Press.

Benton, Richard A., and Lisa A. Keister. 2017. "The Lasting Effect of Intergenerational Wealth Transfers: Human Capital, Family Formation, and Wealth." *Social Science Research* 68: 1–14.

Bernard, Jessie. 1982. *The Future of Marriage*. New Haven, CT: Yale University Press.

Besbris, Max, and William Faber. 2017. "Investigating the Relationship between Real Estate Agents, Segregation, and House Prices: Steering and Upselling in New York State." *Sociological Forum* 32 (4): 850–73.

Besen-Cassino, Yasemin. 2018. *The Cost of Being a Girl: Working Teens and the Origins of the Gender Wage Gap*. Philadelphia: Temple University Press.

Bianchi, Suzanne M., John P. Robinson, and Melissa A. Milke. 2006. *Changing Rhythms of American Family Life*. New York: Russell Sage Foundation.

Bianchi, Suzanne M., Liana C. Sayer, Melissa A. Milkie, and John P. Robinson. 2012. "Housework: Who Did, Does or Will Do It, and How Much Does It Matter?" *Social Forces* 91 (1): 55–63.

Bittman, Michael, Paula England, Liana Sayer, Nancy Folbre, and George Matheson. 2003. "When Does Gender Trump Money? Bargaining and Time in Household Work." *American Journal of Sociology* 109 (1): 186–214.

Blair-Loy, Mary. 2003. *Competing Devotions: Career and Family among Women*. Cambridge, MA: Harvard University Press.

Blau, Francine D., and Lawrence Kahn. 2016. "The Gender Wage Gap: Extent, Trends, and Explanations." Institute of Labor Economics. IZA Discussion Paper #9656. http://ftp.iza.org/dp9656.pdf.

Board of the Governors of the Federal Reserve System. 2019. "What Is the Lowest Level of Unemployment That the U.S. Economy Can Sustain?" https://www.federalreserve.gov/faqs/economy_14424.htm. Accessed July 11, 2019.

Bogle, Kathleen A. 2008. *Hooking Up: Sex, Dating, and Relationships on Campus*. New York: New York University Press.

Bowen, Cathy Faulcon, and Daniel J. Lago. 1997. "Money Management in Families: A Review of the Literature with a Racial, Ethnic and Limited Income Perspective." *Advancing the Consumer Interest* 9 (2): 32.

Bowen, Sarah, Joslyn Brenton, and Sinikka Elliott. 2019. *Pressure Cooker: Why Home Cooking Won't Solve Our Problems and What We Can Do About It*. New York: Oxford University Press.

Branch, Enobong Hannah, and Melissa E. Wooten. 2012. "Suited for Service: Racialized Rationalizations for the Ideal Domestic Servant from the Nineteenth to the Early Twentieth Century." *Social Science History* 36 (2): 169–89.

Brand, Jennie E. 2015. "The Far-Reaching Impact of Job Loss and Unemployment." *Annual Review of Sociology* 41: 359–75.

Brines, Julie. 1994. "Economic Dependency, Gender, and the Division of Labor
at Home." *American Journal of Sociology* 100 (3): 652–88.

Bureau of Labor Statistics. 2016. "Number of Unemployment Spells Experienced by Individuals from Age 18 to Age 46 in 1978–2010 by Educational
Attainment, Sex, Race, and Hispanic or Latino Ethnicity." https://www.bls
.gov/nls/nlsy79r24unempbyedu.pdf. Accessed July 11, 2019.

Bureau of Labor Statistics. 2017. Economic News Release: "Number of Jobs
Held, Labor Market Activity, and Earnings Growth among the Youngest
Baby Boomers: Results from a Longitudinal Survey Summary." https://www
.bls.gov/news.release/nlsoy.nr0.htm. Accessed July 11, 2019.

Bureau of Labor Statistics. 2018. *Women in The Labor Force: A Databook.*
Available at: https://www.bls.gov/opub/reports/womens-databook/2018
/pdf/home.pdf accessed 18 July 2018.

Bureau of Labor Statistics. 2019a. National Longitudinal Surveys: NLSY Round
26 News Release Supplemental Tables. "Number of Jobs Held and Number
of New Jobs Started by Individuals from Age 18 to Age 50 in 1978–2014 by
Age and Sex." https://www.bls.gov/nls/y79supp.htm. Accessed July 11, 2019.

Bureau of Labor Statistics. 2019b. National Longitudinal Surveys: NLSY Round
26 News Release Supplemental Tables. "Distribution of Number of Jobs Held
by Individuals from Age 18 to Age 50 in 1978–2014 by Educational Attainment, Sex, Race, and Hispanic or Latino ethnicity." https://www.bls.gov/nls
/y79supp.htm. Accessed July 11, 2019.

Burgoyne, Carole B., Victoria Clarke, Janet Reibstein, and Anne Edmunds.
2006. "'All My Worldly Goods I Share with You'? Managing Money at
the Transition to Heterosexual Marriage." *Sociological Review* 54 (4):
619–37.

Burgoyne, Carole B., Janet Reibstein, Anne Edmunds, and Valda Dolman.
2007. "Money Management Systems in Early Marriage: Factors Influencing
Change and Stability." *Journal of Economic Psychology* 28 (2): 214–28.

Byron, Reginald, and Vincent J. Roscigno. 2014. "Relational Power, Legitima-
tion and Pregnancy Discrimination." *Gender & Society* 28: 438–62.

Calarco, Jessica McCrory. 2018. *Negotiating Opportunities: How the Middle
Class Secures Advantages in School.* Oxford: Oxford University Press.

Carruthers, Bruce G., and Jeong-Chul Kim. 2011. "The Sociology of Finance."
Annual Review of Sociology 37: 239–59.

Cha, Youngjoo. 2010. "Reinforcing Separate Spheres: The Effect of Spousal
Overwork on Men's and Women's Employment in Dual-Earner Households."
American Sociological Review 75 (2): 202–29.

———. 2019. "Job Mobility and the Great Recession: Wage Consequences by
Gender and Parenthood." *Sociological Science* 1 (May 2): 159–77.

Charles, Nickie, and Emma James. 2005. "'He Earns the Bread and Butter and I Earn the Cream': Job Insecurity and the Male Breadwinner Family in South Wales." *Work, Employment and Society* 19 (3): 481–502.

Chen, Michelle. 2016. "Some Adjunct Professors Earn Just $20,000 a Year." *The Nation*, June 13.

Chesley, Noelle. 2011. "Stay-at-Home Fathers and Breadwinning Mothers: Gender, Couple Dynamics, and Social Change." *Gender & Society* 25 (5): 642–64.

Christopher, Karen. 2012. "Extensive Mothering: Employed Mothers' Constructions of the Good Mother." *Gender & Society* 26 (1): 73–96.

Clawson, Dan, and Naomi Gerstel. 2014. *Unequal Time: Gender, Class, and Family in Employment Schedules*. New York: Russell Sage Foundation.

Cohen, Philip. 2016. "Why Male and Female 'Breadwinners' Aren't Equivalent (in One Chart)." *Family Inequality*. https://familyinequality.wordpress.com/2016/05/31/why-male-and-female-breadwinners-arent-equivalent-in-one-chart/. Accessed July 9, 2018

———. 2018. *Enduring Bonds: Inequality, Marriage, Parenting, and Everything Else That Makes Families Great and Terrible*. Oakland: University of California Press.

Collins, Caitlyn. 2019. *Making Motherhood Work: How Women Manage Careers and Caregiving*. Princeton, NJ: Princeton University Press.

Collins, Patricia Hill. 1990. *Black Feminist Thought: Knowledge, Consciousness, and the Politics of Empowerment*. Boston: Unwin Hyman.

Conger, Rand D., Glen H. Elder, Frederick O. Lorenz, Katherine J. Conger, Ronald L. Simons, Les B. Whitbeck, Shirley Huck, and Janet N. Melby. 1990. "Linking Economic Hardship to Marital Quality and Instability." *Journal of Marriage and Family* 52 (3): 643–56.

Connell, Raewyn C., and James W. Messerschmidt. 2005. "Hegemonic Masculinity: Rethinking the Concept." *Gender & Society* 19 (6): 829–59.

Cooke, Lynn Price. 2008. "'Traditional' Marriages Now Less Stable Than Ones Where Couples Share Work and Household Chores." Council on Contemporary Families. https://contemporaryfamilies.org/traditional-marriages-now-less-stable-ones-couples-share-work-household-chores/. Accessed July 20, 2018.

Coontz, Stephanie. 2016. *The Way We Never Were: American Families and the Nostalgia Trap*. 2nd ed. New York: Basic Books.

Cooper, Marianne. 2000. "Being the 'Go-To Guy': Fatherhood, Masculinity and the Organization of Work in Silicon Valley." *Qualitative Sociology* 23 (4):379–405.

———. 2014. *Cut Adrift: Families in Insecure Times*. Oakland: University of California Press.

Cornwell, Erin York, and Benjamin Cornwell. 2008. "Access to Expertise as a Form of Social Capital: An Examination of Race- and Class-Based Disparities in Network Ties to Experts." *Sociological Perspectives* 51 (4): 853–76.

Correll, Shelley. 2004. "Constraints into Preferences: Gender, Status and Emerging Career Aspirations." *American Sociological Review* 69: 93–113.

Correll, Shelley J., Stephen Benard, and In Paik. 2007. "Getting a Job: Is There a Motherhood Penalty?" *American Journal of Sociology* 112 (5): 1297–1338.

Cottom, Tressie McMillan. 2013. "The Logic of Stupid Poor People." *TMC* (blog). https://tressiemc.com/uncategorized/the-logic-of-stupid-poor -people/. Accessed July 10, 2019.

Crenshaw, Kimberle. 1989. "Demarginalizing the Intersection of Race and Sex: A Black Feminist Critique of Antidiscrimination Doctrine, Feminist Theory and Antiracist Politics." *University of Chicago Legal Forum* 1989 (1): 31.

Damaske, Sarah. 2011. *For the Family? How Class and Gender Shape Women's Work.* New York: Oxford University Press.

Daminger, Allison. 2019. "The Cognitive Dimension of Household Labor." *American Sociological Review* 84 (4). doi: 10.1177/0003122419859007.

Daniels, Arlene Kaplan. 1987. "Invisible Work." *Social Problems* 34 (5): 403–15.

Davies, Andrea Rees, and Brenda D. Frink. 2014. "The Origins of the Ideal Worker: The Separation of Work and Home in the United States from the Market Revolution to 1950." *Work and Occupations* 41 (1): 18–39.

Davis, Gerald F., and Suntae Kim. 2015. "Financialization of the Economy." *Annual Review of Sociology* 41: 203–21.

de Grazia, Victoria, with Ellen Furlough, eds. 1996. *The Sex of Things: Gender and Consumption in Historical Perspective.* Oakland: University of California Press.

Demantas, Ilana, and Kristin Myers. 2015. "Step Up and Be a Man in a Different Manner: Unemployed Men Reframing Masculinity." *Sociological Quarterly* 56 (4): 640–44.

Dernberger, Brittany N., and Joanna R. Pepin. 2020. "Gender Flexibility, but Not Equality: Young Adults' Division of Labor Preferences." *Sociological Science* 7: 36–56. doi: 10.15195/v7.a2.

Deutsch, Francine. 1999. *Halving It All: How Equally Shared Parenting Works.* Cambridge, MA: Harvard University Press.

———. 2007. "Undoing Gender." *Gender and Society* 21 (1):106–27.

DeVault, Marjorie L. 1991. *Feeding the Family: The Social Organization of Caring as Gendered Work.* Chicago: University of Chicago Press.

Dow, Dawn Marie. 2015. "Negotiating 'The Welfare Queen' and 'The Strong Black Woman.'" *Sociological Perspectives* 58 (1): 20.

———. 2016. "Integrated Motherhood: Beyond Traditional Ideologies of Motherhood." *Journal of Marriage and Family* 78 (1): 180–96.

———. 2019. *Mothering while Black: Boundaries and Burdens of Middle-Class Parenthood.* Oakland: University of California Press.

Duffy, Brooke Erin. 2017. *(Not) Getting Paid to Do What You Love: Gender, Social Media, and Aspirational Work.* New Haven, CT: Yale University Press.

Durkheim, Emile. 1984. *The Division of Labor in Society.* Translated by Lewis Coser. New York: The Free Press.

Edin, Kathryn, and Timothy Nelson. 2013. *Doing the Best I Can: Fatherhood in the Inner City.* Oakland: University of California Press.

Edmonds, Dan. 2015. "More Than Half of College Faculty Are Adjuncts: Should You Care?" *Forbes,* May 28.

Ehrenreich, Barbara. 2005. *Bait and Switch: The (Futile) Pursuit of the American Dream.* New York: Metropolitan Books.

Ehrenreich, Barbara, and Arlie Russell Hochschild. 2004. *Global Woman: Nannies, Maids, and Sex Workers in the New Economy.* New York: Holt.

Elliott, Sinikka, Josephine McKelvy, and Sarah Bowen. 2017. "Marking Time in Ethnography: Uncovering Temporal Dispositions." *Ethnography* 18 (4): 556–76.

England, Paula. 2010. "The Gender Revolution: Uneven and Stalled." *Gender & Society* 24 (2): 149–66.

Farber, Henry S. 2015. *Job Loss in the Great Recession and Its Aftermath: U.S. Evidence from the Displaced Workers Survey.* Working Paper 21216. National Bureau of Economic Research.

Fielding-Singh, Priya. 2017a. "A Taste of Inequality: Food's Symbolic Value across the Socioeconomic Spectrum." *Sociological Science* 4: 424–48.

———. 2017b. "Dining with Dad: Fathers' Influences on Family Food Practices." *Appetite* 117: 98–108.

Fingerman, Karen L., Kyungmin Kim, Patrick S. Tennant, Kira S. Birditt, and Steven H. Zarit. 2016. "Intergenerational Support in a Daily Context." *Gerontologist* 56 (5): 896–908.

Folbre, Nancy. 2010. The Declining Demand for Men." *New York Times,* December 13. www.economix.blogs.nytimes.com/2010/12/13/the-declining -demand-for-men/. Accessed October 9, 2019.

Friedan, Betty. 1963. *The Feminine Mystique.* New York: W. W. Norton.

Gaddis, S. Michael. 2015. "Discrimination in the Credential Society: An Audit Study of Race and College Selectivity in the Labor Market." *Social Forces* 93 (4): 1451–79.

Gangl, Markus. 2006. "Scar Effects of Unemployment: An Assessment of Institutional Complementarities." *American Sociological Review* 71 (6): 986–1013.

Garey, Anita Ilta. 1999. *Weaving Work and Motherhood.* Philadelphia: Temple University Press.

Gatta, Mary. 2014. *All I Want Is a Job! Unemployed Women Navigating the Public Workforce System.* Stanford, CA: Stanford University Press.

Gershon, Ilana. 2017. *Down and Out in the New Economy: How People Find (or Don't Find) Work Today.* Chicago: University of Chicago Press.

Gerson, Kathleen. 2009. *The Unfinished Revolution: Coming of Age in a New Era of Gender, Work, and Family.* Oxford: Oxford University Press.

Gerth, H. H., and C. Wright Mills. 1946. *From Max Weber: Essays in Sociology.* New York: Oxford University Press.

Ghayad, Rand. Unpublished paper. "The Jobless Trap." http://www.lexissecuriti esmosaic.com/gateway/FEDRES/SPEECHES/ugd_576e9a_f6cf-3b6661e44621ad26547112f66691.pdf. Accessed July 11 2019.

Glenn, Evelyn Nakano. 2002. *Unequal Freedom: How Race and Gender Shaped American Citizenship and Labor.* Cambridge, MA: Harvard University Press.

Goldrick-Rab, Sara. 2006. "Following Their Every Move: How Social Class Shapes Postsecondary Pathways." *Sociology of Education* 79 (1): 61–79.

Gough, Margaret, and Alexandra Killewald. 2011. "Unemployment in Families: The Case of Housework." *Journal of Marriage and Family* 73 (5): 1085–100.

Granato, Stephani L., Phillip N. Smith, and Candice N. Selwyn. 2015. "Acquired Capability and Masculine Gender Norm Adherence: Potential Pathways to Higher Rates of Male Suicide." *Psychology of Men & Masculinity* 16 (3): 246–53.

Greenhouse, Steven. 2009. *The Big Squeeze: Tough Times for the American Worker.* New York: Anchor Books.

Gu, Chien-Juh. 2017. *The Resilient Self: Gender, Immigration, and Taiwanese Americans.* New Brunswick, NJ: Rutgers University Press.

Guzman, Gloria G. 2017. "Household Income: 2016." *US Census Bureau* 7.

Hacker, Jacob S. 2006. *The Great Risk Shift: The New Economic Insecurity and the Decline of the American Dream.* New York: Oxford University Press.

Hall, Lee. 2015. "I Am an Adjunct Professor Who Teaches Five Classes. I Earn Less Than a Pet-Sitter." *The Guardian*, June 22.

Harris, Adam. 2019. "The Death of an Adjunct." *The Atlantic*, April 8.

Hartmann, Heidi, Jocelyn Fischer, and Jacqui Logan. 2012. "Women and Men in the Recovery: Where the Jobs Are, Women Catching Up in Year Three." Briefing Paper C400, August 1, Institute for Women's Policy Research.

Hays, Sharon. 1996. *The Cultural Contradictions of Motherhood.* New Haven, CT: Yale University Press.

Hoang, Kimberly Kay. 2015. *Dealing in Desire: Asian Ascendancy, Western Decline, and the Hidden Currencies of Global Sex Work.* Oakland: University of California Press.

Hochschild, Arlie Russell 2003. *The Managed Heart: Commercialization of Human Feeling.* Updated edition. Oakland: University of California Press.

Hochschild, Arlie Russell, with Anne Machung. 1989. *The Second Shift.* New York: Penguin Books.

Hook, Jennifer L. 2017. "Women's Housework: New Tests of Time and Money." *Journal of Marriage and Family;* 79 (1): 179–98.

Ilg, Randy. 2010. "Long-Term Unemployment Experience of the Jobless." Retrieved July 9, 2018. https://www.bls.gov/opub/ils/summary_10_05/long_term_unemployment.htm.

Inanc, Hande. 2018. "Unemployment, Temporary Work, and Subjective Well-Being: The Gendered Effect of Spousal Labor Market Insecurity." *American Sociological Review* 83 (3): 536–66.

Jackson, Brandon A., and Adia Harvey Wingfield. 2013. "Getting Angry to Get Ahead: Black College Men, Emotional Performance, and Encouraging Respectable Masculinity." *Symbolic Interaction* 36 (3): 275–92.

Jacobs, Jerry A., and Kathleen Gerson. 2004. *The Time Divide: Work, Family, and Gender Inequality.* Cambridge, MA: Harvard University Press.

Jahoda, Marie. 1982. *Employment and Unemployment: A Social-Psychological Analysis.* Cambridge: Cambridge University Press.

Jahoda, Marie, Paul F. Lazarsfeld, and Hans Zeisel. 1971. *Marienthal: The Sociography of an Unemployed Community.* New York: Routledge.

Jerolmack, Colin, and Shamus Khan. 2014. "Talk Is Cheap: Ethnography and the Attitudinal Fallacy." *Sociological Methods & Research* 43 (2): 178–209.

Kalev, Alexandra. 2014. "How You Downsize Is Who You Downsize: Biased Formalization, Accountability, and Managerial Diversity." *American Sociological Review* 79 (1): 109–35.

Kalleberg, Arne L. 2009. "Precarious Work, Insecure Workers: Employment Relations in Transition." *American Sociological Review* 74 (1): 1–22.

Kanter, Rosabeth Moss. 1993. *Men and Women of the Corporation:* 2nd edition. New York: Basic Books.

Keister, Lisa A. 2004. "Race, Family Structure, and Wealth: The Effect of Childhood Family on Adult Asset Ownership." *Sociological Perspectives* 47 (2): 161–87.

Kenney, Catherine. 2004. "Cohabiting Couple, Filing Jointly? Resource Pooling and U.S. Poverty Policies." *Family Relations* 53 (2): 237–47.

Killewald, Alexandra, and Brielle Bryan. 2018. "Falling Behind: The Role of Inter- and Intragenerational Processes in Widening Racial and Ethnic Wealth Gaps through Early and Middle Adulthood." *Social Forces* 97 (2): 705–40.

Komarovsky, Mirra. (1940) 2004. *The Unemployed Man: The Effect of Unemployment Upon the Status of the Man in Fifty-Nine Families.* Walnut Creek, CA: AltaMira Press.

Kornrich, Sabino. 2016. "Inequalities in Parental Spending on Young Children: 1972 to 2010." *AERA Open* 2 (2). https://doi.org/10.1177/2332858416644180.

Krippner, Greta. 2005. "The Financialization of the American Economy." *Socio-Economic Review* 3: 173–208.

Krivkovich, Alexis, Marie-Claude Nadeau, Kelsey Robinson, Nicole Robinson, Irina Starikova, and Lareina Yee. 2018. *Women in the Workplace.* McKinsey

& Company. https://www.mckinsey.com/featured-insights/gender-equality
/women-in-the-workplace-2018.

Lamont, Ellen. 2014. "Negotiating Courtship: Reconciling Egalitarian Ideals
with Traditional Gender Norms." *Gender & Society* 28 (2): 189–211.

Lamont, Michèle. 2019. "From 'Having' to 'Being': Self Worth and the Current
Crisis of American Society." *British Journal of Sociology* 70 (3): 660–707.

Lan, Pei-Chia. 2018. *Raising Global Families: Parenting, Immigration, and
Class in Taiwan and the US.* Stanford, CA: Stanford University Press.

Lane, Carrie M. 2011. *A Company of One: Insecurity, Independence, and the New
World of White-Collar Unemployment.* Ithaca, New York: Cornell ILR Press.

Landivar, Liana Christin. 2017. *Mothers at Work: Who Opts Out?* Boulder, CO:
Lynne Rienner.

Lareau, Annette. 2011. *Unequal Childhoods: Class, Race, and Family Life.*
2nd ed. Oakland: University of California Press.

Lareau, Annette, and Aliya Hamid Rao. 2016. "It's about the Depth of Your
Data." *Contexts.* https://contexts.org/blog/its-about-the-depth-of-your-data/.

——. Lareau, Annette and Aliya Hamid Rao. (in press). Intensive Family
Observations: A Methodological Guide. Sociological Methods and Research.
https://doi.org/10.1177/0049124120914949.

Legerski, Elizabeth Miklya, and Marie Cornwall. 2010. "Working-Class Job
Loss, Gender, and the Negotiation of Household Labor." *Gender & Society*
24 (4): 447–74.

Levey Friedman, Hilary. 2013. *Playing to Win: Raising Children in a Competitive Culture.* Oakland: University of California Press.

Levine, Judith A., Valerie Bonner, and Joshua Klugman. 2018. "Gender and the
Long Arm of the Job: A Beeper Study Analysis of Work-to-Home Spillover
and Crossover of Emotions." Unpublished manuscript.

Livingston, Gretchen. 2014. "Growing Number of Dads Home with the Kids."
Pew Research Center's Social & Demographic Trends Project. http://www
.pewsocialtrends.org/2014/06/05/growing-number-of-dads-home-with-the
-kids/. Accessed July 9, 2018.

Lopez, Steve H., and Lora A. Phillips. 2019. "Unemployed: White-Collar Job
Searching after the Great Recession." *Work and Occupations* 46 (4):
470–510.

Lundren, Bo. 2006. "Recent Development in Unemployment Insurance in
Sweden." Report for International Experts Workshop of the International
Social Security Association Technical Commission on Unemployment
Insurance and Employment Maintenance. https://www.issa.int/html/pdf
/workshop/bruxelles06/2lundgren.pdf. Accessed: July 11, 2019.

Lunn, Anna, and Sabino Kornrich. 2018. "Family Investments in Education
during Periods of Economic Uncertainty: Evidence from the Great Recession." *Sociological Perspectives* 61 (1): 145–63.

Mallett, Shelley. 2004. "Understanding Home: A Critical Review of the Literature." *Sociological Review* 52 (1): 62–89.

Mandel, Hadas. 2018. "A Second Look at the Process of Occupational Feminization and Pay Reduction in Occupations." *Demography* 55 (2): 669–90.

McKenna, Laura. 2015. "The College President-to-Adjunct Pay Ratio." *The Atlantic*, September 24.

McPherson, J. Miller, Lynn Smith-Lovin, and Matthew E. Brashears. 2006. "Social Isolation in America: Changes in Core Discussion Networks over Two Decades." *American Sociological Review* 71 (3): 353–75.

Michel, Alexandra. 2012. "Transcending Socialization: A Nine-Year Ethnography of the Body's Role in Organizational Control and Knowledge Workers' Transformation." *Administrative Science Quarterly* 56 (3): 325–68.

Mize, Trenton. 2016. "Sexual Orientation in the Labor Market." *American Sociological Review* 81 (6): 1132–60.

Mong, Sherry, and Vincent J. Roscigno. 2010. "African American Men and the Experience of Employment Discrimination. *Qualitative Sociology* 33: 1–21.

Nelson, Margaret K. 2010. *Parenting Out of Control: Anxious Parents in Uncertain Times*. New York: New York University Press.

Newman, Katherine S. 1999. *Falling from Grace: Downward Mobility in the Age of Affluence*. Oakland: University of California Press.

———, ed. 2008. *Laid Off, Laid Low: Political and Economic Consequences of Employment Insecurity*. New York: Columbia University Press.

———. 2012. *The Accordion Family: Boomerang Kids, Anxious Parents, and the Private Toll of Global Competition*. Boston: Beacon Press.

———. 2019. *Downhill from Here: Retirement Insecurity in the Age of Inequality*. New York: Metropolitan Books, Henry Holt & Co.

Norris, Dawn R. 2016. *Job Loss, Identity, and Mental Health*. New Brunswick, NJ: Rutgers University Press.

Ochs, Elinor, and Tamar Kremer-Sadlik, eds. 2013. *Fast-Forward Family: Home, Work, and Relationships in Middle-Class America*. Oakland: University of California Press.

Ocobock, Abigail. 2013. "The Power and Limits of Marriage: Married Gay Men's Family Relationships." *Journal of Marriage and Family* 75 (1): 191–205.

O'Connor, Julia S., Ann Shola Orloff, and Sheila Shaver. 1999. *States, Markets, Families: Gender, Liberalism and Social Policy in Australia, Canada, Great Britain and the United States*. Cambridge: Cambridge University Press.

Oliver, Melvin L., and Thomas M. Shapiro. 2019. "Disrupting the Racial Wealth Gap." *Contexts* 18 (1):16–21.

Orbuch, Terri J., and Sandra L. Eyster. 1997. "Division of Household Labor among Black Couples and White Couples." *Social Forces* 76: 301–22.

Osnowitz, Debra. 2010. *Freelancing Expertise: Contract Professionals in the New Economy.* Ithaca, New York: Cornell University Press.

Ostrander, Susan O. 1984. *Women of the Upper Class.* Philadelphia: Temple University Press.

Pager, Devah. 2003. "The Mark of a Criminal Record." *American Journal of Sociology* 108 (5): 937–75.

Pager, Devah, Bruce Western, and Bart Bonikowski. 2009. "Discrimination in a Low-Wage Labor Market: A Field Experiment." *American Sociological Review* 74: 777–99.

Paik, Leslie. 2017. "Good Parents, Bad Parents: Rethinking Family Involvement in Juvenile Justices." *Theoretical Criminology* 21 (3): 307–23.

Pande, Amrita. 2014. *Wombs in Labor Force: Transnational Commercial Surrogacy in India.* New York: Columbia University Press.

Parreñas, Rhacel Salazar. 2001. *Servants of Globalization: Women, Migration and Domestic Work.* Stanford, CA: Stanford University Press.

Pedulla, David. 2018. "How Race and Unemployment Shape Labor Market Opportunities: Additive, Amplified, or Muted Effects?" *Social Forces* 96 (4): 1477–506.

Pedulla, David S., and Sarah Thébaud. 2015. "Can We Finish the Revolution? Gender, Work-Family Ideals, and Institutional Constraint." *American Sociological Review* 80 (1): 116–39.

Pepin, Joanna R. 2019. "Beliefs about Money in Families: Balancing Unity, Autonomy, and Gender Equality." *Journal of Marriage and Family* 81 (2): 361–79.

Pepin, Joanna, and David Cotter. 2017. "Trending Towards Traditionalism? Changes in Youths' Gender Ideology." *Council on Contemporary Families.* Retrieved July 17, 2018. https://contemporaryfamilies. org/2-pepin-cotter-traditionalism/.

Pepin, Joanna R., Liana C. Sayer, and Lynne M. Casper. 2018. "Marital Status and Mothers' Time Use: Childcare, Housework, Leisure, and Sleep." *Demography* 55 (1): 107–33.

Pew Research Center. 2015. Social and Demographic Trends. "Raising Kids and Running a Household: How Working Parents Share the Load." November 4. https://www.pewsocialtrends.org/2015/11/04/raising-kids-and-running-a -household-how-working-parents-share-the-load/. Accessed July 11, 2019.

Pfeffer, Carla A. 2010. "'Women's Work'? Women Partners of Transgender Men Doing Housework and Emotion Work." *Journal of Marriage and Family* 72 (1): 165–83.

———. *Queering Families: The Postmodern Partnership of Cisgender Women and Transgender Men.* New York: Oxford University Press.

Pugh, Allison. 2015a. *The Tumbleweed Society: Working and Caring in an Age of Insecurity.* New York: Oxford University Press.

———. 2015b. "Men at Work: The Age of Austerity Has Transformed Work, but What It Means to Be a Man Has Not Caught Up." *Aeon*, December 4. https://aeon.co/essays/what-does-it-mean-to-be-a-man-in-the-age-of-austerity.

———. 2018. "Parenting in an Insecure Age: Class, Gender and the Flexible Child." *SocioLogica: Italian Journal of Sociology*. https://sociologica.unibo.it/article/view/9082/9037.

Putnam, Robert D. 2001. *Bowling Alone: The Collapse and Revival of American Community*. New York: Simon and Schuster.

Quadlin, Natasha. 2018. "The Mark of a Woman's Record: Gender and Academic Performance in Hiring." *American Sociological Review* 83 (2): 331–60.

Quadlin, Natasha, and Long Doan. 2018. "Sex-Typed Chores and the City: Gender, Urbanicity, and Housework." *Gender & Society* 32 (6): 789–813.

Rao, Aliya Hamid. 2017a. "Stand by Your Man: Wives' Emotion Work during Men's Unemployment." *Journal of Marriage and Family* 79(3): 636–56.

Rao, Aliya Hamid. 2017b. "'You Don't Dare Plan Much': Contract Work and Personal Life for International Early-Career Professionals." *Research in the Sociology of Work* 31: 429–53.

———. 2018. "Parenting and Inequality in Insecure Times: A Comment to the Symposium." *SocioLogica* 12(3): 59–65.

———. 2019a. "From Professionals to Professional Mothers? How College-Educated, Married Mothers Experience Unemployment in the US." *Work, Employment and Society*. Online First (November 26). https://doi.org/10.1177/0950017019887334.

———. 2019b. "Raising the Secure Child: Parenting in Affluent Families Experiencing Unemployment." American Sociological Association, annual Conference. New York, NY.

Rao, Aliya Hamid, and Megan Tobias Neely. 2019. "What's Love Got to Do with It? Passion and Inequality at Work." *Sociology Compass* 13 (12): 1–14.

Ravenelle, Alexandrea J. 2019. *Hustle and Gig: Struggling and Surviving in the Sharing Economy*. Oakland, CA: University of California Press.

Ray, Raka, and Seemin Qayum. 2009. *Cultures of Servitude: Modernity, Domesticity, and Class in India*. Stanford, CA: Stanford University Press.

Reich, Jennifer. 2005. *Fixing Families: Parents, Power, and the Child Welfare System*. New York: Routledge.

Ridgeway, Cecilia L. 2011. *Framed by Gender: How Gender Inequality Persists in the Modern World*. New York: Oxford University Press.

Risman, Barbara J. 2009. "From Doing to Undoing: Gender as We Know It." *Gender & Society* 23 (1): 81–84.

Risman, Barbara, Ray Sin, and William Scarborough. 2017. "Millennials: Not Pushing the Envelope, Not Rejecting the Gender Revolution—Council on Contemporary Families." *The Society Pages*, April 18. https://thesociety

pages.org/ccf/2017/04/18/millennials-not-pushing-the-envelope-not
-rejecting-the-gender-revolution/. Accessed July 20, 2018.

Rivera, Lauren A. 2012. "Hiring as Cultural Matching: The Case of Elite
Professional Service Firms." *American Sociological Review* 77 (6): 999–1022.

———. 2015. *Pedigree: How Elite Students Get Elite Jobs.* Princeton, NJ:
Princeton University Press.

Rivera, Lauren A., and András Tilcsik. 2016. "Class Advantage, Commitment
Penalty: The Gendered Effect of Social Class Signals in an Elite Labor
Market." *American Sociological Review* 81 (6): 1097–131.

Rivers-Moore, Megan. 2016. *Gringo Gulch: Sex, Tourism, and Social Mobility
in Costa Rica.* Chicago: University of Chicago Press.

Roscigno, Vincent, Sherry Mong, Reginald Byron, and Griff Tester. 2007. "Age
Discrimination, Social Closure, and Employment." *Social Forces* 86 (1):
313–34.

Rosenblat, Alex. 2018. *Uberland: How Algorithms Are Rewriting the Rules of
Work.* Oakland, CA: University of California Press.

Roy, Kevin, Anisa Zvonkovic, Abbie Goldberg, Elizabeth Sharp, and Ralph
LaRossa. 2015. "Sampling Richness and Qualitative Integrity: Challenges for
Research with Families." *Journal of Marriage and Family* 77 (1): 243–60.

Ruddick, Sara. 1980. "Maternal Thinking." *Feminist Studies* 6 (2): 342.

Ruppanner, Leah, Francisco Perales, and Janeen Baxter. 2019. "Harried and
Unhealthy? Parenthood, Time Pressure, and Mental Health." *Journal of
Marriage and Family* 81 (2): 308–26.

Sanders, Jasmine. 2019. "A Black Legacy, Wrapped Up in Fur." *New York Times,*
January 31.

Sarkisian, Natalia, and Naomi Gerstel. 2004. "Kin Support among Blacks and
Whites: Race and Family Organization." *American Sociological Review* 69
(6): 812–37.

Sayer, Liana C. 2010. "Trends in Housework." In *Dividing the Domestic: Men,
Women, and Household Work in Cross-National Perspective,* edited by Judith
K. Treas and Sonja Drobnić, 19–38. Stanford, CA: Stanford University Press.

Sayer, Liana C., and Leigh Fine. 2011. "Racial-Ethnic Differences in U.S.
Married Women's and Men's Housework." *Social Indicators Research* 101 (2):
259–65.

Schafer, Markus H., and Nicholas Vargas. 2016. "The Dynamics of Social
Support Inequality: Maintenance Gaps by Socioeconomic Status and Race?"
Social Forces 94 (4): 1795–822.

Schneider, Daniel. 2012. "Gender Deviance and Household Work: The Role of
Occupation." *American Journal of Sociology* 117 (4): 1029–72.

Schneider, Daniel, and Kristen Harknett. 2019. "Consequences of Routine
Schedule Instability for Worker Health and Wellbeing." *American Sociological Review* 84 (1): 82–114.

Schneider, Daniel, Kristin Harknett, and Sara McLanahan. 2016. ""Intimate Partner Violence in the Great Recession." *Demography* 53 (2): 471–505.

Schor, Juliet B. 1991. *The Overworked American: The Unexpected Decline of Leisure*. New York: Basic Books.

Schwartz, Christine R., and Robert D. Mare. 2005. "Trends in Educational Assortative Marriage from 1940 to 2003." *Demography* 42 (4): 621–46.

Seamster, Louise. 2019. "Black Debt, White Debt." *Contexts* 18 (1): 30–35.

Sharone, Ofer. 2013. *Flawed System / Flawed Self: Job Searching and Unemployment Experiences*. Chicago: University of Chicago Press.

Silva, Jennifer. 2013. *Coming Up Short: Working-Class Adulthood in an Age of Uncertainty*. New York: Oxford University Press.

Silva, Jennifer, and Kaisa Snellman. 2018. "Salvation or Safety Net? Meanings of 'College' among Working- and Middle-Class Young Adults in Narratives of the Future." *Social Forces* 97 (2): 559–82.

Small, Mario Luis. 2009. "'How Many Cases Do I Need?': On Science and the Logic of Case Selection in Field-Based Research." *Ethnography* 10 (1): 5–38.

Smith, Vicki. 2001. *Crossing the Great Divide: Worker Risk and Opportunity in the New Economy*. Ithaca, NY: ILR Press.

Stone, Pamela. 2007. *Opting Out? Why Women Really Quit Careers and Head Home*. Oakland: University of California Press.

Stuart, Forrest. 2016. *Down, Out, and Under Arrest: Policing and Everyday Life in Skid Row*. Chicago: University of Chicago Press.

Swidler, Ann. 1986. "Culture in Action: Symbols and Strategies." *American Sociological Review* 51 (2): 273–86.

Thébaud, Sarah, Sabino Kornrich, and Leah Ruppanner. 2019. "Good Housekeeping, Great Expectations: Gender and Housework Norms." *Sociological Methods & Research* (May 30). Online. doi: 10.1177/0049124119852395.

Thoits, Peggy A. 1986. "Multiple Identities: Examining Gender and Marital Status Differences in Distress." *American Sociological Review* 51 (2): 259–72.

Thomeer, Mieke Beth, Corinne Reczek, and Debra Umberson. 2015. "Gendered Emotion Work around Physical Health Problems in Mid- and Later-Life Marriages." *Journal of Aging Studies* 32: 12–22.

Thomeer, Mieke Beth, Debra Umberson, and Tetyanna Pudrovska. 2013. "Marital Processes around Depression: A Gendered and Relational Perspective." *Society and Mental Health* 3 (3): 151–69.

Thompson, Derek. 2009. "It's Not Just a Recession. It's a Mancession!" *The Atlantic*, July 9.

Thorne, Deborah. 2010. "Extreme Financial Strain: Emergent Chores, Gender Inequality and Emotional Distress." *Journal of Family and Economic Issues* 31 (2): 185–97.

Treas, Judith. 1993. "Money in the Bank: Transaction Costs and the Economic Organization of Marriage." *American Sociological Review* 58 (5): 723–34.

Vallas, Steven Peter. 2011. *Work: A Critique*. New York: Polity.

van der Zwan, Natascha. 2014. "Making Sense of Financialization." *Socio-Economic Review* 12 (1): 99–129.

Villalobos, Ana. 2014. *Motherload: Making it all Better in Insecure Times*. Oakland, CA: University of California Press.

Walzer, Susan. 1998. *Thinking about the Baby: Gender and Transitions into Parenthood*. Philadelphia: Temple University Press.

Weinberger, Michelle F., Jane R. Zavisca, and Jennifer M. Silva. 2017. "Consuming for an Imagined Future: Middle-Class Consumer Lifestyle and Exploratory Experiences in the Transition to Adulthood." *Journal of Consumer Research* 44 (2): 332–60.

Weiss, Robert Stuart. 1994. *Learning from Strangers: The Art and Method of Qualitative Interview Studies*. New York: Free Press.

Weisshaar, Katherine. 2018. "From Opt Out to Blocked Out: The Challenges for Labor Market Re-entry after Family-Related Employment Lapses." *American Sociological Review* 83 (1): 34–60.

Wendt, Douglas, and Kevin Shafer. 2016. "Gender and Attitudes about Mental Health Help Seeking: Results from National Data." *Health & Social Work* 41 (1): e20–28.

West, Candace, and Don H. Zimmerman. 1987. "Doing Gender." *Gender & Society* 1 (2): 125–51.

Whillans, Ashley. 2019. "Time for Happiness." *Harvard Business Review*, January 31.

Williams, Joan. 1999. *Unbending Gender: Why Family and Work Conflict and What to Do about It*. Oxford: Oxford University Press.

Wooten, Melissa E., and Enobong H. Branch. 2012. "Defining Appropriate Labor: Race, Gender, and Idealization of Black Women in Domestic Service." *Race, Gender & Class* 19 (3–4): 292–308.

Wynn, Alison T., and Shelley J. Correll. 2017. "Gendered Perceptions of Cultural and Skill Alignment in Technology Companies." *Social Sciences* 6 (2): 45.

Wynn, Alison, and Aliya Hamid Rao. 2020. "Failures of Flexibility: How Perceived Control Motivates the Individualization of Work-Life Conflict." *Industrial and Labor Relations Review* 73 (1): 61–90.

Yang, Yang, Nitesh V. Chawla, and Brian Uzzi. 2019. "A Network's Gender Composition and Communication Pattern Predict Women's Leadership Success." *PNAS: Proceedings of the National Academy of Sciences of the United States of America* 116 (6): 2033–38.

Yavorsky, Jill, Lisa A. Keister, Yu Quian, and Michael Nau. 2019. "Women in the One Percent: Gender Dynamics in Top Income Positions." *American Sociological Review* 84 (1): 54–81.

Young, Cristobal. 2012. "Losing a Job: The Nonpecuniary Cost of Unemployment in the United States." *Social Forces* 91: 609–33.

Zelizer, Viviana. 2015. "Paying Wives: Bonus, Gift, or Allowance?" *Huffington Post*. https://www.huffingtonpost.com/viviana-a-zelizer/paying-wives -bonus-gift-or-allowance_b_7493142.html. Accessed January 15, 2019.

———. 2017. *The Social Meaning of Money: Pin Money, Paychecks, Poor Relief, and Other Currencies*. 2nd edition. Princeton, NJ: Princeton University Press.

Index

Founded in 1893,
UNIVERSITY OF CALIFORNIA PRESS
publishes bold, progressive books and journals
on topics in the arts, humanities, social sciences,
and natural sciences—with a focus on social
justice issues—that inspire thought and action
among readers worldwide.

The UC PRESS FOUNDATION
raises funds to uphold the press's vital role
as an independent, nonprofit publisher, and
receives philanthropic support from a wide
range of individuals and institutions—and from
committed readers like you. To learn more, visit
ucpress.edu/supportus.